ICAS 2017

The Thirteenth International Conference on Autonomic and Autonomous Systems

May 21 - 25, 2017

Barcelona, Spain

ICAS 2017 Editors

Carlos Becker Westphall, University of Santa Catarina, Brazil

Márcio Mendonça, Federal University of Technology of Paraná, Brazil

Rafael Oliveira Vasconcelos, Pontifical Catholic University of Rio de Janeiro (PUC-Rio) / University Tiradentes (UNIT), Brazil

Printed from e-media with permission by:

Curran Associates, Inc.
57 Morehouse Lane
Red Hook, NY 12571

Some format issues inherent in the e-media version may also appear in this print version.

Printed by Curran Associates, Inc. (2017)

International Academy, Research, and Industry Association (IARIA)
412 Derby Way
Wilmington, DE 19810

Phone: (408) 893-6407
Fax: (408) 527-6351

petre@iaria.org

Additional copies of this publication are available from:

Curran Associates, Inc.
57 Morehouse Lane
Red Hook, NY 12571 USA
Phone: 845-758-0400
Fax: 845-758-2633
Email: curran@proceedings.com
Web: www.proceedings.com

TABLE OF CONTENTS

ICAS 1: AUTONOMIC COMPUTING

ICAS 2: ALGORITHMS AND THEORY FOR CONTROL AND COMPUTATION

ICAS 3: ADVANCES IN SYSTEM AUTOMATION

ICAS 4 / FUCOMA: FUZZY COGNITIVE MAPS

ICAS 5 / IOIT I: INTERNET OF INTELLIGENT AND AUTONOMIC THINGS I

ICAS 6 / IOIT II: INTERNET OF INTELLIGENT AND AUTONOMIC THINGS II

ICAS 2017

Foreword

The Thirteenth International Conference on Autonomic and Autonomous Systems (ICAS 2017), held between May 21 - 25, 2017 - Barcelona, Spain, was a multi-track event covering related topics on theory and practice on systems automation, autonomous systems and autonomic computing.

The main tracks referred to the general concepts of systems automation, and methodologies and techniques for designing, implementing and deploying autonomous systems. The next tracks developed around design and deployment of context-aware networks, services and applications, and the design and management of self-behavioral networks and services. We also considered monitoring, control, and management of autonomous self-aware and context-aware systems and topics dedicated to specific autonomous entities, namely, satellite systems, nomadic code systems, mobile networks, and robots. It has been recognized that modeling (in all forms this activity is known) is the fundamental for autonomous subsystems, as both managed and management entities must communicate and understand each other. Small-scale and large-scale virtualization and model-driven architecture, as well as management challenges in such architectures are considered. Autonomic features and autonomy requires a fundamental theory behind and solid control mechanisms. These topics gave credit to specific advanced practical and theoretical aspects that allow subsystem to expose complex behavior. We aimed to expose specific advancements on theory and tool in supporting advanced autonomous systems. Domain case studies (policy, mobility, survivability, privacy, etc.) and specific technology (wireless, wireline, optical, e-commerce, banking, etc.) case studies were targeted. A special track on mobile environments was indented to cover examples and aspects from mobile systems, networks, codes, and robotics.

Pervasive services and mobile computing are emerging as the next computing paradigm in which infrastructure and services are seamlessly available anywhere, anytime, and in any format. This move to a mobile and pervasive environment raises new opportunities and demands on the underlying systems. In particular, they need to be adaptive, self-adaptive, and context-aware.

Adaptive and self-management context-aware systems are difficult to create, they must be able to understand context information and dynamically change their behavior at runtime according to the context. Context information can include the user location, his preferences, his activities, the environmental conditions and the availability of computing and communication resources. Dynamic reconfiguration of the context-aware systems can generate inconsistencies as well as integrity problems, and combinatorial explosion of possible variants of these systems with a high degree of variability can introduce great complexity.

Traditionally, user interface design is a knowledge-intensive task complying with specific domains, yet being user friendly. Besides operational requirements, design recommendations refer to standards of the application domain or corporate guidelines.

Commonly, there is a set of general user interface guidelines; the challenge is due to a need for cross-team expertise. Required knowledge differs from one application domain to another, and the core knowledge is subject to constant changes and to individual perception and skills.

Passive approaches allow designers to initiate the search for information in a knowledge-database to make accessible the design information for designers during the design process. Active approaches, e.g., constraints and critics, have been also developed and tested. These mechanisms deliver information (critics) or restrict the design space (constraints) actively, according to the rules and guidelines. Active and passive approaches are usually combined to capture a useful user interface design.

We take here the opportunity to warmly thank all the members of the ICAS 2017 Technical Program Committee, as well as the numerous reviewers. The creation of such a high quality conference program would not have been possible without their involvement. We also kindly thank all the authors who dedicated much of their time and efforts to contribute to ICAS 2017. We truly believe that, thanks to all these efforts, the final conference program consisted of top quality contributions.

Also, this event could not have been a reality without the support of many individuals, organizations, and sponsors. We are grateful to the members of the ICAS 2017 organizing committee for their help in handling the logistics and for their work to make this professional meeting a success.

We hope that ICAS 2017 was a successful international forum for the exchange of ideas and results between academia and industry and for the promotion of progress in the fields of autonomic and autonomous systems.

We are convinced that the participants found the event useful and communications very open. We also hope that Barcelona provided a pleasant environment during the conference and everyone saved some time for exploring this beautiful city.

ICAS 2017 Chairs:

Satoshi Kurihara, University of Electro-Communications, Japan
Ljubo Vlacic, Griffith University, Australia
Roy Sterritt, Ulster University, UK
Mark J. Balas, Embry-Riddle Aeronautical University, USA
Elisabetta Di Nitto, Politecnico di Milano, Italy
Radu Calinescu, University of York, UK
Karsten Böhm, Fachhochschule Kufstein, Austria
S.G. Ponnambalam, Monash University Malaysia, Malaysia
Richard Anthony, University of Greenwich, UK
Jacques Malenfant, UPMC, France
Wladyslaw Homenda, Warsaw University of Technology, Poland
Albert M. K. Cheng, University of Houston, USA

ICAS Industry/Research Advisory Committee
Loris Penserini, Informatica e Società Digitale - IES, Italy
Stefanos Vrochidis, Centre for Research and Technology Hellas - Thermi-Thessaloniki, Greece
Tsuyoshi Ide, IBM T. J. Watson Research Center, USA
Petr Skobelev, Knowledge Genesis Group / Samara Technical University, Russia
Rajat Mehrotra, Desert Research Institute, USA
Andreas Kercek, Lakeside Labs GmbH, Austria
Claudius Stern, biozoom services GmbH - Kassel | FOM University of Applied Sciences - Essen, Germany

ICAS 2017

Committee

ICAS Steering Committee

Satoshi Kurihara, University of Electro-Communications, Japan
Ljubo Vlacic, Griffith University, Australia
Roy Sterritt, Ulster University, UK
Mark J. Balas, Embry-Riddle Aeronautical University, USA
Elisabetta Di Nitto, Politecnico di Milano, Italy
Radu Calinescu, University of York, UK
Karsten Böhm, Fachhochschule Kufstein, Austria
S.G. Ponnambalam, Monash University Malaysia, Malaysia
Richard Anthony, University of Greenwich, UK
Jacques Malenfant, UPMC, France
Wladyslaw Homenda, Warsaw University of Technology, Poland
Albert M. K. Cheng, University of Houston, USA

ICAS Industry/Research Advisory Committee

Loris Penserini, Informatica e Società Digitale - IES, Italy
Stefanos Vrochidis, Centre for Research and Technology Hellas - Thermi-Thessaloniki, Greece
Tsuyoshi Ide, IBM T. J. Watson Research Center, USA
Petr Skobelev, Knowledge Genesis Group / Samara Technical University, Russia
Rajat Mehrotra, Desert Research Institute, USA
Andreas Kercek, Lakeside Labs GmbH, Austria
Claudius Stern, biozoom services GmbH - Kassel | FOM University of Applied Sciences - Essen, Germany

ICAS 2017 Technical Program Committee

Sherif Abdelwahed, Mississippi State University, USA
Jose Aguilar, Universidad de Los Andes, Venezuela
Alba Amato, Institute for High-Performance Computing and Networking (ICAR), Napoli, Italy
Razvan Andonie, Central Washington University, USA
Richard Anthony, University of Greenwich, UK
Markus Bader, Technische Universität Wien, Austria
Mark J. Balas, Embry-Riddle Aeronautical University, USA
Julita Bermejo-Alonso, Universidad Politécnica de Madrid (UPM), Spain
Karsten Böhm, Fachhochschule Kufstein, Austria
Radu Calinescu, University of York, UK
Paolo Campegiani, University of Roma Tor Vergata, Italy
Valérie Camps, Paul Sabatier University | IRIT, France
José Manuel Castro Torres, University Fernando Pessoa / LIACC - Artificial Intelligence and Computer Science Laboratory / ISUS - Intelligent Sensing and Ubiquitous Systems, Portugal
Albert M. K. Cheng, University of Houston, USA
Feng Chu, University of Evry, France

Siobhan Clarke, Trinity College Dublin, Ireland
Prithviraj (Raj) Dasgupta, University of Nebraska, USA
Angel P. del Pobil, Jaume I University, Spain
Elisabetta Di Nitto, Politecnico di Milano, Italy
Sotirios Diamantas, Athens Information Technology, Greece
Larbi Esmahi, Athabasca University, Canada
Anna Esposito, Seconda Università di Napoli & IIASS, Italy
Lukas Esterle, Vienna University of Technology, Austria
Thaddeus Eze, University of Chester, UK
Luis Fernando Orleans, Universidade Federal Rural do Rio de Janeiro, Brazil
Maurizio Fiasché, Politecnico di Milano, Italy
Manuel Filipe Santos, Universidade do Minho | Research Centre Algoritmi, Portugal
Ziny Flikop, Scientist, USA
Stefano Franchi, University of Texas A&M, USA
Matjaz Gams, Jozef Stefan Institute, Slovenia
Fabio Gasparetti, ROMA TRE University, Italy
Marie-Pierre Gleizes, University Paul Sabatier of Toulouse | IRIT, France
Fatemeh Golpayegani, Trinity College Dublin, Ireland
Teodor Lucian Grigorie, University of Craiova, Romania
William Grosky, University of Michigan-Dearborn, USA
Jordi Guitart, Universitat Politècnica de Catalunya (UPC), Spain
Maki K. Habib, The American University in Cairo, Egypt
Gerold Hoelzl, University of Passau, Germany
Wladyslaw Homenda, Warsaw University of Technology, Poland
Wei-Chiang Hong, Nanjing Tech University, China
Marc-Philippe Huget, Polytech Annecy-Chambery-LISTIC | University of Savoie, France
Jinho Hwang, IBM T.J. Watson Research Center, USA
Tsuyoshi Ide, IBM T. J. Watson Research Center, USA
Luis Iribarne, University of Almería, Spain
Michael Jenkin, York University, Canada
Richard Jiang, Northumbria University, UK
Paulo Jorge Sequeira Goncalves, Instituto Politecnico de Castelo Branco, Portugal
Imed Kacem, Université de Lorraine, France
Alexey Kashevnik, St. Petersburg Institute for Informatics and Automation of the Russian Academy of Sciences (SPIIRAS), Russia
Andreas Kercek, Lakeside Labs GmbH, Austria
Won-jong Kim, Texas A&M University, USA
Ah-Lian Kor, Leeds Beckett University, UK
Igor Kotenko, St. Petersburg Institute for Informatics and Automation of the Russian Academy of Sciences (SPIIRAS), Russia
Boris Kovalerchuk, Central Washington University, USA
Satoshi Kurihara, University of Electro-Communications, Japan
Noel Lopes, Polytechnic of Guarda, Portugal
José Machado, University of Minho, Portugal
Prabhat Mahanti, University of New Brunswick, Canada
Jacques Malenfant, UPMC, France
Pushparaj Mani Pathak, Indian Institute of Technology, Roorkee, India
Jerusa Marchi, Universidade Federal de Santa Catarina, Brazil

Konrad Andrzej Markowski, Warsaw University of Technology, Poland
Goreti Marreiros, Polytechnic of Porto, Portugal
Rajat Mehrotra, Desert Research Institute, USA
René Meier, Lucerne University of Applied Sciences and Arts, Switzerland
Márcio Mendonça, Federal University of Technology of Paraná, Brazil
Yasser F. O. Mohammad, KDDI Laboratories, Japan / Assiut University, Egypt
Masayuki Murata, Osaka University Suita, Japan
Adnan Abou Nabout, Bergische Universität Wuppertal, Germany
Kai Nagel, TU Berlin, Germany
Nicol Naidoo, University of KwaZulu-Natal, South Africa
Vivek Nallur, Trinity College Dublin | University of Dublin, Ireland
Roberto Nardone, University of Naples Federico II, Italy
Rafael Oliveira Vasconcelos, Pontifical Catholic University of Rio de Janeiro (PUC-Rio) / University Tiradentes (UNIT), Brazil
Chiemela Onunka, Mangosuthu University of Technology, South Africa
Flavio Oquendo, IRISA - University of South Brittany, France
Eros Pasero, Politecnico of Turin, Italy / Tongji University, Shanghai, China
Loris Penserini, Informatica e Società Digitale - IES, Italy
Agostino Poggi, DII - University of Parma, Italy
S.G. Ponnambalam, Monash University Malaysia, Malaysia
José Ragot, Université de Lorraine, France
Douglas Rodrigues, University of Sao Paulo (USP), Brazil
Fariba Sadri, Imperial College London, UK
Lakhdar Sais, CRIL - CNRS, University of Artois, France
Jagannathan Sarangapani, Missouri University of Science and Technology, USA
Jurek Z. Sasiadek, Carleton University, Canada
Madhavan Shanmugavel, Monash University Malaysia Campus, Malaysia
Pietro Siciliano, Institute for Microelectronics and Microsystems IMM-CNR, Italy
Fábio Silva, University of Minho, Portugal
Maria Silvia Pini, University of Padova, Italy
David Sislak, Czech Technical University in Prague, Czech Republic
Petr Skobelev, Knowledge Genesis Group / Samara Technical University, Russia
Antonino Staiano, University of Naples, Parthenope, Italy
Bernd Steinbach, University of Mining and Technology, Germany
Claudius Stern, biozoom services GmbH - Kassel | FOM University of Applied Sciences - Essen, Germany
Roy Sterritt, Ulster University, UK
Ryszard Tadeusiewicz, AGH University of Science and Technology, Poland
Giorgio Terracina, Università della Calabria, Italy
Emanuele Tonucci, IES - Informatica e Società Digitale, Italy
Viviane Torres da Silva, IBM Research, Brazil
Ali Emre Turgut, Middle East Technical University (METU), Turkey
Paulo Urbano, Universidade de Lisboa, Portugal
Egon L. van den Broek, Utrecht University, The Netherlands
Pierluigi Vellucci, Università di Roma "La Sapienza", Italy
Ramon Vilanova i Arbos, Escola d'Enginyeria - UAB, Spain
Ljubo Vlacic, Griffith University, Australia
Stefanos Vrochidis, Centre for Research and Technology Hellas - Thermi-Thessaloniki, Greece
Yu Weiwei, Northwestern Polytechnical University, China

Reuven Yagel, Azrieli - Jerusalem College of Engineering, Israel
Linda Yang, University of Portsmouth, UK
Xin-She Yang, Middlesex University, UK
Mingyi Zhang, Huawei US R&D Research Center, USA
Saman Zonouz, Rutgers University, USA

Copyright Information

Towards a Framework for Applying the Visualization of Smart Monitoring Architectures to a Distributed Ubiquity Mobility Platform

Djamel Khadraoui and Christophe Feltus
Luxembourg Institute of Science and Technology (LIST)
E-mail: djamel.khadraoui@list.lu

***Abstract*—Smart Mobility is proved to be a high priority topic in regard to arising European societal challenges. Deploying smart mobility required both technological and monitoring knowledge, and one important key features of the initiative stay in the multiplicity of the final users. Its goal is, depending on the type of users, to provide the required accurate data through a dynamic monitoring application. This implies to collect data coming from physical sensors deployed in all the parking areas of a region. Those sensors are simple, meaning that the information that they can collect is limited to an entry or exit signal of a vehicle. This paper presents an architecture for applying the visualization of smart monitoring architecture to a distributed ubiquity mobility platform and show a deployment in the frame of a use case. The later has been developed in a European region and consists in a smart mobility monitoring project.**

Keywords-Mobility; Visualisation; Model; Self-adaptability; Self-management; Monitoring; Automatic Context-aware system.

I. Introduction

Smart Mobility is proved to be a high priority topic in regard to arising societal challenges. Deploying smart mobility required both technological and monitoring knowledge. In the frame of a use case, which has actually been developed in a European region, and which consists in a mobility monitoring project (actually implemented), one important key feature of the initiative stay in the multiplicity of the final users. Its goal is, depending on the type of users, to give the wanted data through a dynamic monitoring application. This implies to collect data coming from physical sensors deployed in all the parking areas of a region. Those sensors are simple, meaning that the information that they can collect is limited to an entry or exit signal of a vehicle. Another data that has to be collected in this scenario is the live traffic data from the same geographical region; once again, the type of data is simple; the number of passing vehicles for each road of the region is collected in a predefined and fixed period of time. The need of monitoring is not a new challenge in computer science since a lot of solutions are proposed until this day. The fact is that the monitoring can be effective for a project only if it is completely applied for the problem while it should give the right information to a specific user (physical or not). For our case, a famous delivery company needs an effective and complete monitoring for all its parking spots around a big urban center. So, in collaboration with the city administration, this company needs a platform to handle a large amount of data and transform it into valuable information for their daily operations, optimizing their routines. This platform aims at monitoring the trips of their employees around the urban area and to give them an exact live situation. The solution responds to the business needs of an organization and provides to the different users a dynamic monitoring of the data combined with specific business rules. Using one deployed platform, collected and analyzed data are accessible from different final users with distinctive needs. In parallel to the monitoring of their employees, the targeted system is also able to provide important information to the city administration around live traffic levels and parking availability. Another view of the system could also be the notification to citizens about the roads congestion of the city. However, the interfaces must be readjusted for each case and administration solutions have to be adapted to the user and his rights among the system. Therefore, it is obvious that the current solution must be extended with new functionalities that should be able to be added without any new implementation of the gathering platform.

Smart monitoring systems consists in solutions which monitor, control and support the decision making related to security issue of complexes and critical systems (and information systems) spread out over disseminated areas. Hence, smart monitoring architecture seems to be the most relevant approach for the monitoring and decision making provided that they are designed to deal with increasingly sensitive and crucial situations for an economy or country (like the healthcare, the power distribution, the telecom, etc.) and consists in complex, sophisticated and integrated systems which support people in governing and monitoring a plethora of knowledge generated by critical infrastructures (CI – in military, energy, transport, industries, and healthcare) [1]. In our previous work, we have first defined a metamodel for the components of the smart monitoring architecture [2]. This metamodel has been elaborated acknowledging traditional enterprise architecture metamodel (EAM) and it allows modelling each component according to a similar structure. Afterwards, we have proposed a complement [2] to explore the enterprise architecture model ArchiMate® and to redesign its structure in order to comply with component software actors' characteristics, specificities and domain constraints. The principal focus of this paper concerns the design and the consideration of the policies that are centric concepts related to the activation of component's comportment. Our new contribution consists in the modeling of the monitoring system platform and the definition of the policies according to these models.

The paper is structured as following: next section presents the OCTOPUS platform (model and software) that we designed. Section III presents the OCTOPUS platform augmented with a smart monitoring solution. Section IV illustrates the monitoring interface for Smart Mobility in the frame of the augmented OCTOPUS platform and discusses the approach. Section V presents related works and last section concludes the paper and presents futures works.

II. OCTOPUS PLATFORM

OCTOPUS is a multi-agent platform; all the technologies related to agents are combined to provide a system for solving a data gathering and monitoring problem in an adaptive way. Being a multi-agent system, OCTOPUS has basic MAS characteristics as autonomy, local view and decentralization.

All the agents are autonomous and partially independent: the shutdown of an agent does lead to a platform's deactivation. Furthermore, the agents can continue their execution if the system has to reboot for any reason in order to ensure that their behavior is unchanged and that the data gathering is operational even if the remote communication is temporary deactivated.

No local agent has a global view of the platform and the main behavior aside from data gathering of the agents is to communicate to remote agents. In this way, a decentralization of the processes is effective; all the agents collect specific data and spread information to a controlling component of the system. This controlling component and its particular communication with the remainder of the system is the main defining characteristic of OCTOPUS.

OCTOPUS defines several components to achieve the deployment of an adaptive multi-agent system with different views of monitoring data and a particular communication routine to implement the constraints of the problem. Those constraints are the rules that each agent has to follow and depending on them, each agent changes his behavior.

OCTOPUS platform presents a hierarchy between the sub-platforms; containers grouping agents that are remotely connected. Throughout this hierarchy, the system defines types of agents that have a specific role. Each agent's sub-platform has an implemented behavior and specific role. A *Brain* agent is implemented, which is the management component, connected to all the agents of the sub-platform. All data gathering agents are waiting for rules from this *Brain* agent and are sending feedback in return. When necessary, *Brain* agents can also be part of a global hierarchy, in which a *Super-Brain* takes care of their organization and management. This way, each *Brain* can provide a view for a specific level of work; a main, administration view of the entire system is provided by the *Super-Brain* (see Figure 1). The P_n components represent agent's sub-platform containing *P* type agents while the T_n components represent implemented *T* type agent's sub-platform. In this case, the system is composed of a single *Brain*, a communication and organizing instance sub-platform.

This *Brain* is a sub-platform containing agents which remotely connects all the agents existing in its network. These agents are waiting for information collected from the *T* and *P* sub-platforms. The Brain is able to send this data to a monitoring interface through messages. The selection of the view and the type of data to be sent to the monitoring component remains at the sole discretion of the *Brain*. The main purpose of the *Brain* is to send rules to the connected sub-platforms of agents and receiving data from them. This way, the untreated data is sent from lower levels (*T* and *P* sub-platforms) to higher (*Brain*). Finally, this system example is a lower level of OCTOPUS itself; it is only one of the "*tentacles*" of the final architecture.

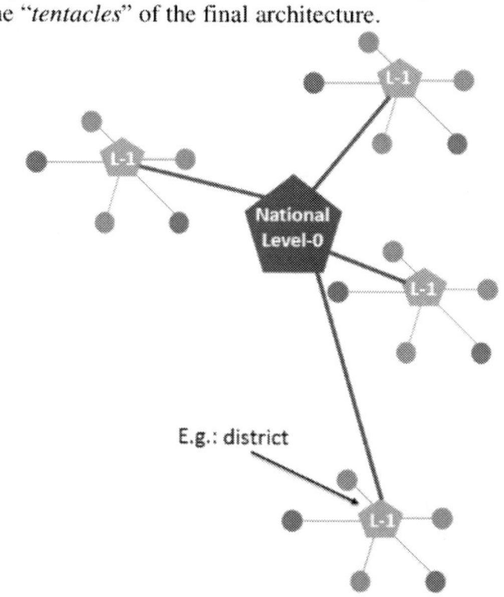

Figure 1. OCTOPUS global architecture

Obtaining a complete OCTOPUS instance is possible with adding one hierarchical level to the previous example. Figure 1 presents an architecture, in which all the *Brains* (with their *T* and *P* connected sub-platforms) are linked to a *Super-Brain*. Such a component has the same role as a *Brain*, but the collected data is coming from *Brain* sub-platforms. In this case, a global monitoring of the platform is possible and the rules are sent to the *Brains* of the network. The architecture is typically the same but with one higher level of hierarchy.

Finally, such architecture introduces a two-way data and rules flow: data collected from *T* and *P* type agents is sent to

Brain sub-platforms and after analysis, forwarded to the *Super-Brain*.

In return, rules are pushed from *Super-Brain* to the others *Brains* and their establishment inside *T* and *P* sub-platforms (through the agents). This bi-directional data flow is yet another key functionality of OCTOPUS platform. The generic examples presented in this section are only possible instances of OCTOPUS, the system can be adapted to different scenarios, data type and number of agents following the same hierarchical architecture. The *T* and *P* agents' type is an example of generic implementation of agents gathering data. Specific characteristics of agents and their types are descripted in next sections.

III. OCTOPUS PLATFORM AUGMENTED WITH A MONITORING SOLUTION

This section introduced the monitoring approach proposed by our OCTOPUS framework.

A. *Smart monitoring platform metamodelling insights*

The smart monitoring platform metamodel has been largely, and with many details, presented in [2]. This section recalls and summarizes the theoretic foundation and premise of our research in this area. The goal in modelling the monitoring system into a layered architecture metamodel is to furnish CI actors with solutions for governing the platform (monitoring and decision making support mechanism). In our previous work [3], extended smart monitoring platform metamodel using the *ArchiMate*® metamodel was elaborated to provide and support the use of a multiple layered approach of a monitoring component based on dynamic and autonomous policies.

To generate the OCTOPUS platform, we realized a specialization of the original *ArchiMate*® metamodel for the monitoring components. First, we redefined and structure the *Core* of the metamodel in order to figure out the semantic of the *Policy* [14] [17] (see Figure 2). The *Core* represents the handling of *Passive Structures* by *Active Structures* along the realization of *Behaviors*.

Concerning the *Active Structures* and the *Behavior*, the *Core* differentiates between external concepts which represent the way, in which the architecture is being perceived by the external elements (as a *Sub-Brain of a type T or P* attainable by means of an *Interface* or communicating with the *Brain*), and the internal elements which is composed of *Structure Elements* (*Roles, Components*) and linked to a *Policy Execution* concept. *Passive Structures* contains *Object* (e.g., *data or organizational object),* which represents architecture knowledge. Secondly, the concept of *Policy* has been defined in accordance to the platform metamodeling approach. The proposed representation is composed of three elements which allow defining the *Policy structure*: (1) the "Event" that is defined as a trigger generated by a *Structural component* that generates the realization of a *Policy*, (2) the "Context" whish symbolizes a configuration of *Passive Structure* that allows the *Policy* to be realized. In the case of Octopus, the context includes the sub-region environment specificities (3) the "Responsibility" [4][5][12][13][16] which is the more rich semantic concept and which is defined as a state assigned to a component (human or software) to specify obligations and rights in a specific context (Feltus et al., 2014).

Thereby, the responsibility corresponds to a set of behaviors that have to be realized by means of *Structure Elements*. That behavior may also use *Objects* of y type *Passive Structure* or modify values. With these three elements, we generate an auxiliary *Policy artefact* that mirrors the fulfilment of a set of *Responsibilities* [2] in a specific monitoring *Context* and in response to a predefined *Event*. Through the *Policy Concept*, we show that each operation done by the monitoring components can be transferred into a *Policy Execution*.

Although there is a clear semantic difference in *ArchiMate*® between the business user (human or machine) which exploits an application, and the application itself, in the smart monitoring field, we consider that actors and roles are played by components that we define as being a specific *Structure Elements* acting in Critical Infrastructure environment. As a result, three level are necessary to structure the metamodel for the monitoring domain: (1) The *Organizational Layer* offers services and products to external customers that are represented in the organization by organizational processes performed by *Organizational Roles* according to *Organizational Policies*. (2) The *Application Layer* supports the *Organizational Layer* with *Application Services* which are realized by *Applications* according to *Application Policies*. (3) The *Technology Layer* which offers *Infrastructure Services* needed to run applications, performed by system software, computer and communication hardware.

Concepts and colors were taken from the original *ArchiMate*® language, except for *Organizational Function* and the *Application Function* which were switched with the *Organizational Policy* component and the *Application Policy* component. Based on the following analysis, we have defined the *Organizational Policy* as "*the rules which define the organizational responsibilities and govern the execution of behaviors, at the organization domain, that serve the product domain in response to a process domain occurring in a specific context, which is symbolized by a configuration of the information domain*"

And we have defined the *Application Policy* as "*the rules that define the application responsibilities and govern the execution, at the application domain, of behaviors that serve the data domain to achieve the application strategy.*"

B. *Smart monitoring system metamodel layers*

The three layers which structure the smart monitoring platform metamodel (see Figure 2) are from down to top: the *technical level*, the *applicative level* and the *organization* or *business level*.

The *Technical Layer* is used to represent the structural aspect of the system and highlights the links between the *Technical Layer* and the *Application Layer* and how physical pieces of information called *Artefacts* are produced or used. The main concept of the *Technical layer* is the *Node* which represents a computational resource, on which *Artefacts* can be deployed and executed. The *Node* can be accessed by other *Nodes* or by components of the *Application Layer*. A *Node* is composed of a *Device* and a *System Software* [6]. *Devices* are physical computational resources where *Artefacts* are deployed when the *System Software* represents a software environment for types of components and objects. Communication between the *Nodes* of the *Technology Layer* is defined logically by the *Communication Path* and physically by the *Network*.

An *Organizational Object* defines unit of information which relates to an aspect of the organization. At the *Application layer*, this is used to represent the *Application Components* and their interactions with the *Application Service* derived from the *Organizational Policy* of the *Organizational Layer*. The concept of the components in the metamodel is very similar to the components concept of *UML* (UML 2) and allows representing any part of the program. Components use *Data Object*, which is a modelling concept of objects and object types of *UML*. Interconnection between components is modelled by the *Application Interface* in order to represent the availability of a component to the outside [3] (implementing a part or all of the services defined in the *Application Service*). The concept of *Collaboration* from the *Organizational Layer* is present in the *Application Layer* as the *Application Collaboration* and can be used to symbolize the cooperation (temporary) between components for the realization of behavior. *Application Policy* represents the behavior that is carried out by the components.

The *Organizational Layer* highlights the organizational processes and the associations with the *Application Layer*. Firstly, the *Organizational Layer* is defined as an *Organizational Role* (e.g.: *Alert Detection Concept*). This role, accessible from outside the monitoring behavioral structure through an *Organizational Interface*, performs behavior based on and according to organization's policy (*Organizational Policy component*), which are associated with the role. Afterwards, the components are able (depending on their roles – but also *function* is some cases) to interact with other roles to perform behavior; this is symbolized by the concept of *Role Collaboration* outside.

Organizational Policies are behavioral components of

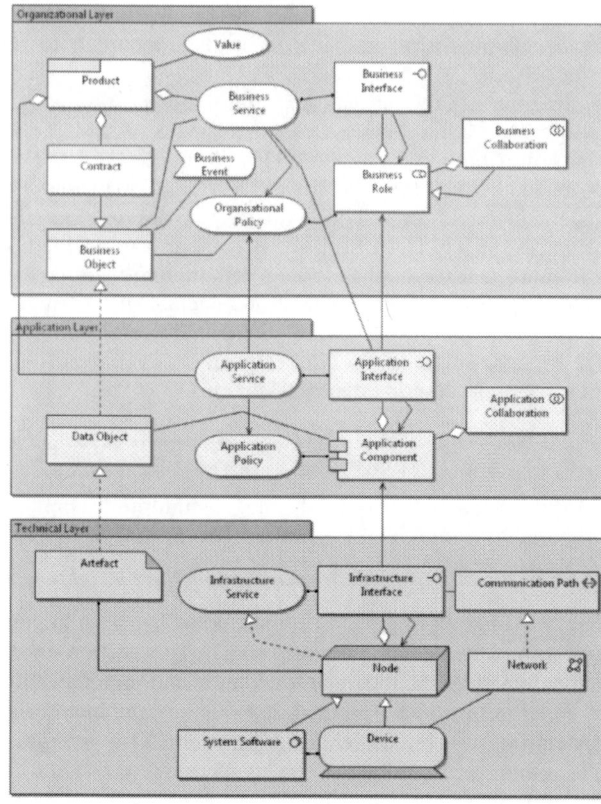

Figure 2. Smart monitoring platform metamodel

the organization whose goal is to achieve an *Organizational Service* to a role following *Events*. *Organizational Services* are contained in *Products* accompanied by *Contracts*. *Contracts* are formal or informal specifications of the rights and obligations associated with a *Product*. *Values* are defined as an appreciation of a *Service* or a *Product* that the *Organization* attempts to provide or acquire. The complete smart monitoring platform metamodel is the union of the three layers. As shown below, new connections between the layers have appeared.

For the *Passive Structure,* we observe that *Artefact* of the *Technical Layer* realizes *Data Object* of the *Application Layer* which, itself, realizes *Organizational Object* of the *Organizational layer*.

The *Behaviour* concept association shows that the *Application Service* uses the *Organizational Policy* to determine the services that it sustain. In the same manner, the *Technical Layer* bases its *Infrastructure Service* upon the *Application Policy* of the *Application Layer*. Concerning the *Active Structure* connections, the *Role* concept determines, together whit the *Application Component,* the *Interface* provided in the Application layer. The Interface of the Technical Layer is also based on the components of the Application Layer. The modelling language related to the above artefact is available in The Open Group [19].

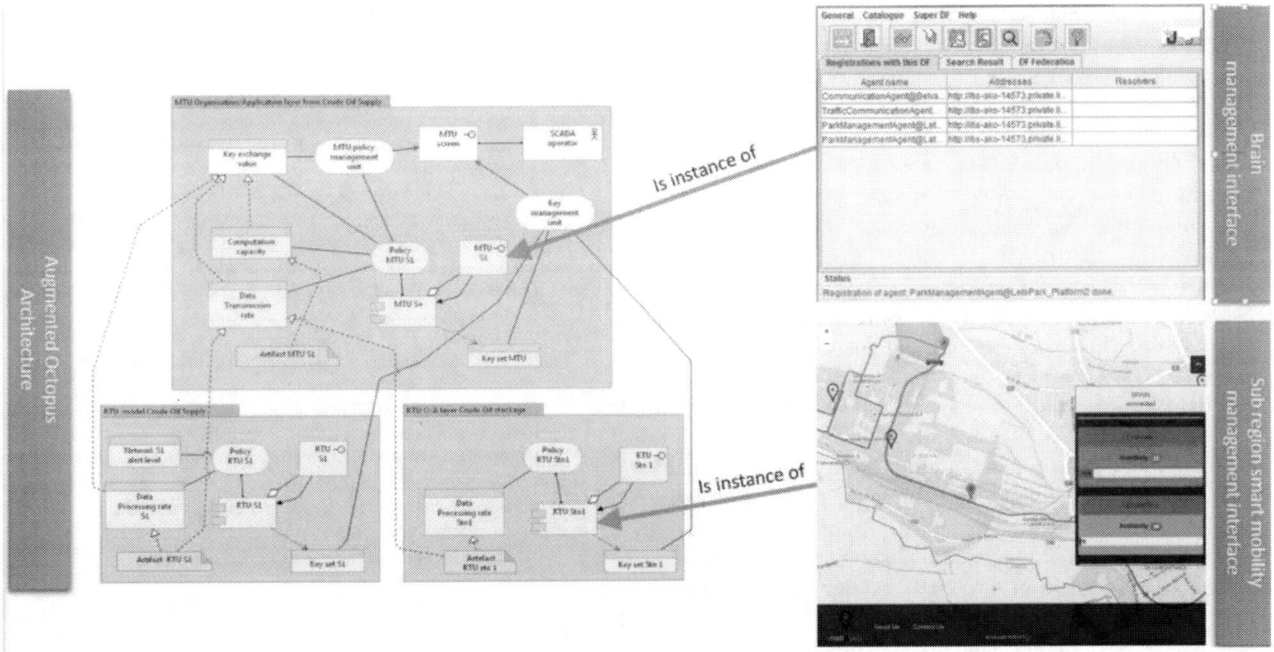

Figure 3. Smart Mobility management and sub-region interfaces

IV. VALIDATION IN THE FRAME OF A MONITORING INTERFACE AUGMENTED FOR SMART MOBILITY

This section aims at reporting and evaluating how OCTOPUS augmented has been designed for a specific Mobility management steering interface. Therefore, we review and validate the advantages and the improvements provided by the implementation that has been specifically required for this use case in the mobility domain.

As explained earlier, the monitoring architecture is defined based on generic agents easily instantiable for whatever cases, but steering interface is always dependent of the type of monitoring developed. Figure 3 shows the interface for the implementation of the smart mobility solution in the region. This interface content a monitoring frame including static information (e.g., map of the region, frames for the parking monitoring, etc.) and dynamic information (e.g., level of traffic jam on specific road, amount of places available at each parking, etc.)

Aside the monitoring interface, additional management functionalities are also available. These functionalities are not presented in the paper. They concern the management of the users of the solution, the creation of specialized viewpoints for each type of user requirements, the dynamic definition of "business rules" in order to configure the behavior of the different agents and hence, to suggest user mobility decisions.

This needs to be put in parallel with the three constraints related to the key management broadcasting mechanism related to the smart monitoring platform architecture have been defined by Bailey et al., 2003 [7] and need to be considered along the modelling of the policies: (1) the computational capacity limit, which may be represented as an artefact of a type data object at the application layer of the MTU, (2) the low data transmission rate which is also a concept related to the MTU by means of a data object, and (3) the real-time processing that needs to be consider to prevent data processing delay and which may be represented as a data object from the RTUs structures.

The definition and the exploitation of the proposed augmented OCTOPUS framework in the mobility area has demonstrate to what extend the solution offers flexibility and usability to the business administrators. Indeed, most of the manipulations (e.g., traffic decisions, road optimization, informed communication, etc.) performed by the platform operators has been realized more intuitively and with more accuracy than with previous version of the frameworks.

V. RELATED WORKS

Literatures explain methodologies to model Multi-Agent System (MAS) [18] and their environments as a one layer model and give complete solutions or frameworks. Gaia [8] is a framework for the development of agent architectures based on a lifecycle approach. AUML (http://www.auml.org), and MAS-ML [9] are extensions of the UML language for the modelling of MAS but do no longer exist following the release by the OMG of UML 2.0 supporting MAS. Prometheus defines a metamodel of the application layer and allows generating organizational diagrams, roles diagrams, classes' diagrams, sequences diagrams and so forth.

The Prometheus approach permits hence to generate codes but does not provide links between diagrams and therefore makes it difficult to use for alignment purposes or with other languages (e.g., MOF, DSML4MAS [10]). CARBA provides a dynamic architecture for MAS similar to the middleware CORBA based on the role played by the agent. Globally, we observe that these solutions aim at modelling the application layer of MAS [11]. CARBA goes one step further introduces the concept of Interface and Service. This approach is closed to the solution based on *ArchiMate*® that we design in our proposal but offers less modelling features. As we have notice that agent systems are organized in a way close to the enterprises system, our proposal analyses how an enterprise architecture model may be slightly reworked and adapted for MAS. Therefore, we exploit *ArchiMate*® which has the following advantages to be supported by The Open Group. It has a large community and proposes a uniform structure to model enterprise architecture. Another advantage of *ArchiMate*® is that it uses referenced existing modelling languages like UML.

As a conclusion of the related work, we may consider that our approach may be used in parallel to existing solutions while, in the same time, complete their added value in a set of business driven dimensions like the visualization of the system or the elaboration of integrated and self-contain two types of policies. The evolution of our approach may also be regarded following the performance generated at the metric level. Indeed, contrarily to solutions presented through the state of the art, our proposal fit fully with the measurement theory requirement and, hence, may be more pragmatically devoted to performance based design of critical and highly sensitive infrastructures.

VI. CONCLUSIONS AND FUTURE WORKS

Monitoring systems are important solutions to secure critical infrastructures against traditional and cyber-attacks threats. Those systems need to be accurately managed and protected in terms of interconnection, homogeneity and real time reaction. Therefore, the paper proposes an integrated approach for modelling the monitoring architecture based on the enterprise architecture modelling language and more specially ArchiMate® which has been particularly tailored for smart monitoring systems.

Based on a dedicated metamodel, the paper has demonstrated how technical, application and organization policies could be designed and metamodeled, especially regarding the policy management for interconnected monitoring systems for two of its functions. All along the modelling of the platform model and the definition of the policies according to these models, we have illustrated the theory with a business case study related to the petroleum supply chain, and more specially the specific functions of crude oil supply and crude oil storage and distribution.

REFERENCES

[1] L. Briesemeister, S. Cheung, U. Lindqvist, and A. Valdes, "Detection, correlation, and visualization of attacks against critical infrastructure systems," In Privacy Security and Trust (PST).

[2] C. Feltus and D. Khadraoui,."Designing security policies for complex SCADA systems management and protection," International Journal of Information Technology and Management, 15(4), pp. 313-332.

[3] C. Feltus, M. Ouedraogo, and D. Khadraoui, "Towards cyber-security protection of critical infrastructures by generating security policy for SCADA systems," in Information and Communication Technologies for Disaster Management (ICT-DM), 2014. IEEE.

[4] G. Neumann and M. Strembeck, "A scenario-driven role engineering process for functional RBAC roles," In Proceedings of the seventh ACM symposium on Access control models and technologies, 2002, pp. 33-42, ACM.

[5] C. Feltus and M. Petit, "Building a responsibility model including accountability, capability and commitment," in Availability, Reliability and Security, 2009. ARES'09. International Conference on, pp. 412-419. IEEE, 2009

[6] G. Beydoun, C. Gonzalez-Perez, G. Low, and B. Henderson-Sellers, "Synthesis of a generic MAS metamodel". In ACM SIGSOFT Software Engineering Notes, 30(4), 2005, pp. 1-5.

[7] D. Bailey and E. Wright, "Practical SCADA for industry". Elsevier, 2003, Newnes, 288 pages.

[8] L. Cernuzzi, T. Juan, L. Sterling, and F. Zambonelli, "The gaia methodology. In Methodologies and Software Engineering for Agent Systems", 2004, pp. 69-88.

[9] V. T. da Silva, R. Choren, C. J. De Lucena, "A UML based approach for modeling and implementing multi-agent systems," in Proceedings of the Third International Joint Conference on Autonomous Agents and Multiagent Systems-Volume 2, 2004, pp. 914-921. IEEE Computer Society.

[10] S. Warwas, C. and Hahn, C, "The DSML4MAS development environment," in Proceedings of The 8th International Conference on Autonomous Agents and Multiagent Systems-Volume 2, 2009.

[11] J. J. Gomez-Sanz, J. Pavon, and F. Garijo, "Metamodels for building multi-component systems," Proceedings of ACM symposium on Applied computing. ACM, New York, NY, USA,2002 pp. 37-41.

[12] C. Feltus, M. Petit, and E. Dubois, "Strengthening employee's responsibility to enhance governance of IT: COBIT RACI chart case study". In Proceedings of the first ACM workshop on Information security governance, 2009, pp. 23-32. ACM

[13] J. Zachman, "The zachman framework for enterprise architecture". Zachman International, 2002.

[14] C. Feltus, D. Khadraoui, B. de Rémont, and A. Rifaut, "Business Gouvernance based Policy regulation for Security Incident Response," In IEEE GIIS 2007 Global Infrastructure Symposium, Vol. 6, 2007.

[15] G. Guemkam, C. Feltus, P. Schmitt, C. Bonhomme, D. Khadraoui, and Z. Guessoum, "Reputation based dynamic responsibility to agent assignement for critical infrastructure, " in Proceedings of the IEEE/WIC/ACM International Conferences on Web Intelligence and Intelligent Agent Technology-Volume 02, 2011, pp. 272-275.

[16] C. Feltus, M. Petit, and E. Dubois, "ReMoLa: Responsibility model language to align access rights with business process requirements, " in Research Challenges in Information Science (RCIS), 2011.

[17] A. Rifaut and C. Feltus, "Improving Operational Risk Management Systems by Formalizing the Basel II Regulation with Goal Models and the ISO/IEC 15504 Approach", in ReMo2V, 2006.

[18] B. Gâteau, D. Khadraoui, and C. Feltus, "Multi-agents system service based platform in telecommunication security incident reaction," in Information Infrastructure Symposium, 2009, pp. 1-6.

[19] http://pubs.opengroup.org/architecture/archimate2-doc/ (last access: February 2017)

OptPLAN: Improving the Optimal Plan Calculation on Relational Databases

Luís Fernando Orleans*, Miguel Mendes de Brito†, Egberto Caetano Araújo da Silva‡
*Departamento de Ciência da Computação
Instituto Multidisciplinar - UFRRJ, Rio de Janeiro, Brazil
†Email: lforleans@ufrrj.br, mmdebrito@ufrrj.br, egbertocaetano@ufrrj.br

***Abstract*—In order to find the best execution plan for an SQL query, a DBMS uses information regarding the cost of disk operations, notably the cost of a sequential page reading (seq_page_cost or just *spc*) and the cost of random pages reading (random_page_cost or just *rpc*). Such information is predefined by DBMS vendors and are rarely changed - although it can cause inaccuracies in the optimization phase. This paper lists some typical scenarios where disk access costs miscalculations can lead to sub-optimal query plans and presents the OptPLAN, a tool for the PostgreSQL DBMS that calculates the correct relationship between *spc* and *rpc* and automatically set their values at the configuration properties. In our experiments, we obtained up to 69% of query speed up after *spc* and *rpc* adjustment.**

***Keywords*—OptPlan; Query Optimization; Autonomous RDBMS.**

I. INTRODUCTION

Because Relational Database Management Systems (RDBMS) provide a convenient and secure way to store and retrieve data, they became crucial components for many modern systems [1]. Also, RDBMS are a result of decades of joint efforts from both scientific and industry research teams [2], which provides a solid and well-formed theory behind them.

The Structured Query Language (SQL) is the most used tool for manipulating data stored by RDBMS [3]. Commands written in SQL are first parsed and validated. If no errors are found, the commands are then translated to an internal logical tree representation of the query, denoted as *execution plan* or just *plan*.

Several plans can be derived from a single SQL statement [3], each using different strategies and algorithms for performing relational operations, e.g., a joint operation could be represented using a Nested Loop Join algorithm in one tree and using a Hash Join in another tree. While the algorithm choosing process does not impact on query's semantics, it does directly impact on query's *cost*, i.e., the amount of disk blocks the RDBMS will transfer from/to memory during query execution.

Finding the cheapest tree is not a trivial task – in fact, [4] claims this problem is NP-complete. Each RDBMS has one or more optimization algorithms implemented for this specific problem and they vary greatly from one vendor to another. The open-source RDBMS PostgreSQL, for instance, uses a genetic query optimization approach. In addition, PostgreSQL provides a classic optimization engine based on Dynamic Programming [5]. Regardless the optimization strategy, the RDBMS server hardware configuration influences the search for the optimal plan. For instance, the same SQL statement might result in different plans depending where data is stored: in a fast SSD or in a slow HDD. Ignoring this hardware dependency can result in sub-optimal execution plans due to inefficient optimizations phases which, in turn, can result in poor query performance.

This paper presents OptPLAN, a tool that calculates both sequential and random disk read costs for a PostgreSQL RDBMS host and set those values on the configurations file, providing the optimization algorithm correct costs which results in better optimal plan search. Our results show that all example queries presented reduced costs after OptPLAN adjust the configurations file when compared to default values provided by RDBMS vendor.

The remainder of this paper is as following: Section II describes a few related works we found most relevant, while Section III reviews the steps taken by a query executor engine from a typical RDBMS. Our tool OptPLAN is defined in Section IV, the experiments we conducted along with their results are described in Section V. Finally, Section VI lists our conclusions and possible future works.

II. RELATED WORK

The research presented in [6] discusses self-adaptable database systems based on Microsoft's AutoAdmin project. That work focuses primarily on the design of automatized databases. Other approaches for query optimization are described in [7], where the authors describe a log inspection tool, which provides several statistics for the database administrator (DBA). Those statistics are collected through Machine Learning techniques. Also using changes in the query optimizer, the work on [8] explains ORACLE 10g's capability of optimize SQL queries automatically. Such optimization is possible due to longer than usual SQL statement analysis, validating statistics used on the search for the optimal plan. Finally, Chaudhuri et al. [9] describe the advances made on self-adjustment on Microsoft's SQL Server RDBMS, which is achieved through automatic indexes creation and more efficient memory management and dynamic resource allocation approaches.

All those works do not pursuit finding the correct values for sequential and random page disks reads, neither do they have an open implementation that can be used on more than one DBMS. Our work exploits hardware-related factors from the DBMS host, enhancing the searching for the optimal plan for the SQL queries without the need of any modifications at the DBMS core.

III. Query Processing

Data is typically manipulated on a RDBMS through a series of SQL statements issued by a user or a system. Upon its arrival, each SQL statement is checked for syntax correctness and, whether no errors are found, an internal representation (using a tree format) of the statement is created. Each node of the tree represents a Logic Relational Operator (LGO) that can have several implementations, one for each specific scenario. For instance, a Join LGO can be implemented physically as Nested Loop Join (NLJ), Hash Join (HJ) or Sort-Merge Join (SMJ). The decision of which implementation should be picked is responsibility of the Query Optimizer, that searches for the cheapest execution plan that physically represents the tree. After the optimal plan is found, it gets executed by the Query Executor Engine (Figure 1).

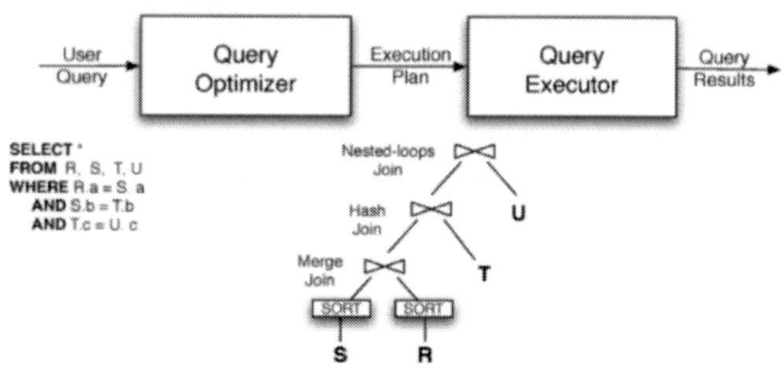

Fig. 1: Query Execution [3]

Internally, the most widespread implementation of an execution plan is through the Iterator pattern, described in [10]. Also, each LGO includes an annotation regarding which physical implementation shall be used.

A. *Query Optimization*

A typical query optimizer relies on host hardware information and relations statistics to find the cheapest execution plan for an SQL statement. RDBMSs often store those metadata within an internal structure called *catalog*. It is a common practice to store information about *column values*, such as histograms, ordering, among others. When combined with some hardware information, such as sequential page read cost (SPC), random page read cost (RPC), data transfer rate, etc. The Query Optimizer can correctly determine which physical relational operator should be used in order to find the cheapest plan. It is important to notice that hardware information are often represented as normalized cost values instead of absolute values, i.e., the amount of time for the hardware to process a task.

As an example, consider the following database schema:

```
CLIENT(id_client, name, email, gender,
age, id_address);
ADDRESS(id_address, street_name, number,
borough, city, state, zip);
```

Consider there is an B-Tree index on column 'Address.city'. The following SQL statement is used to retrieve the names of all clients that live in the city of 'Nova Iguaçu':

```
SELECT C.name
FROM CLIENT C, ADDRESS A
WHERE C.id_address = A.id_address
AND A.city = "Nova Iguacu";
```

One of the possible plans that represents the SQL statement in Section III-A is shown in Figure 2(a). Now consider the Figure 2(b) is the histogram that counts how many clients live on each city.

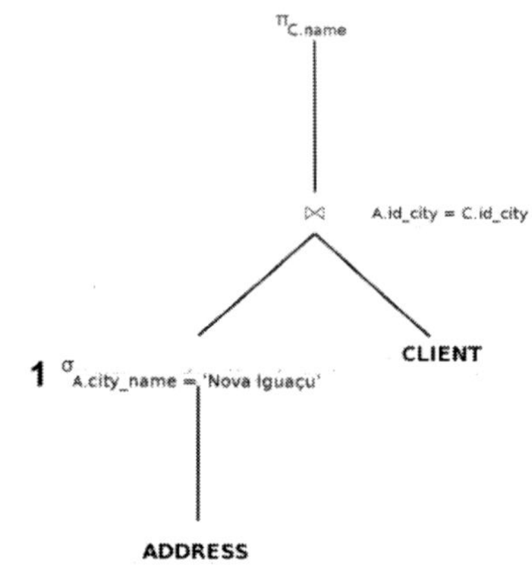

(a) Execution Query Plan.

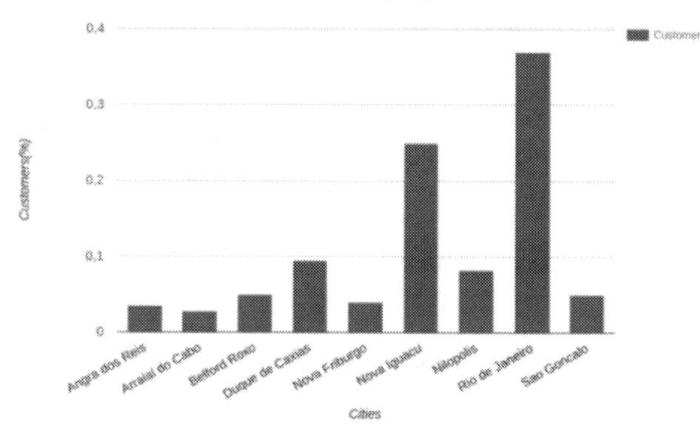

(b) Clients distribution among cities.

Fig. 2: Information used by the Query Optimizer.

Finally, consider that there are 1000 tuples in each table.

The cost for reading a whole table – sequentially or randomly – can be expressed by:

$$C = (blc * cl) + (t * cc), \quad (1)$$

where C is the total cost; blc is the total number of disk blocks where tuples are stored; cl is the cost for a block read. The read can be performed sequentially (cl_s) or randomly (cl_r); t is total tuples of a relation; and cc is the CPU cost for processing each tuple [11]. It is worth noting cl_s, cl_r and cc are hardware related parameters.

For the first example, let us assume the following values for the variables (the variable blc has the same value for both tables):

$$cl_s = 1; cl_r = 4; blc = 10. \tag{2}$$

Worth noting that those are default values for clean PostgreSQL installations.

When the process of selecting all Address tuples that have city values equal to 'Nova Iguaçu' (point 1 at 2(a)) is evaluated, both sequential ($C_{Sequential}$) and random (C_{Random}) reads are considered. The cost for $C_{Sequential}$ is computed as follows:

$$C_{Sequential} = (blc * cl_s) + (t * cc) \tag{3}$$

$$C_{Sequential} = (10 * 1) + (1000 * 0.01) = 20 \tag{4}$$

On the other hand, to compute the cost for C_{Random}, the Query Optimizer can use the histogram depicted in Figure 2(b) to retrieve an estimate of how many tuples will be read, as random reads use indexes to perform direct access to the data. As the frequency of Address tuples having city equals to 'Nova Iguaçu' is 0.25, hence $f_{NovaIguaçu} = 0,25$. So, $t = 1000 * 0,25 = 250$ and the expression is as follows:

$$C_{Random} = (blc * cl_r) + (t * cc) \tag{5}$$

$$C_{Random} = (10 * 4) + (250 * 0.01) = 42.5 \tag{6}$$

which is 4 times greater than $C_{Sequential}$. Hence, the Optimizer will prefer to perform a table scan instead of random reads using the index.

However, let us consider that cl_r variable value is 1.5, i.e. a random read is one and a half times slower than a sequential read. Hence:

$$C_{Random} = (10 * 1.5) + (250 * 0.01) = 17.5 \tag{7}$$

and the Optimizer now should prefer using the index instead of a full table scan to perform the query! It becomes clear that inaccuracies on both SPC and RPC values can cause the Query Optimizer to choose a suboptimal execution plan for any SQL statement.

B. PostgreSQL Hardware Specific Variables

Among PostgreSQL configuration files, *postgresql.conf* is the one that holds default values for SPC (seq_page_cost) and RPC (random_page_cost) [5]. The first parameter refers to reading a single page from disk sequentially and its value is normalized to 1. On the other hand, the second parameter refers to randomly reading a single page from disk and its value defaults to 4 – which means that RPC is 4 times greater than SPC by default. As those are normalized values, increasing SPC and RPC values proportionally will not change the execution plan.

However, as PostgreSQL can be used on a plethora of different platforms, those variables should be adjusted to reflect the host's hardware. Whether the PostgreSQL server is attached to a Storage Area Network or using a conventional HDD, those relative values will vary from one configuration to another. In the next section, we present OptPLAN, a tool that computes the correct values for both SPC and RPC and sets them in the configuration file.

IV. OptPLAN

We developed a tool named OptPLAN that executes a series of tests on the hardware where the PostgreSQL is being installed and determines the up-to-date relative values for SPC and RPC, setting those values on *postgresql.conf* file. The Query Optimizer will then use correct values when searching for optimal plans, avoiding query slow down. In addition, OptPLAN is invoked periodically to detect hardware changes.

A. Implementation

OptPLAN was written in C, taking advantage of low-level capabilities provided by the Operating System for that language. As the Linux Kernel is also written in C, its API opens room for using disk read functions with very little overhead [12]. Hence, OptPLAN creates two test files (one for sequential reads and the other for random reads) with the same number of pages but with different contents, a strategy planned to avoid the Operating System caching mechanism. Those files are split in contiguous blocks with 512 bytes each – which are the same size of a standard disk page on Ext4, the file system used in our experiments. Nevertheless sequential reads or random reads are in use, the system reads one page at a time.

The second step in OptPLAN is to read those files. The sequential scan is performed first, by positioning the read pointer to the file beginning, i.e., to the first byte of the file. Sequential read operations are performed within a loop and the system halts when all pages were read.

Random read tests are more complex, because the pointer should not read contiguous pages. To simulate this behaviour, OptPLAN uses a array with the same number of positions that the number of pages kept in the file. That array is then shuffled and is seen as holding the positions to where the pointer should be moved. After the shuffle process is over, the array is scanned sequentially and, for each iteration, the page corresponding to the value kept on the current position is read. This process successfully simulates a table scan using a complete index transverse.

V. Experiments

This section explains how the experiments were conducted, their setup and the obtained results.

A. Setup

We conducted the experiments on 3 different hardware configurations, denoted here as Maq1, Maq2 and Maq 3 (All computers were running the Ubuntu Linux OS, version 14.04 LTS):

TABLE I: TEST RESULTS OF OPTPLAN READS.

File \Server	Maq1	Maq2	Maq3
102.4MB	1.359	1.332	1.334
204.8MB	1.419	1.417	1.551
307.2MB	1.423	1.429	1.556
409.4MB	1.461	1.467	1.650
512MB	1.491	1.483	1.605
1024MB	1.540	1.522	1.707
Mean	1.449	1.441	1.567

- Maq 1: a notebook with an Intel Core i7 Quad Core Mobile Processor i7-4700MQ, clocked at 2.40GHz 6MB of cache, 8GB RAM DDR3 (1600MHz) and with a 120GB Samsung SSD 120GB;
- Maq 2: a desktop with AMD Phenom(tm) II X4 955 Quad Core with 512KB cache, 4GB RAM and a 1TB Seagate HDD 7200 RPM;
- Maq 3: a desktop with an Intel Core i5 Dual-Core Processor 4210U clocked at 1.7GHz, 3MB cache, 4GB RAM DDR (1600MHz) and a 500GB HD Seagte 5400 RPM.

Each server was running a stable version of PostgreSQL 9.4 and populated with the sample database DVD Rental [13].

We used three SQL statements on our experiments, each one with different complexity. Query Q1 returns all clients that rented any movies starring the actor with name Nick Stallone (a simple query example). On the other hand, Query Q2 retrieves the tuples containing clients that never rented any movies where the actor Nick Stallone starred (A subquery example). Finally, Query Q3 returns the names of those clients that rented all movies where actor Nick Stallone starred (a complex DIVIDE example). All SQL statements were analyzed using the PostgreSQL's EXPLAIN command, which prints the chosen execution plan calculated by the RDBMS along with the best and worst costs.

In order to detect the correct values for SPC and RPC, we conducted a series of experiments on each hardware configuration. The size of files used on our experiments varied from 102.4MB to 1024MB. Those values correspond to the number of pages in each file: the 102.4MB file has a total of 200,000 512 bytes pages. Each file was read 5 times, using both sequential and random reads strategies. At the end, the we calculated the median for each round to avoid anomalies on the final result. Finally, the mean of the values obtained using all files were used on *postgresql.conf* to replace the default values of seq_page_cost and random_page_cost.

B. Results

The results of our experiments comparing the execution plans generated using PostgreSQL default values for SPC and RPC against those values corrected by OptPLAN appear on the next graphics and table below. Table I describes the ratio between random and sequential reads median values in each server. We used 6 different files to simulate accessing tables of different sizes. The mean is calculated and the updated *random_page_cost* value is set at *postgresql.conf*.

Figure 3 shows the results we obtained for the best case for Q1. Note that the costs for executing the query after updating RPC value is lower than the default in all hardware configurations. Also, note that for different hardware configurations, OptPLAN calculated different RPC values, which leads to different costs. That is not true whether the default value of RPC is used, where all hardware configurations calculated the same execution plan.

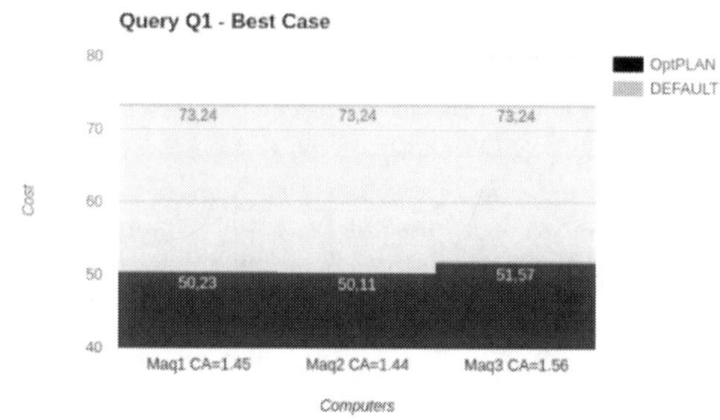

Fig. 3: Q1 - Best case

Figure 4 shows the cost values for the worst cases, where updated configurations have up to 15.3% of cost drop.

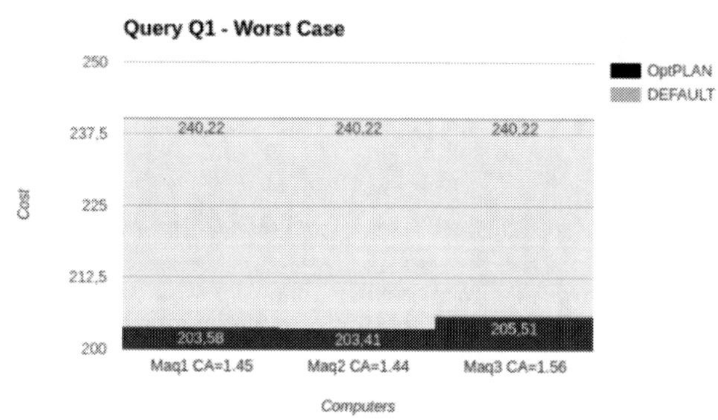

Fig. 4: Q1 - Worst case

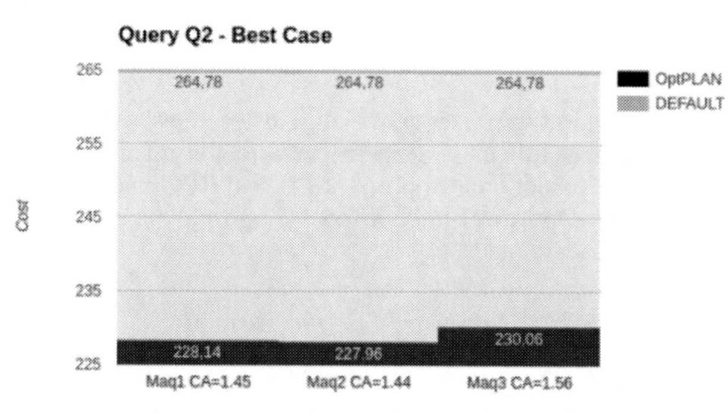

Fig. 5: Q2 - Best case

Figure 5 compares the costs for executing Q2 in the best case. Again, the scenarios where OptPLAN were used obtained better results – up to 13.9% of cost drop. Figure 6 compares

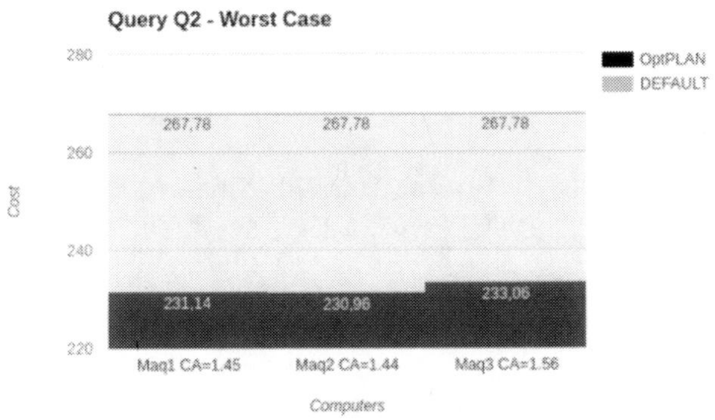

Fig. 6: Q2 - Worst case

the costs for the worst case, where OptPLAN caused a drop of up to 13.75% on the costs.

Finally, Figure 7 compares the results for the best cases on each server when executing Q3. Once again, OptPLAN utitlization resulted on better, (up to 33.4%) cheaper plans. The worst cases of Q3 plans are compared in Figure 8 and the modified RPC values resulted in up to 69% of cost drop.

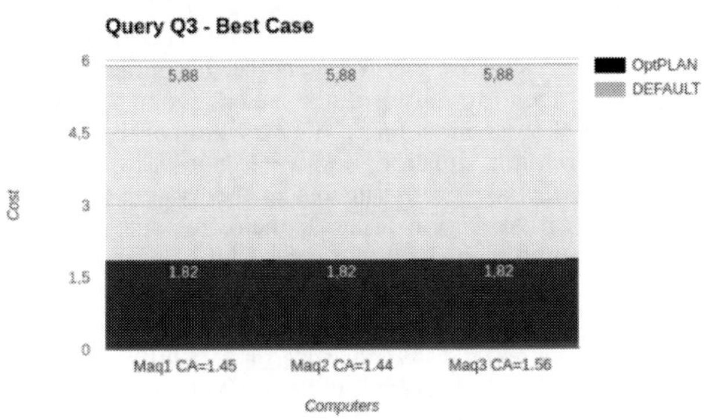

Fig. 7: Q3 - Best case

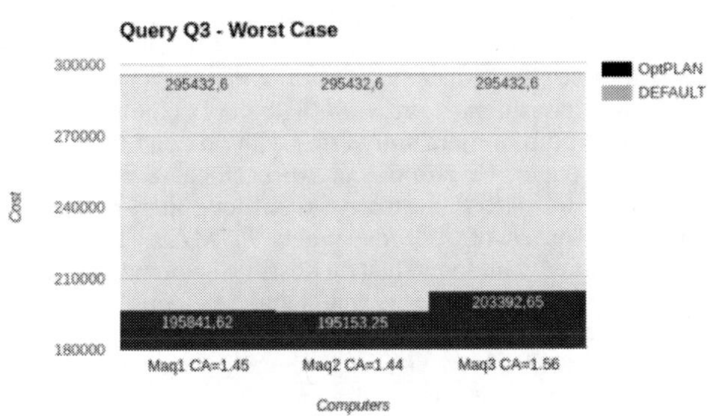

Fig. 8: Q3 - Worst case

VI. Conclusions and Future Works

In this paper, we discussed how the search for the best execution plan, i.e., the optimization of an SQL statement is affected by the hardware configurations where the RDBMS is deployed, as cost-based Query Optimizers highly depends on the capacity of that hardware to transfer data from disk to memory sequentially and randomly, execute in-memory comparisons, etc.. We focused our discussion on the PostgreSQL RDBMS due to its open source nature.

In that direction, we developed a tool called OptPLAN, that computes the speed that data is read from disk both sequentially and randomly – permitting to compute their normalized values that are used by PostgreSQL, seq_page_cost (SPC) and random_page_cost (RPC). Afterwards, we compared the costs of three SQL queries using both default and rectified SPC and RPC values in three RBDMS servers using different hardware configurations. Our results showed a performance gain of up to 69% and confirmed that is possible to obtain cheaper costs for SQL queries only by adjusting hardware related parameters.

As future works, we intend to implement a hybrid read approach, where sequential reads and random reads are performed in the same OptPLAN run. The main advantage of this combined method would be representing a more real behaviour of disk access. Also, we plan to better examine the effect of cache mechanisms on file access patterns and their impacts on OptPLAN. Finally, as our tool is tightly coupled to some functions provided by the Kernel of the Linux Operating System, we are currently evaluating the possibility to provide alternate OptPLAN implementations that work with MacOS and Windows.

References

[1] R. Elmasri and S. B. Navathe, *Fundamentals of Database Systems*, 7th ed. Pearson, 6 2015.

[2] J. M. Hellerstein, M. Stonebraker, and J. Hamilton, *Architecture of a database system*. Now Publishers Inc, 2007.

[3] A. Deshpande, Z. Ives, and V. Raman, "Adaptive query processing," *Found. Trends databases*, vol. 1, no. 1, pp. 1–140, Jan. 2007. [Online]. Available: http://dx.doi.org/10.1561/1900000001

[4] Y. E. Ioannidis, "Query optimization," *ACM Comput. Surv.*, vol. 28, no. 1, pp. 121–123, Mar. 1996. [Online]. Available: http://doi.acm.org/10.1145/234313.234367

[5] PostgreSQL, "Query planning - planner cost constants," http://www.postgresql.org/docs/9.3/static/runtime-config-query.html, 2016, [Online; acessado em 22 de Maio de 2016].

[6] S. Chaudhuri and V. Narasayya, "Self-tuning database systems: a decade of progress," in *Proceedings of the 33rd international conference on Very large data bases*. VLDB Endowment, 2007, pp. 3–14.

[7] B. Mozafari, C. Curino, and S. Madden, "Dbseer: Resource and performance prediction for building a next generation database cloud." in *CIDR*, 2013.

[8] B. Dageville, D. Das, K. Dias, K. Yagoub, M. Zait, and M. Ziauddin, "Automatic sql tuning in oracle 10g," in *Proceedings of the Thirtieth international conference on Very large data bases-Volume 30*. VLDB Endowment, 2004, pp. 1098–1109.

[9] S. Chaudhuri, E. Christensen, G. Graefe, V. R. Narasayya, and M. J. Zwilling, "Self-tuning technology in microsoft sql server," *IEEE Data Eng. Bull.*, vol. 22, no. 2, pp. 20–26, 1999.

[10] G. Graefe, "Query evaluation techniques for large databases," *ACM Computing Surveys (CSUR)*, vol. 25, no. 2, pp. 73–169, 1993.

[11] PostgreSQL, "Using explain," http://www.postgresql.org/docs/9.3/static/using-explain.html, 2016, [Online; Accessed: 2016-05-22].

[12] R. Love, *Linux System Programming: Talking Directly to the Kernel and C Library*, 2nd ed. O'Reilly Media, 6 2013.

[13] "Dvd rental database," http://www.postgresqltutorial.com/postgresql-sample-database/, 2016, [Online; Accessed: 2016-05-22].

Detection of Runtime Normative Conflict based on Execution Scenarios

Mairon Belchior
Computer Science Department
Fluminense Federal University
Niteroi - RJ, Brazil
email: mbelchior@ic.uff.br

Viviane Torres da Silva
IBM Research (on leave from UFF)
Rio de Janeiro - RJ, Brazil
email: vivianet@br.ibm.com

***Abstract* — Norms in multi-agent systems are used as a mechanism to regulate the behavior of autonomous and heterogeneous agents and to maintain the social order of the society of agents. Norms describe actions that must be performed, actions that can be performed and actions that cannot be performed by a given entity in a certain situation. One of the challenges in designing and managing systems governed by norms is that they can conflict with another. Two norms are in conflict when the fulfillment of one causes the violation of the other. When that happens, whatever the agent does or refrains from doing will lead to a social constraint being broken. Several researches have proposed mechanisms to detect conflicts between norms. However, there is a kind of normative conflict not investigated yet in the design phase, here called runtime conflicts, that can only be detected if we know information about the runtime execution of the system. This paper presents an approach based on execution scenarios to detect normative conflicts that depends on execution order of runtime events in multi-agent systems. The designer are able to provide examples of execution scenarios and evaluate the conflicts that may arise if those scenarios would be executed in the system. The conflict verification proposed in this paper occurs in the design phase.**

Keywords-Norms; Normative Conflict; Multi-agent Systems; OWL; SWRL.

I. Introduction

Norms have been used in open multi-agent systems (MAS) as a mechanism to regulate the behavior of autonomous and heterogeneous agents without directly interfering with their autonomy. They are system-level constraints that are independent from the implementation of specific agents and represent the ideals of behavior of these agents [1]. They represent a way for agents to understand their responsibilities and the responsibilities of the others. Norms define what is permitted, prohibited and obligatory. Norm's specification relates entities, the actions that they execute, and the period during while the actions are being regulated [4].

An important issue that must be considered while specifying the norms is the conflicts that may arise between them. Due to the numeral norms that may be necessary to govern a normative MAS, the normative conflict might not be immediately obvious to the system designer. Two norms are in conflict when the fulfillment of one causes the violation of the other, and vice-versa. In other words, the agent will be in a position in which whatever it does (or refrains from doing) will lead to a social constraint being broken [14]. For example, there is a conflict when a norm prohibits an agent from performing a particular action and another that requires the same agent to perform the same action at the same period of time.

There are many approaches in the literature that deal with conflicts between norms in MAS. However, there is another kind of normative conflict not investigated yet in the design phase that can only be detected when we know information about the runtime execution of the system. We will call this kind of conflict as *runtime conflict*. This kind of conflict depends on events that only happen at runtime. For example, let us suppose that *N1* is a norm that prohibits an agent *Ag* from performing the action *Ac* after the execution of action *X*. Moreover, suppose that *N2* is another norm that obligates the same agent to perform the same action before the execution of another action *Y*. The execution of the actions *X* and *Y* are runtime situations and we do not know when they will be performed by the agents in the system. However, analyzing the execution order of them, we can say that if event *Y* would happen first compared to event *X*, we could assert that *N1* and *N2* will be not in conflict. Otherwise, there will be a conflict between *N1* and *N2*. Therefore, if we have information about the time of when the conditions that make the norms active will happen in the system, i.e., information about the moment the events will occur in the systems, it would be possible to detect the existence of the conflict. In this paper, we defined six types of conditions that define the activation period of a norm, which are (i) the execution of an action by an agent, (ii) a fact that become true for an agent, (iii) the fulfillment or (iv) violation of a norm and (v) the activation or (vi) deactivation of a norm. The proposed approach considers norms with before condition, after condition, both of them and norms with no condition.

In this paper, we propose an approach based on execution scenarios to detect normative conflicts that depend on execution order of runtime events in MAS. The system designer may want to evaluate a possible sequence of actions in the system and know if that sequence would cause any normative conflict. The conflict detection approach identifies normative conflicts in case such scenario would be executed in the system. The proposed approach uses Semantic Web technologies, such as, Semantic Web Rule Language (SWRL) rules, OWL DL and SPARQL query language. The Web Ontology Language (OWL) is an expressive knowledge representation language endorsed by the World Wide Web

Consortium (W3C). OWL DL is a sublanguage of OWL that is based on Description Logic (DL), a decidable fragment of the first-order logic [9]. The SWRL is a Horn clause rules extension to OWL [6]. One of the most powerful features of SWRL is its support for built-ins functions to perform operations for comparisons, mathematical, strings, date, and others.

This paper is organized as follows. Section II presents the related work. Section III formalizes the ontology-based norm definition adopted in this paper and, in Section IV, the execution scenario ontology are presented. Section V describes the normative conflict detection approach and gives an example of detection of this kind of conflict. The conclusions and future works are presented in Section VI.

II. Related Work

Several researchers have investigated mechanisms to detect normative conflicts in multi-agent systems. Some of them deals with the identification of direct conflicts, such as in [3][8][12][13]. Direct conflict involves two norms that are associated with the same entity, regulate the same behavior, have contradictory deontic concepts, and are defined in the same context. The detection of this conflict can be done by simply comparing the norm elements (i.e., entity, behavior, context of the norm) in order to check if they apply to the same elements. There are other mechanisms that also detect indirect conflicts, such as in [1][2][7][10][11]. Indirect conflict involves two norms whose elements are not the same but are related. The detection of indirect conflicts can be done only when the relationships among elements of the norms are identified. However, to the best of our knowledge, none of them is able to detect in the design phase normative conflicts that may occur depending on execution order of runtime events.

Lam et al. [7] proposed an approach that uses SWRL and OWL DL to represent norm-governed organizations, including roles and their relationship and various kinds of normative notions, such as permissions, prohibitions, obligations, power and norm violation detection. A conditional norm with deadlines was specified where the condition is only a *xsd:dateTime* associated with either *before* or *after* object properties. However, the authors did not show how to detect a conflict between norms with conditions. Their approach does not allowed a norm to have a relationship with both *before* and *after* properties. Moreover, runtime conditions, such as those described in this paper are not supported. Their approach can only detect direct and indirect conflicts.

Sensoy et al. [11] developed a framework for representing OWL-based policies for distributed agent-based systems called OWL-POLAR. The activation and expiration conditions of a norm in OWL-POLAR are represented by a conjunctive semantic formula, which are facts in the knowledge base. However, the authors did not take into account before and after conditions and their approach cannot detect normative conflicts that may occur in runtime.

Uszok et al. [12] developed a policy framework called KAoS that uses OWL ontology-based representation and reasoning to specify, deconflict, and enforce policies. KAoS supports two main types of norms: (positive and negative) authorization and (positive and negative) obligation. However, KAoS does not provide mechanisms to represent deactivation condition of a norm. Also, before and after conditions are not supported and their framework only detects direct conflicts.

III. Norm Definition

The main classes represented in the norm ontology are *Norm*, *Context*, *DeonticConcept*, *Entity*, *Action*, *Condition*, *FulfillmentStatus* and *ActivationStatus*. The class *Norm* represents a norm definition used as a mechanism to regulate the behavior of agents in MAS and is defined in DL in Figure 1, as follows.

```
Norm ≡ ∀ hasContext.Context ⊓
  =1 hasDeonticConcept.DeonticConcept ⊓
  =1 hasEntity.Entity ⊓
  =1 hasAction.Action ⊓
  ≤1 hasBefore.Condition ⊓
  ≤1 hasAfter.Condition ⊓
  =1 hasActivationStatus.ActivationStatus ⊓
  =1 hasFulfillmentStatus.FulfillmentStatus ⊓
  ∀ hasConflict.Norm
```

Figure 1. Definition of the *Norm* class

According to the definition above, a norm can be related to instances of the classes *Context*, *DeonticConcept*, *Entity*, *Action*, *ActivationStatus* and *FulfillmentStatus* through the object properties *hasContext*, *hasDeonticConcept*, *hasEntity*, *hasAction*, *hasActivationStatus* and *hasFulfillmentStatus*, respectively. It also can be connected to the *Condition* class via two object properties: *hasBefore* and *hasAfter*. Moreover, a norm can have a relationship to order instances of norm by using the *hasConflict* property. The symbol "=" stands for cardinality restriction and "≤" represents the maximum cardinality restriction. The first one specifies the *exact* number of relationships that an individual must participate in for a given property, while the second specifies the *maximum* number of relationships that an individual can participate in for a given property. The symbol "∀" represents universal restriction. It constrains the relationship along a given property to individuals that are members of a specific class. It does not specify the existence of a relationship, i.e., the universal restriction also describes the individuals that do not participate in any relationship.

The class *Context* determines the application area of a norm. Norms can be defined usually in two different contexts: *Environment* and *Organization* contexts. They are defined in the norm ontology as subclasses of the *Context* class, as shown in Figure 2.

```
Organization ⊑ Context
Environment ⊑ Context
```

Figure 2. Subclasses of Context

The class *DeonticConcept* describes behavior restrictions for agents in the form of obligations, permissions and prohibitions. Thus, the individuals *Obligation*, *Permission* and *Prohibition* were introduced in the norm ontology, and the class *DeonticConcept* was defined as the enumeration of its members using Nominals in DL, as shown in Figure 3.

```
DeonticConcept ≡
  {Obligation,Permission,Prohibition}
```

Figure 3. Definition of the *DeonticConcept* class

The *Entity* class describes the entities whose behavior is being controlled by a norm. An entity is the subject of a norm-controlled action. It has a relationship with a context, via the *actsIn* object property, to determine in which context an entity is acting. The entities represented in this paper are single agents. Instances of the *Entity* class can perform an action in the MAS. Thus, they can have a relationship along the object property *perfomAction* to individuals that are members of the *Action* class. An entity can also participate in a situation, instance of *Situation* class. A situation is one kind of activation condition that represents a fact in the knowledge base (e.g., an agent has a car, lives in New York or is graduated from a college). An agent can participate in zero, one or many situations by using the object property *participateIn*. Activation conditions will be explained latter in this section. The class *Entity* is defined in DL in Figure 4.

```
Entity ⊑ ∀ actsIn.Context ⊓
  ∀ perfomAction.Action ⊓
  ∀ participateIn.Situation
```

Figure 4. Definition of the *Entity* class

The behavior been controlled by the norm is defined by the *Action* class. An action can be performed by individuals that are members of the *Entity* class via *isPerformedBy* object property, which is the inverse property of the *perfomAction* property. The *Action* class is defined in Figure 5.

```
Action ⊑ ∀ isPerformedBy.Entity
```

Figure 5. Definition of the *Action* class

The class *Condition* determines the period during which a norm is active. A norm has a relationship with a condition via two object properties, namely, *hasBefore* and *hasAfter*, which are used to delimitate its activation period. For example, let *n1* and *n2* be two norms, and *n1* is defined to be activated *after* norm *n2* has been fulfilled. Thus, the fulfilment of *n2* is the condition of norm *n1* and the activation period of *n1* is whenever norm *n2* is fulfilled until +infinite.

A norm can have no relationship with any condition. When that happens, its activation period is since the beginning of the system's execution until +infinite, i.e., the norm is always active. There are six types of conditions defined in the norm ontology as subclasses of the *Condition* class. They are *ExecutionOfAction*, *ActivationOfNorm*, *DeactivationOfNorm*, *FulfillmentOfNorm*, *ViolationOfNorm* and *Situation*, and are defined in Figure 6.

```
ActivationOfNorm ⊑ Condition ⊓
    =1 hasRelatedNorm.Norm
DeactivationOfNorm ⊑ Condition ⊓
    =1 hasRelatedNorm.Norm
FulfillmentOfNorm ⊑ Condition ⊓
    =1 hasRelatedNorm.Norm
ViolationOfNorm ⊑ Condition ⊓
    =1 hasRelatedNorm.Norm
ExecutionOfAction ⊑ Condition ⊓
    =1 hasRelatedAction.Action ⊓
    =1 hasRelatedEntity.Entity
Situation ⊑ Condition
```

Figure 6. Definition of the six types of norm condition

Individuals that are members of any of the classes *ActivationOfNorm*, *DeactivationOfNorm*, *FulfillmentOfNorm* and *ViolationOfNorm* must specify a norm that is related to the condition through the object property *hasRelatedNorm*. The class *ExecutionOfAction* was defined as subclass of *Condition* that has exactly one relationship to *Action* and *Entity* classes through *hasRelatedAction* and *hasRelatedEntity* object properties, respectively. The *Situation* class is one type of condition that represents a fact in the knowledge base.

The class *ActivationStatus* represents the activation status of a norm and can be either *activated*, *deactivated* or *none*. When a norm is *activated*, it means the norm becomes active and must be somehow fulfilled. Once a norm is activated, it can be *deactivated* at some time and no action is required anymore. The *none* activation status means that the norm has not been neither *activated* nor *deactivated* yet. All instance of *Norm* are started in the system with *none* value for its activation status. This status is useful to let the agents know about the existences of the norms. The individuals *Activated*, *Deactivated* and *None* were introduced in the ontology, and the class *ActivationStatus* was defined as the enumeration of its members, as shown in Figure 7.

```
ActivationStatus ≡
    {Activated,Deactivated,None}
```

Figure 7. Definition of the *ActivationStatus* class

The class *FulfillmentStatus* describes the fulfillment status of a norm, which can be either *fulfilled*, *violated* or *unknown*. The *unknown* fulfillment status means that the norm has not been neither *fulfilled* nor *violated* yet. For example, let us suppose we have an activated obligation norm stating that a given action must be performed, but that action has not been execute yet. Hence, in that case, the fulfillment status is *unknown*. However, if that action is executed, the fulfillment status will become fulfilled. But, if that norm turns into deactivated and the action has not been executed yet, then the fulfillment status would be violated. All norms are started with *unknown* value for its fulfillment status. The individuals *Fulfilled*, *Violated* and *Unknown* were introduced in the ontology, and the class *FulfillmentStatus* was defined as the enumeration of its members, as shown in Figure 8.

```
FulfillmentStatus ≡
    {Fulfilled,Violated,Unknown}
```

Figure 8. Definition of the *FulfillmentStatus* class

A norm can have a relationship to individuals that are members of the *Norm* class by using the object property *hasConflict*, which represents a normative conflict between two instances of norms.

In order to classify the norms regarding their compliance, the *FulfilledObligationNorm*, *ViolatedObligationNorm*, *FulfilledProhibitionNorm*, *ViolatedProhibitionNorm* and *ViolatedPermissionNorm* classes were introduced in the norm ontology as subclasses of the *Norm* class (Figure 9).

```
FulfilledObligationNorm ⊑ Norm ⊓
    hasDeonticConcept.(Obligation) ⊓
    hasFulfillmentStatus.(Fulfilled)
ViolatedObligationNorm ⊑ Norm ⊓
    hasDeonticConcept.(Obligation) ⊓
    hasActivationStatus.(Deactivated) ⊓
    ¬ FulfilledObligationNorm
FulfilledProhibitionNorm ⊑ Norm ⊓
   hasDeonticConcept.(Prohibition) ⊓
   hasActivationStatus.(Deactivated) ⊓
   ¬ ViolatedProhibitionNorm
ViolatedProhibitionNorm ⊑ Norm ⊓
    hasDeonticConcept.(Prohibition) ⊓
    hasFulfillmentStatus.(Violated)
ViolatedPermissionNorm ⊑ Norm ⊓
    hasDeonticConcept.(Permission) ⊓
    hasFulfillmentStatus.(Violated)
```

Figure 9. Classes used to classify the norms according to their compliance

Due to the open word assumption of OWL, in order to the classification of the classes *ViolatedObligationNorm*, *FulfilledProhibitionNorm* work properly, it is necessary to explicitly limit the universe of known individuals of the *FulfilledObligationNorm* and *ViolatedProhibitionNorm* classes by setting them equivalent to the enumeration of their members. Suppose that the *FulfilledObligationNorm* class has two individuals, called *oblig1* and *oblig2*. Thus, the following axiom is added to the norm ontology (Figure 10).

```
FulfilledObligationNorm ≡ {oblig1, oblig2}
```

Figure 10. Limiting the universe of known individuals of the *FulfilledObligationNorm* class

IV. EXECUTION SCENARIO ONTOLOGY

The norm ontology allows to represent an agent performing an action, participating in a situation, and a norm being fulfilled, violated, activated and deactivated. However, in order to detect normative conflict that depends on execution order of runtime events in MAS, it is not enough to know only that those events occurred in the system. More them that, it is necessary to know when such events were executed in the system and if they happened before or after another one. In other words, if we know the moment when each condition of the system norms happens in the system, then it will be possible to ensure if such norms are in conflict or not.

Therefore, the execution scenario ontology extends the norm ontology in order to add the notion of *time*. The moment when a condition of a norm happens in the system is captured by the *hasConditionTime* datatype property and is represented by an integer value. The range of this property is an xsd:integer. The following axiom was added to the *Condition* class (Figure 11).

```
Condition ⊑ ∀ hasConditionTime.Integer
```

Figure 11. Datatype property *hasConditionTime* added to Condition class

The execution scenario ontology also introduced the class *Time* to represent the moment when an action is performed by an agent and when a situation becomes true in the system for an agent. The *Time* class is related to *hasTime* datatype property, which range is an xsd:integer. The following axioms were added to the classes *Entity*, *Action* and *Situation*, and the *Time* class is defined as follows (Figure 12).

```
Entity ⊑ ∀ entityTime.Time
Action ⊑ ∀ actionTime.Time
Situation ⊑ ∀ situationTime.Time
Time ⊑ ∀ hasTime.Integer ⊓
    (∀ timeEntity.Entity ⊔
    ∀ timeAction.Action ⊔
    ∀ timeSituation.Situation)
```

Figure 12. Definion of *Time* class

As described in section III, a norm is activated during a period of time, which is determined by the *Condition* class along with *hasBefore* and *hasAfter* object properties. An agent can perform an action at any time in the system. However, in order to an obligation norm to be fulfilled by the agent, the regulated action must be performed only while the norm is active, i.e., during the period of time where the norm is active. It is necessary to know when the activation period of the norm starts and ends. Therefore, the datatype properties *hasStart* and *hasEnd* were included to the execution scenario ontology. Their domain and range are the *ActivationPeriod* class and xsd:integer, respectively. The class *ActivationPeriod* represents the timeline period during which a norm is active. The following axiom was added to the *Norm* class and the *ActivationPeriod* class is defined as follows (Figure 13).

```
Norm ⊑ ∀hasActvPrd.ActivationPeriod
ActivationPeriod ⊑
  ∀ hasStart.Integer ⊓
  ∀ hasEnd.Integer
```

Figure 13. Definition of *ActivationPeriod* class

In this paper, we are considering that a norm can have at most one before condition and one after condition. Therefore, a norm can have one of the five types of activation intervals showed in Figure 14. The first type is when a norm has no condition and is always active, i.e., its activation interval starts at time zero and lasts until +infinite. The second type refers to a norm associated with only one before condition. This interval starts from zero and lasts until whenever that condition happens in the system. The third type represents a norm with only one after condition and the interval starts whenever that condition happens and lasts until +infinite. The fourth and fifth types refer to a norm associated with both before and after conditions. They differ each other by the moment the conditions happen in the system. If the before condition happens first, then the norm activation period is characterized by the fourth interval type. Otherwise, the norm activation period is represented by the fifth interval type.

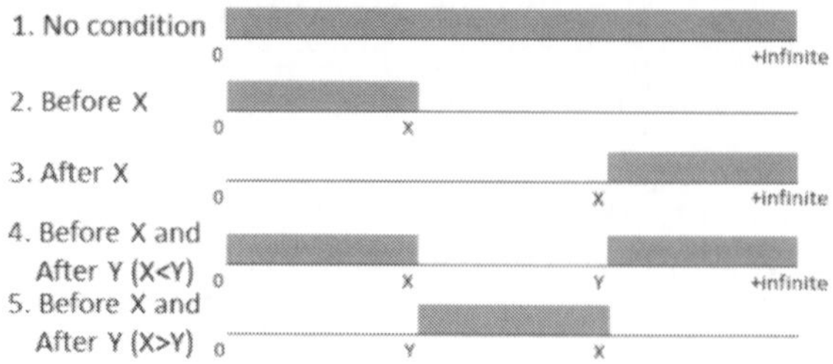

Figure 14. Five types of activation intervals.

The fourth interval type is the only one which a norm has two activation periods, i.e., from zero to whenever the before condition happens and from whenever the after condition happens to +infinite. Therefore, the norms can have one or at most two activation intervals. The classes and properties of the execution scenario ontology are graphically represented in Figure 15.

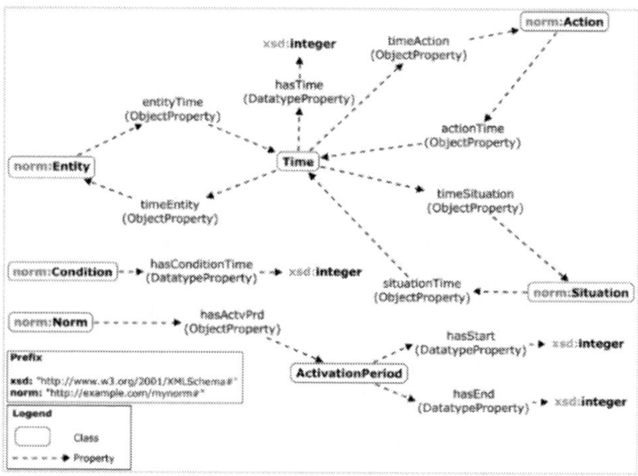

Figure 15. Graphical representation of the execution scenario ontology.

In the norm ontology, six conditions were defined as subclass of *Condition* class, which were the classes *ExecutionOfAction*, *ActivationOfNorm*, *DeactivationOfNorm*, *FulfillmentOfNorm*, *ViolationOfNorm* and *Situation*. The time when such conditions happen in the system can be inferred automatically from the normative system, if the time when an action was performed by an agent and the time when a situation became true to an agent are known in advance. Assuming these times are known, the remaining times can be inferred by using SWRL rules, as follows.

The times of the *ExecutionOfAction* and *Situation* conditions can be easily inferred by using the rules 1 and 2, respectively. These rules verify, respectively, the actions executed and the situations participated by an entity, and check whether the times of those events were provided by the designer. If so, the value of the *hasConditionTime* object property is updated.

```
Rule1: ExecutionOfAction(?c) ∧
hasRelatedAction(?c, ?a) ∧ Action(?a) ∧
hasRelatedEntity(?c, ?e) ∧ Entity(?e) ∧
entityTime(?e, ?t) ∧ Time(?t) ∧
timeAction(?t, ?a) ∧ hasTime(?t, ?ti)
→ hasConditionTime(?c, ?ti)
```

```
Rule2: Situation(?c) ∧ participateIn(?e, ?c) ∧
Entity(?e) ∧ entityTime(?e, ?t) ∧ Time(?t) ∧
timeSituation(?t, ?c) ∧ hasTime(?t, ?ti)
→ hasConditionTime(?c, ?ti)
```

The norm's fulfillment depends on its deontic concept, i.e., if the norm is an *obligation*, *prohibition* or *permission*. As described in section III, the fulfillment can be *unknown*, *fulfilled* or *violated*. When the norm is an *obligation*, it becomes *fulfilled* when the agent performed the action while the norm is active. If the norm was deactivated, but the agent did not perform the action, then the norm becomes *violated*. If the norm is a *prohibition*, then the opposite behavior can be observed. It becomes *violated* when the agent performed the action while the norm is active, and *fulfilled* when the norm was deactivated, but the agent did not perform the action. When the norm is a *permission*, it becomes *violated* when the agent performed the action, but it has no permission to do that, i.e., the norm is not active. A *permission* norm never becomes *fulfilled* because a permission is an authorization and it is not expected to be perform by the agent.

The condition's time for fulfilment and violation of an obligation norm are shown in rules 3 and 4, respectively. Rule 3 tests whether the *FulfillmentOfNorm* condition is satisfied, i.e., whether an action *?a* was executed by an entity *?e*, both defined by an obligation norm *?n*, and whether *?a* happened during which *?n* was active. In other words, it checks whether *?ti* happened after *?ts* and before *?te* by using the SWRL comparison built-in functions *swrlb:greaterThanOrEqual(?ti, ?ts)* and *swrlb:lessThan(?ti, ?te)*, where *?ti* is the time when action *?a* happened and *?ts* and *?te* are the start and end times of the norm activation period, respectively. As a result, the value of the *hasConditionTime* object property is updated to *?ti*.

```
Rule3: FulfillmentOfNorm(?c) ∧
hasRelatedNorm(?c, ?n) ∧ Norm(?n) ∧
hasDeonticConcept(?n, Obligation) ∧
hasAction(?n, ?a) ∧ Action(?a) ∧
hasEntity(?n, ?e) ∧ Entity(?e) ∧
entityTime(?e, ?t) ∧ Time(?t) ∧
timeAction(?t, ?a) ∧ hasTime(?t, ?ti) ∧
hasActvPrd(?n, ?ap) ∧ hasStart(?ap, ?ts) ∧
hasEnd(?ap, ?te) ∧
swrlb:greaterThanOrEqual(?ti, ?ts) ∧
swrlb:lessThan(?ti, ?te)
→ hasConditionTime(?c, ?ti) ∧
hasFulfillmentStatus(?n, Fulfilled)
```

Rule 4 tests whether the related norm of a *ViolationOfNorm* condition was classified as *ViolatedObligationNorm*. If so, the value of the *hasConditionTime* object property is updated with the *?te* value, which is the end time of the norm activation period.

```
Rule4: ViolationOfNorm(?c) ∧
hasRelatedNorm(?c, ?n) ∧
ViolatedObligationNorm(?n) ∧
hasActvPrd(?n, ?ap) ∧ hasEnd(?ap, ?te)
→ hasConditionTime(?c, ?te) ∧
hasFulfillmentStatus(?n, Violated)
```

In a similar manner, the condition's time for fulfilment and violation of a prohibition norm can be inferred, but in the opposite way. The rules 5 and 6 calculate the condition's time for activation and deactivation of a norm. These rules get the time when a norm starts and ends its activation period, respectively, and update the value of the *hasConditionTime* object property.

```
Rule5: ActivationOfNorm(?c) ∧
hasRelatedNorm(?c, ?n) ∧ Norm(?n) ∧
hasActvPrd(?n, ?ap) ∧ hasStart(?ap, ?ts)
→ hasConditionTime(?c, ?ts)
```

```
Rule6: DeactivationOfNorm(?c) ∧
hasRelatedNorm(?c, ?n) ∧ Norm(?n) ∧
hasActvPrd(?n, ?ap) ∧ hasEnd(?ap, ?te)
→ hasConditionTime(?c, ?te)
```

The start and end times of a norm activation period cannot be inferred by using SWRL, because in SWRL there is no way to check the existence of these relationships: *hasBefore* and *hasAfter*. This verification can be done by using NOT EXISTS filter expression in SPARQL queries [5]. For example, suppose that *n1* is a norm that has only a relationship with *hasBefore* condition, named *c1*. The activation interval of that norm starts at time zero and the end time will depend on whether or not the condition *c1* was satisfied. If not, the end time is unknown. Otherwise, the end time is the time when the condition *c1* became true in the knowledge base.

V. Conflict Detection

The execution scenario ontology can be used by the system designer as a means for providing an example of execution scenario performed by the agents in the system. The system designer may want to evaluate a possible sequence of actions in the system and know if that sequence would cause any normative conflict. The conflict detection rule uses the times provided by the execution scenario ontology in order to detect conflicts between the norms in case such execution scenario would be executed in the system. As described in section IV, the designer only needs to provide the time when an action would be performed by an agent and when a situation would become true to an agent. The remaining times are automatically calculated.

Two norms are said to be in conflict when they are active, have contradictory deontic concepts (i.e., prohibition *versus* permission or prohibition *versus* obligation), are defined in the same context, govern the same behavior and are executed by the same entity. To detect conflict between two norms that depends on execution order of runtime events, we have to compare the activation periods two by two in order to find intersections between them. Rule 7 shows the detection of normative conflict between an obligation and a prohibition.

```
Rule7: Norm(?n1) ∧ Norm(?n2) ∧ hasEntity(?n1,
?e) ∧ hasEntity(?n2, ?e) ∧ hasAction(?n1, ?a)
∧ hasAction(?n2, ?a) hasContext(?n1, ?c) ∧
hasContext(?n2, ?c) ∧ hasDeonticConcept(?n1,
Obligation) ∧ hasDeonticConcept(?n2,
Prohibition) ∧ hasActvPrd(?n1, ?ac1) ∧
hasStart(?ac1, ?st1) ∧ hasEnd(?ac1, ?ed1) ∧
hasActvPrd(?n2, ?ac2) ∧ hasStart(?ac2, ?st2)
∧ hasEnd(?ac2, ?ed2) ∧ swrlb:lessThan(?st1,
?st2) ∧ swrlb:greaterThanOrEqual(?ed1, ?st2)
→ hasConflict(?n1, ?n2)
```

This rule verifies if any activation periods of two norms intersects each other by comparing the initial and final times of their activation intervals. If that happen, then they are in conflict. A similar rule must be created in order to identify conflicts between a permission and a prohibition. The consistencies of the norm and execution scenario ontologies and the SWRL rules were checked by making use of existing DL reasoners such as Pellet [15].

A. Conflicting Norms Example

This section presents an example of the detection of this kind of conflict. Let us assume a daily home rules for a family with a child called Riley. The following norms are defined for him.

Norm1 (N1): Agent *Riley* is obligated to perform the action *doHomework*.

Norm2 (N2): Agent *Riley* is permitted to perform the action *playGame* after fulfill the norm *Norm1*.

Norm3 (N3): Agent *Riley* is prohibited to perform *playGame* after he performs *haveLunch* action and before the situation *doneLunching* becomes true for him.

Norm4 (N4): Agent *Riley* is obligated to perform the action *cleanRoom* before he performs *haveLunch*.

Norm5 (N5): Agent *Riley* is prohibited to perform the action *playGame* if he violates the norm *norm4*.

Let us suppose now that the designer provided the following execution scenario and wanted to know if there is any normative conflict in case this scenario would be executed in the system.

- *Riley* performs action *doHomework* at time 10;
- *Riley* performs action *haveLunch* at time 20, and;
- The situation *doneLunching* becomes true for *Riley* at time 30.

The activation periods for each norm are depicted in Figure 16. Since *norm1* does not have activation condition, its activation period starts at the beginning of the system's execution and lasts until +infinite, i.e., the norm is always active. The time of the *fulfilment of Norm1* is inferred by *rule 3*, when *Riley* performs the *doHomework* action at time 10. Thus, the activation of *norm2* starts at time 10. According to the execution scenario, *norm3* prohibits *Riley* to perform the action *playGame* from time 20 to 30, and *norm4* obligates him to perform *cleanRoom* action until time 20. The times of the conditions *ExecutionOfAction haveLunch* and *Situation doneLunching* are inferred by rules 1 and 2, respectively.

Since no information about the execution of *cleanRoom* action was mentioned in the execution scenario during which *norm4* was active, the fulfillment status of *norm4* became violated at time 20, when it became deactivated, and it is captured by rule 4. Therefore, the activation of *norm5* starts at this time.

According to the proposed conflict detection approach, *rule7* identifies two normative conflicts, one between the norms *N2* and *N3*, and the other between norms *N2* and *N5*, because they are applied to the same agent and action, have contradictory deontic concept, and their activation intervals intersect each other. Thereby, it provides to the system designer a way to reevaluate the system norms according to an example of an expected execution scenario of the system.

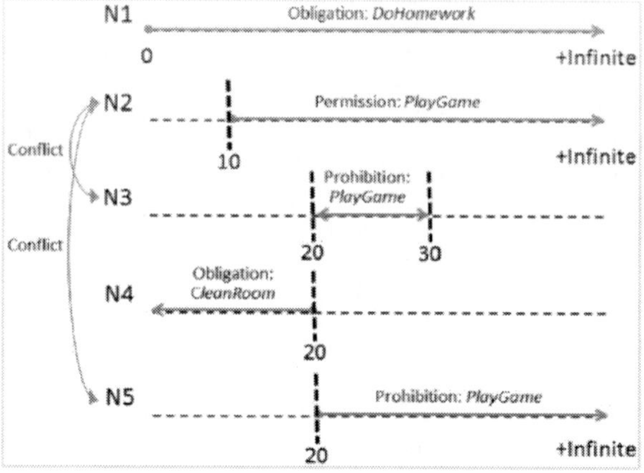

Figure 16. Example of norms in conflict.

VI. CONCLUSIONS

Norms have been used to guide and model the behavior of software agents, without restricting their autonomy. However, conflicts between the norms may occur. A normative conflict arises when the fulfilment of one norm causes the violation of another. In this paper, we have presented an approach based on execution scenarios to deal with the detection of normative conflicts that depends on information about the runtime execution of the system. The designer are able to provide examples of execution scenarios and evaluate the conflicts that may arise if those scenarios would be executed in the system. The conflict verification proposed in this paper occurs in the design phase.

There are several extensions we continue to work on. Since multi-agent systems are composed of multiple autonomous and heterogeneous agents, there is a huge amount of possibilities of execution scenarios to happen in the system. We would like to investigate how the proposed approach can be extended in order to generate automatically the execution scenarios and provide to the designer potential normative conflicts in the system. We also want to extend the proposed approach to support repetition of before and after conditions. Moreover, we are investigating mechanisms for resolution of this kind of normative conflict.

REFERENCES

[1] M. S. Aphale, T. J. Norman, and M. Sensoy, "Goal directed conflict resolution and policy refinement," In 14th International Workshop on Coordination, Organizations, Institutions and Norms in Agent Systems, Valencia, Spain, 2012, pp. 87-104.

[2] V. T. Da Silva, C. Braga, and J. Zahn, "Indirect Normative Conflict: Conflict that Depends on the Application Domain," In International Conference on Enterprise Information Systems (ICEIS), 2015, Barcelona, pp. 452-561.

[3] B. F. Dos Santos Neto, V. T. Da Silva, and C. J. P. De Lucena, "Developing goal-oriented normative agents: The NBDI architecture," In Filipe, J. and Fred, A., editors, Agents and Artificial Intelligence, volume 271 of Communications in Computer and Information Science, pp. 176–191. Springer Berlin Heidelberg, 2013.

[4] K. S. Figueiredo, V. T. Da Silva, and C. O. Braga, "Modeling norms in multi-agent systems with NormML," In Coordination, Organizations, Institutions, and Norms in Agent Systems VI, volume 6541 of Lecture Notes in Computer Science, pp. 39–57. Springer, Berlin, 2011.

[5] S. Harris, A. Seaborne, and E. Prud'hommeaux, SPARQL 1.1 query language. W3C recommendation, vol. 21, no. 10, 2013.

[6] I. Horrocks et al. SWRL: A semantic web rule language combining OWL and RuleML. W3C Member submission, vol. 21, pp. 79, 2004.

[7] J. S. C. Lam, F. Guerin, W. Vasconcelos, and T. J. Norman, "Representing and Reasoning about Norm-Governed Organisations with Semantic Web Languages," In Sixth European Workshop on Multi-Agent Systems. Bath, UK. December, pp. 18-32, 2008.

[8] T. Li et al. "Contextualized institutions in virtual organizations," In Coordination, Organizations, Institutions, and Norms in Agent Systems IX. Springer International Publishing, pp. 136-154, 2014.

[9] S. Rudolph, "Foundations of description logics," Reasoning Web. Semantic Technologies for the Web of Data. Springer Berlin Heidelberg, 2011, pp. 76-136.

[10] J. S. Santos, and V. T. Silva, "Identifying Indirect Normative Conflicts using the WordNet Database," In Proceedings of the 18th International Conference on Enterprise Information Systems - Volume 2: ICEIS, ISBN 978-989-758-187-8, 2016 pp. 186-193.

[11] M. Sensoy, T. J. Norman, W. W. Vasconcelos, and K. Sycara, "Owl-polar: A framework for semantic policy representation and reasoning," Web Semantics: Science, Services and Agents on the World Wide Web, vol. 12, pp. 148–160, 2012.

[12] A. Uszok et al. "New developments in ontology-based policy management: Increasing the practicality and comprehensiveness of KAoS," In: POLICY '08: Proceedings of IEEE Workshop on Policies for Distributed Systems and Networks, pp. 145-152, 2008.

[13] W. Vasconcelos, A. García-Camino, D. Gaertner, J. A. Rodríguez-Aguilar, and P. Noriega, "Distributed norm management for multi-agent systems," Expert Systems with Applications, vol. 39, no. 5, pp. 5990–5999, 2012.

[14] W. W. Vasconcelos, M. J. Kollingbaum, T. J. Norman, "Normative conflict resolution in multi-agent systems," Autonomous Agents and Multi-Agent Systems, v. 19, n. 2, pp. 124-152, 2009.

[15] E. Sirin, B. Parsia, B. C. Grau, A. Kalyanpur, and Y. Katz, "Pellet: A practical owl-dl reasoner," Web Semantics: science, services and agents on the World Wide Web, vol. 5, no. 2, pp. 51-53, 2007.

Discrete Time LQG Controller for Speed Control in a Steam Turbine Coupled to DC Generator

Hernando González Acevedo, Hernan González Acuña
Universidad Autónoma de Bucaramanga
UNAB
Bucaramanga, Colombia
e-mails: hgonzalez7@unab.edu.co, hgonzalez3@unab.edu.co

***Abstract*— This paper proposes a discrete-time Linear Quadratic Gaussian controller (LQG) for speed control in a steam turbine coupled to a DC generator. The goal is to keep the speed constant despite the changes of pressure in the steam pipeline and the field resistance of DC generator. In the first part, the mathematical model that describes the dynamic behavior of a steam turbine coupled to a DC generator and their parameters are calculated using an optimization algorithm. In the second part, the discrete LQG controller is designed to eliminate the influence of the disturbance in the output signal. Finally, in the last part the controller was implemented on a distributed control system (DCS), called Delta V (Emerson), and tested for different set points.**

Keywords- LQG Controller; steam turbine; distributed control system (DCS)

I. INTRODUCTION

Industrial steam turbines have many applications such as driving electric generators, small and large ship propellers, pumps and compressors. A steam turbine extracts thermal energy from pressurized steam to convert it into mechanical work using a shaft to drive an electrical generator. The steam turbine is a kind of heat engine that derives much of its improvement in thermodynamic efficiency through the use of multiple stages in the expansion of the steam, which results in a closer approach to the most efficient reversible process. An ideal steam turbine is considered an isentropic process or a constant entropy process, in which the entropy of the steam entering the turbine is equal to the entropy of the steam leaving the turbine, however, based on the steam turbine application, it's considered a typical isentropic efficiency ranges from 20% to 90%.

The interior of a turbine is composed of several sets of blades, commonly named buckets. One set of stationary blades is connected to the casing and one set of rotating blades is connected to the shaft. The efficiency of the turbine can vary depending on the size and configuration of the sets. This inner structure of the steam turbine allows it tasks that require high rotational speeds, even with widely fluctuating loads.

The mechanical speed control of the turbine, the governor, is essential, as turbines need to be run up slowly to prevent damage in some applications (such as the generation of alternating current electricity). Uncontrolled acceleration of the turbine rotor can lead to an overspeed, which causes the nozzle valves that control the flow of steam to the turbine to close. If this fails, the turbine may continue accelerating until the governor can break. Instead of that, an electronic controller and a control valve can be implemented to regulate the amount of steam that is going to the turbine. Some techniques for regulating the speed of shaft in a steam turbine are PID [1][2], FUZZY [3][4] and MPC [5][6].

This paper is structured as follows: in Section 2, dynamic models of steam turbine and DC generator are presented. Section 3 presents the design of the LQG control. In Section 4, the experimental validation of the control system is presented, and Section 5 resumes the conclusions of this research.

II. DYNAMIC MODEL

The dynamic model of the system relates the differential equations of the steam turbine and the separately excited Dc generator.

A. Steam turbine

In many cases, the steam turbine models are simplified, many intermediate variables are omitted and only map input variables to outputs as outlined in [7]. In these conditions, the input-output mathematical model (the transfer function) of a steam turbine and the expression for mechanical power developed by a turbine are based on the continuity equation:

$$\frac{\partial W}{\partial t} = V\frac{\partial \rho}{\partial t} = F_{in}(t) - F_{out}(t) \qquad (1)$$

where W is the weight of steam in turbine $[kg]$; V – volume of turbine $[m^3]$; ρ – density of steam $[kg/m^3]$; F – steam mass flow rate $[kg/s]$; t – time $[sec.]$.

Assuming the flow out of the turbine to be proportional to pressure in the turbine:

$$F_{out} = P\frac{F_0}{P_0} \qquad (2)$$

where P – pressure of steam in the turbine $[kPa]$; P_0 – rated pressure; F_0 – rated flow out of turbine. With constant temperature in the turbine:

$$\frac{\partial \rho}{\partial t} = \frac{\partial P}{\partial t}\frac{\partial \rho}{\partial P} \tag{3}$$

From (1)-(3), it results the differential equation:

$$F_{in}(t) - F_{out}(t) = V\frac{\partial P}{\partial t}\frac{\partial \rho}{\partial P} = V\frac{\partial \rho}{\partial P}\frac{P_0}{F_0}\frac{\partial F_{out}}{\partial t} = T_T\frac{\partial F_{out}}{\partial t} \tag{4}$$

$$T_T\frac{\partial F_{out}}{\partial t} + F_{out}(t) = F_{in}(t) \tag{5}$$

and, after a Laplace transform, the transfer function of a steam turbine unit:

$$\frac{F_{out}(s)}{F_{in}(s)} = \frac{1}{T_T s+1} \tag{6}$$

where $T_T = V\frac{P_0}{F_0}\frac{\partial \rho}{\partial P}$ is the time constant [seconds.]. The turbine torque is proportional to the steam flow rate:

$$T_m(t) = kF_{out}(t) \tag{7}$$

where k is a proportional constant. The change in density of steam respecting to pressure $(\partial \rho/\partial P)$ at a given temperature may be determined from tables. The steam flow $(F_{in}(t))$ is regulated by a proportional valve:

$$F_{in}(t) = k_p e^{-T_d s}u(t) \tag{8}$$

where k_p is a proportional constant, T_d is time delay [seconds] and $u(t)$ is percentage of valve opening.

B. Separately excited Dc generator

Separately excited DC generators are those whose field magnets are energized by some external DC source, such as a battery. The dynamic of this type of machines is represented by the following differential equations:

$$V_f(t) = R_f I_f(t) + L_f\frac{dI_f(t)}{dt} \tag{9}$$

$$K_v\omega(t) = (R_a + R_L)I_a(t) + L_a\frac{dI_a(t)}{dt} \tag{10}$$

$$T_m(t) = J\frac{d\omega(t)}{dt} + B_m\omega(t) + K_I I_f(t)I_a(t) \tag{11}$$

where V_f is the voltage applied to field coil, I_f is the current in field coil, R_f is the resistance in the field coil, L_f is the inductance of the field coil, K_v is the speed constant, ω is the shaft speed, R_a is the resistance in the armature coil, L_a is the inductance in the armature coil, I_a is the armature current, R_L is the load resistor connected to generator, T_m is the mechanical torque of the steam turbine, J is the inertia of shaft that joins the DC generator to the steam turbine, B_m is the viscous friction coefficient and K_I is the torque constant.

C. Parameters of the mathematical model

The following transfer function corresponds to the type Terry steam turbine coupled to a DC generator with a power of 1 kW:

$$\frac{T_m(s)}{u(s)} = \frac{k_p k e^{-T_d s}}{T_T s+1} \tag{12}$$

$$\frac{\omega(s)}{T_m(s)} = \frac{L_a s + R_T}{(Js+B_m)(L_a s+R_T)+K_v K_I I_{f\_ss}} \tag{13}$$

where R_T is the sum of the armature resistance and load resistance, $I_{f\_ss} = V_f/R_f$ is the current in the field coil in stable state. The following parameters are given by the technical sheet of the generator: $R_f = 367\,\Omega$, $L_f = 20.6\,H$, $R_a = 7.4\,\Omega$, $L_a = 11.38\,mH$, $R_L = 20.8\,\Omega$ y $V_f = 213$. To evaluate the unknown parameters of the model, an optimization algorithm was programmed, the algorithm is based on Sequential Quadratic Programming (SQP) method. The optimization function is the mean square error between experimental data and simulated data, for a control signal $u(t)$. Figure 1 shows the data used for optimization algorithm: generator speed (revolutions per minute - RPM) and percentage of valve opening. Table 1 presents the values obtained for each parameter.

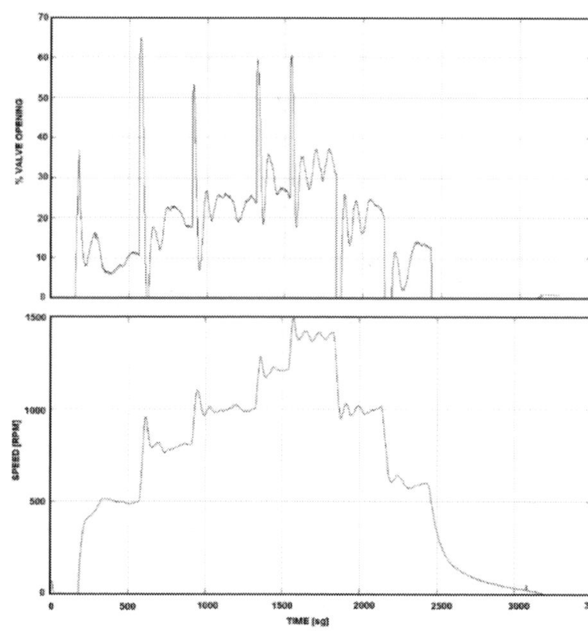

Figure 1. Experimental data. a) Percentage of valve opening, b) Generator speed

The transfer function of the system is:

$$\frac{\omega(s)}{T_m(s)} = \frac{(0.01879s+46.56)e^{-9s}}{0.02574s^3+63.8s^2+124.5s+1.036} \quad (14)$$

To simplify the model, the delay was approximated to a transfer function of first order (Pade approximation).

$$e^{-9s} = \frac{-s+2/9}{s+2/9} \quad (15)$$

TABLE I. PARAMETERS OF MATHEMATICAL MODEL

T_T	119.7 $[sg]$
$k_p k$	0.055031$[^{Nm}/_{\%}]$
T_d	9 $[sg]$
J	0.006015527721586 $[Kg \cdot m^2]$
K_i	0.843524807917543 $[^{N \cdot m}/_{A^2}]$
K_v	0.620330916257256 $[^{N \cdot m}/_{A^2}]$
B_m	0.000922377688340 $\left[\frac{N \cdot m}{rad/sg}\right]$

The model of the steam turbine coupled to DC generator was discretized with a sampling period of one second and represented in state space.

$$x(k+1) = G_L x(k) + H_L u(k) \quad (16)$$
$$y(k) = C_L x(k)$$

where

$$G_L = \begin{bmatrix} -0.000117 & -0.004559 & -0.000102 & -0.000003 \\ 0.001424 & 0.055065 & -0.042968 & -0.001370 \\ 0.039239 & 1.519927 & 0.880884 & -0.003809 \\ 0.006815 & 0.264122 & 0.238425 & 0.999629 \end{bmatrix} \quad (17)$$

$$H_L = \begin{bmatrix} 0.000089 \\ 0.039239 \\ 0.109044 \\ 0.010605 \end{bmatrix} \quad (18)$$

$$C = [0 \quad -0.002851 \quad -1.766304 \quad 1.570189] \quad (19)$$

III. LINEAR QUADRATIC GAUSSIAN (LQG) CONTROLLER

For plants with no integrator, the basic principle of the design is to insert an integrator in the feedforward path between the error comparator and the plant [8], as shown in Figure 2.

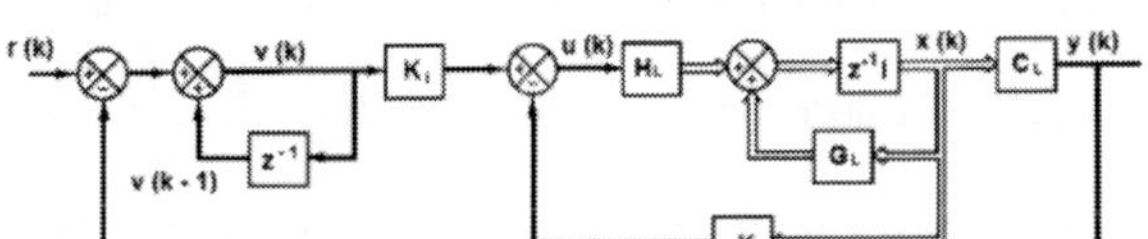

Figure 2. Block diagram of tracking system

Assume that a reference input (step function) is applied at $t = 0$ where t is the time [seconds]. Then, for $t > 0$, the system dynamic can be described by:

$$\begin{bmatrix} x(k+1) \\ v(k+1) \end{bmatrix} = \begin{bmatrix} G_L & 0 \\ -C_L G_L & 1 \end{bmatrix} \begin{bmatrix} x(k) \\ v(k) \end{bmatrix} + \begin{bmatrix} H_L \\ -C_L H_L \end{bmatrix} u(k) + \begin{bmatrix} 0 \\ 1 \end{bmatrix} r(k+1) \quad (20)$$

Remark that $r(k)$ is a step input, so we have $r(k) = r(k+1) = r$. When k approaches to infinity:

$$\begin{bmatrix} x(\infty) \\ v(\infty) \end{bmatrix} = \begin{bmatrix} G_L & 0 \\ -C_L G_L & 1 \end{bmatrix} \begin{bmatrix} x(\infty) \\ v(\infty) \end{bmatrix} + \begin{bmatrix} H_L \\ -C_L H_L \end{bmatrix} u(\infty) + \begin{bmatrix} 0 \\ 1 \end{bmatrix} r(\infty) \quad (21)$$

By subtracting (20) from (21), we obtain:

$$\begin{bmatrix} x_e(k+1) \\ v_e(k+1) \end{bmatrix} = \begin{bmatrix} G_L & 0 \\ -C_L G_L & 1 \end{bmatrix} \begin{bmatrix} x_e(k) \\ v_e(k) \end{bmatrix} + \begin{bmatrix} H_L \\ -C_L H_L \end{bmatrix} u_e(k) \quad (22)$$

where

$$x_e(k) = x(k) - x(\infty) \quad (23)$$
$$v_e(k) = v(k) - v(\infty) \quad (24)$$
$$u_e(k) = -\boldsymbol{K} x_e(k) + \boldsymbol{K_I} v_e(k) \quad (25)$$

Define a new $(n+1)$ th-order error vector $\xi(k)$ by:

$$\xi(k) = \begin{bmatrix} x_e(k) \\ v_e(k) \end{bmatrix} = (n+1) - vector \quad (26)$$

Then (22) becomes:

$$\xi(k+1) = \hat{\boldsymbol{G}}\xi(k) + \hat{\boldsymbol{H}} u_e(k) \quad (27)$$
$$u_e(k) = \hat{\boldsymbol{K}}\xi(k) \quad (28)$$

where

$$\hat{G} = \begin{bmatrix} G_L & 0 \\ -C_L G_L & 1 \end{bmatrix} \quad \hat{H} = \begin{bmatrix} H_L \\ -C_L H_L \end{bmatrix} \quad \hat{K} = [K \quad -K_I] \quad (29)$$

The LQG regulator consists in an optimal state-feedback gain and a Kalman state estimator [9]. The first design step is to seek a state-feedback law that minimizes the cost function of regulation performance, (30), it is measured by a quadratic performance criterion with user-specified weighting matrices, Q and R, which define the trade-off between regulation performance and control effort, respectively. The gain matrix $\hat{\boldsymbol{K}}$, to minimize the function J, is obtained by solving an algebraic Riccati equation.

$$J = \frac{1}{2}\sum_{K=0}^{\infty}(\xi^T Q \xi + u_e{}^T R u_e) \quad (30)$$

The next design step is to derive a state estimator using a Kalman filter because the optimal state feedback cannot be implemented without full state measurement. Since the Kalman filter is an optimal estimator when dealing with Gaussian white noise, it minimizes the asymptotic covariance of the estimation error. Mathematically, the Kalman state estimator can be expressed by (31), with two inputs, controls u(k) and measurements y(k). The gain matrix L of the Kalman filter is determined solving the Riccati algebraic equation.

$$\hat{x}(k+1) = G_L\hat{x}(k) + H_L u(k) + L(y(k) - C_L\hat{x}(k)) \quad (31)$$

The following values are assumed for the controller design: $Q = \text{diag}(1, 1, 1, 8.5, 0.009)$ and $R = 5$. By solving the Riccati equation gives $\hat{K}$ = [0.061111, 2.367096, 1.369298, 1.786684, -0.037269]. To design the observer, the variance of experimental data of the control signal and the generator speed are determined. The values are $Q_n = 176.9876$ and $R_n = 21225$, respectively. By solving the Riccati equation gives L = 10-8 [37.59397, -1129.21097, -51464.655, 1617969.98].

Figure 3 shows the block diagram of the control strategy. An anti-windup gain is implemented because integral term accumulates a significant error during the rise (windup), this creates a large overshoot, a slow settling time, and, sometimes, even instability in the speed response. A method used to compensate this phenomenon is tracking back calculation [10]. In the linear range, the error is integrated and the difference between the saturated and the unsaturated control signal is used to generate a feedback signal. This signal can control properly the integral state in the saturation range. It may seem advantageous to choose a very large value for the anti-windup gain K_a because the integrator can be limited quickly. If the anti-windup gain is big, a spurious error can cause input saturation and accidentally reset the integrator. For the design of the control system, it is assumed an anti-windup gain of $K_a = 10$. Evaluating closed loop response to a step input, it gets an overshoot of 2.22 % and a setting time of 130 seconds.

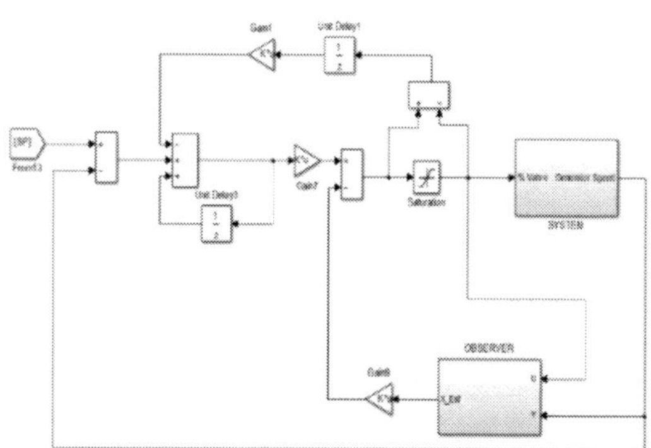

Figure 3. Block diagram of the control strategy

IV. RESULTS

The LQG controller is implemented in Delta V DCS. The pseudocode that depicts the operating principle of the algorithm is shown in Table 2, where the matrices G_L, H_L and C_L correspond to the state space representation of the mathematical model.

TABLE II. PSEUDOCODE LQG CONTROLLER

```
SP = Read Setpoint
PV = Read process value
en = SP – PV
% Anti-windup gain
Vk = en + Vk_1 – Ka*Du
un = Ki*Vk – K*Xob_1
if un > Umax
    U = Umax
If un > Umin & U<Umax
    U = un
If un < Umin
    U = Umin
% Observer
Xob = (G_L – L*C_L)*Xob_1 + H_L*U + L*PV
Vk_ 1 = Vk
Du = un - U
Xob_1 = Xob
```

The strategy of control is suitable for startup procedure and it can be applied for nominal work point (the range of speed is 0 RPM to 1500 RPM). Figure 4 shows the transient response of the generator speed and the signal control for different values of the reference signal. As seen in Figure 4, the signal that corresponds to generator speed, oscillates around the set point when steady state value is reached, this oscillations are due to changes of steam pressure in the pipeline as shown in Figure 5.

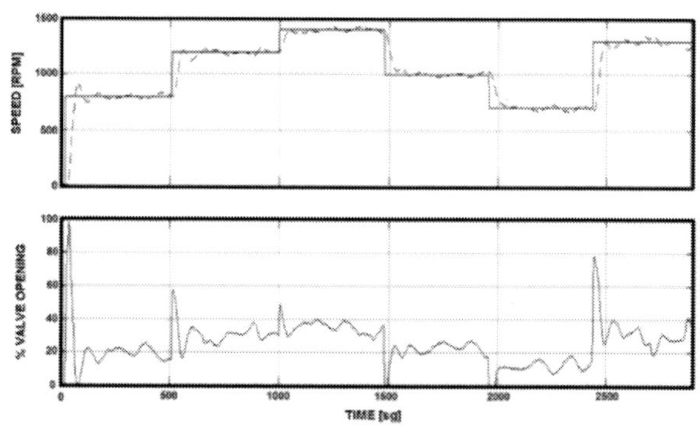

Figure 4. Transient response of LQG control. a) Speed generator b) Control signal

The transient response of the LQG controller is analyzed by making variations in the field resistance of the DC generator. By decreasing this parameter, the mechanical speed of the turbine increases, therefore, it is expected that the proportional valve should decrease its opening percentage. As seen in Figure 6, for a set point of 1000 RPM, at the 120 seconds, the field resistance is changed to 60 % over its nominal value and the controller stabilizes the signal in 70 seconds. At the 950 seconds, the resistance value is changed to 20 % over its nominal value and the signal stabilizes in 120 seconds. At the 1400 seconds, the resistance is set to its nominal value and the speed has a strong transient response, then the controller stabilizes the signal in 200 seconds.

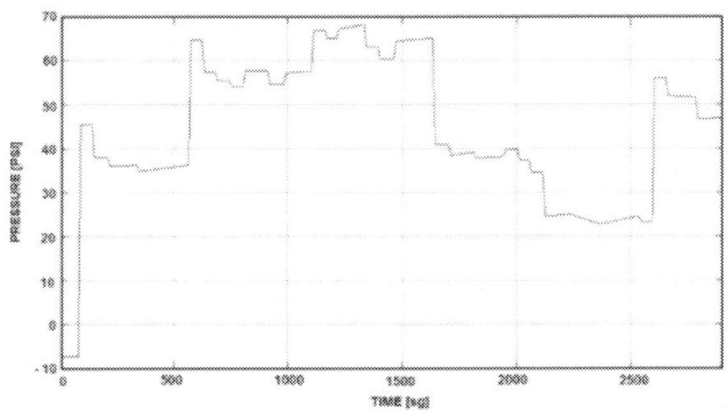

Figure 5. Steam pressure in pipeline

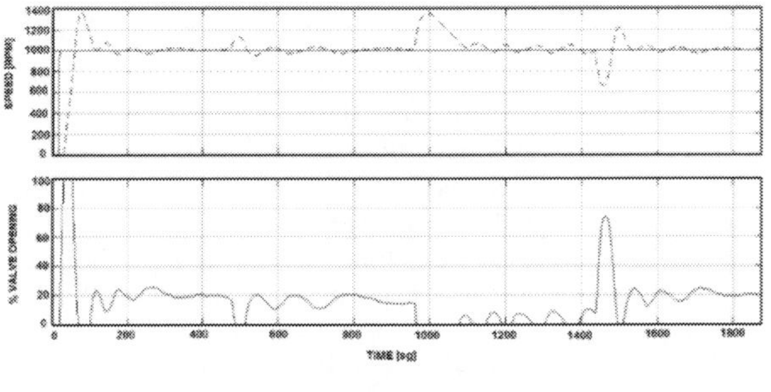

Figure 6. Transient response of the speed generator due to changes of field resistance in the generator

A proportional integral (PI) controller (32) was designed based on the dynamic model of steam turbine coupled to the DC generator. Figure 7 shows the transient response of generator speed and the control action, for the same speed range. The PI controller has a greater overshoot than the LQG control and the changes in the steam pressure in the pipeline considerably affect the speed around the reference point.

$$G_c(z) = 0.1188 + \frac{0.0012}{1-z^{-1}} \quad (32)$$

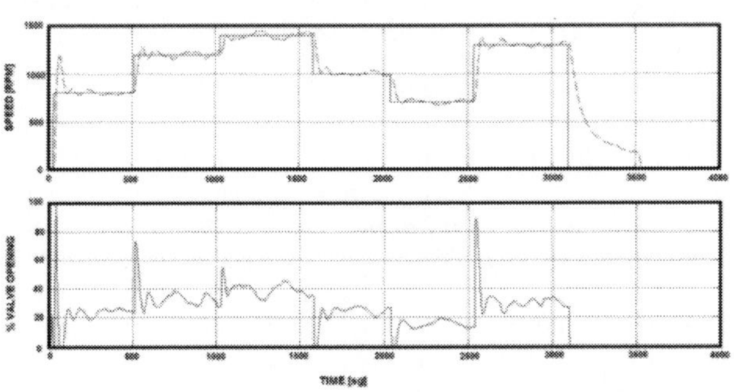

Figure 7. Transient response of PID control. a) Speed generator b) Control signal

V. CONCLUSION

In this paper, it was presented the design, test and comparison of two different control strategies applied to a steam turbine coupled to a DC generator. The dynamic model of the system was obtained using an optimization algorithm that is based on the quadratic sequential programming method. The turbine model was approached to a first order system with delay and the DC generator model was approached to a second order transfer function. Then, two control strategies were designed based on the dynamic model: PI control and LQG control. The obtained results show that the LQG controller has a better performance than the PI controller considering three main points: changing the set point, the transient response is quicker and smoother with the LQG controller; if the pressure changes in the steam line, the speed variations around the set point are smaller with the LQG controller; making changes in the value of the field resistance of the DC generator, results in oscillations in the speed, such oscillations are smaller with the LQG controller. For further research, it can develop a dynamic model that contemplates the thermal effects present in the elements inside the turbine and test other control strategies like fuzzy logic and predictive control.

REFERENCES

[1] M. Ismail, "Adaptation of PID controller using AI technique for speed control of isolated steam turbine", Proc. IEEE Symp. Electronics, Communications and Computers (JEC-ECC), IEEE Press, March 2012, doi: 10.1109/JEC-ECC.2012.6186962.

[2] F. Wang, Z. Yao, W. Wang, J. Huo, X. Zhao, "Research on Steam Turbine Speed Fuzzy Self-Tuning PID Control during Island Formation", Proc. IEEE Symp. Electrical and Control Engineering (ICECE), IEEE Press, June 2010, doi: 10.1109/iCECE.2010.435.

[3] Q. Zhu, Y. Zhang, J. Zhang, "Design Of Fuzzy Neural Network Controller For Marine Steam Turbine System", Proc. IEEE Symp. Fourth International Conference on Natural Computation (ICNC'08), IEEE Press, Oct. 2008, doi: 10.1109/ICNC.2008.637.

[4] F. A. Alturki, A. B. Abdennour, "Neuro-fuzzy control of a steam boiler-turbine unit", Proc. IEEE Symp. International Conference on Control Applications, IEEE Press, Aug. 1999, doi: 10.1109/CCA.1999.801041.

[5] M. Kordestani, M. S. Khoshro; A. Mirzaee, "Predictive control of large steam turbines", Proc. IEEE Symp. Control Conference ASCC. IEEE Press, June. 2013, doi: 10.1109/ASCC.2013.6606366.

[6] M. Gyun; Y. Rok, Y. Joon, "Design of an adaptive predictive controller for steam generators", Proc. IEEE Symp. IEEE Transactions on Nuclear Science, IEEE Press, Feb. 2003, doi: 10.1109/TNS.2002.807854.

[7] M. Dulau, D. Bica. "Mathematical modelling and simulation of the behaviour of the steam turbine". The 7th International Conference Interdisciplinarity in Engineering (INTER-ENG), ScienceDirect, vol. 12, pp. 723–729, 2014, doi: 10.1016/j.protcy.2013.12.555.

[8] K. Ogata. "Sistemas de control en tiempo discrete". Ed. Pearson Educacion, ISBN 0-13-034281-5, pp. 596 – 609, 1995.

[9] R. Burns. "Advanced Control Engineering". Ed. Butterworth Heinemann, ISBN 0750651008, pp. 288 – 299, 2001

[10] X. Lan Li, J. Gyu Park, H. Beom Shin. "Comparison and evaluation of anti-windup PI Controllers", Journal of Power Electronics, vol. 11, January 2011, doi: 10.6113/JPE.2011.11.1.045.

A Control Method for Bipedal Trunk Spring Loaded Inverted Pendulum Model

Jongwoo Lee[1], Minh Nhat Vu[1,2], Yonghwan Oh[1,2]

[1]Center for robotics research, Korea Institute of Science and Technology
Seoul 02792, Korea
Email: {jongwoo, oyh}@kist.re.kr
[2]HCI and Robotics, University of Science and Technology KIST Campus
Seoul 02792, Korea
Email: minh.vunhat@gmail.com

Abstract—**In this paper, we present a control method for bipedal robotic walking with compliant legs and upright trunk. The proposed method is validated with dynamic simulation of a planar, reduced-order biped walking model, consisting of a rigid trunk and compliant legs. Existing literatures have found that simple mass-spring model can describe dynamic characteristics of bipedal locomotion, in terms of Ground Reaction Force (GRF) and the Center of Mass (CoM) profile. In order to explain trunk-upright walking mechanics, a control method named the Virtual Pivot Point (VPP) method based on the Virtual Pendulum (VP) concept has been previously introduced. In this method, the axial force of a compliant leg is redirected towards the VPP of the model, which is located above the CoM of the model, in order to provide restoring moment about trunk motion. The resulting behaviour of the model would resemble a virtual pendulum rotating about the VPP, thus upright trunk while walking is pursued. However, we have found that for some cases this method provides upsetting moment, instead of restoring moment, which degrades the performance of the control. Inspired from this analysis, we propose a new force-redirecting method as a controller for robotic biped walking. We consider a dynamic simulation of a simple, planar simple walking model to validate the performance of the proposed method under random initial condition and under the presence of force disturbance. The proposed method shows stable and robust walking performance compared to the VPP method.**

Keywords–Bipedal walking control; compliant leg; reduced-order walking model; force redirection rule.

I. Introduction

Bipedal robotic locomotion has been an extensive field of research for many years in robotics research community. Zero-moment-point (ZMP) approaches have been successful in demonstrating robust and versatile bipedal locomotion due to its mathematical tractability [1]–[4]. The joint trajectories are planned assuming level-height motion of the center of mass (CoM) of the robot with zero angular momentum and fully-actuated legs (i.e., at least one foot is always flat on the ground with ankle actuation), while in practice under-actuation is common in bipedal robot. In order to handle nonlinear, underactuated, hybrid dynamics of bipedal robot, a formal method such as hybrid zero dynamics (HZD)-based approaches [5]–[7], or model-based trajectory optimization and stabilization [8] have been studied deeply. However, these methods usually require precise dynamic models. They also require to compute periodic trajectories based on the model and transition among different trajectories for versatile locomotion is not a trivial problem [9]. On the other hand, some end up with an idea that the bipedal walking controller does not need to be complex and one can find proper target physical behaviours based on simple reduced-order models; then, joint trajectories will be determined by dynamic interaction of the robot, controller, and the environment [10]–[13].

Traditionally, the mechanics of walking and running have been modelled with different paradigm, i.e., inverted pendulum model for walking [14] and spring-mass model for running [15]. After many evidences that the inverted pendulum model cannot reproduce mechanical characteristics of walking ([10], [16], [17]), Geyer et al. [18] have suggested the spring-mass model as a unifying template for bipedal locomotion; both the fundamental characteristics of walking and running could be reproduced by the same model with different set of parameters. However, the point-mass conceptual models cannot explain the upright posture of walking with non-zero angular momentum. Therefore, robots based on the spring-mass model concept controlled trunk position be zero and this control was independent from the compliant leg behavior [9], [19], [20].

Regarding this issue, Maus et al. [21] and Gruben and Boehm [22] have investigated experimental results of different animals and propose that the ground reaction forces (GRF) are intersecting a single fixed point above the CoM. This point is called either the virtual pivot point (VPP) [21], or the divergent point (DP) [22]. According to these studies, the GRFs directing to this point generate uprighting torque to trunk, thus upright posture is maintained while walking or running. As the force direction could be calculated by geometrical property only, without global orientation of the trunk, the upright posture could be achieved with inherent mechanical property without complex control algorithms. The concept affected controller for biped hopping [23] but required a high-level stabilizing controller around a pre-computed periodic trajectory as in the formal method. Stable robotic walking with a simple controller based on the VPP method seems hard to achieve yet [24].

In this paper, we propose a very simple form of control for bipedal walking with trunk, inspired by the Virtual Pendulum (VP) concept. We first argue that having GRF towards a single fixed point such as VPP or DP is not sufficient for maintaining upright posture, even in a simple model with massless legs; a

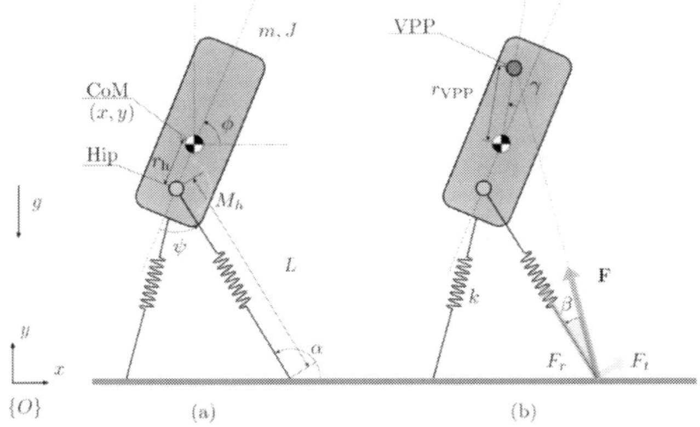

Figure 1. BTSLIP model (a). The VPP model suggested by [21] (b). Notations for parameters and variables are redefined in this paper.

simple analysis supports this argument. Based on this analysis, we propose a new GRF-redirecting control method for hip torques; the law no longer constrains the direction of GRF towards a single point but to the direction which is always providing a restoring moment to the body. A dynamic simulation result demonstrates the effectiveness of the proposed method. Here, we only consider a planar simple bipedal model with massless springy legs. The simulation results indicate that the proposed method is a promising method for achieving stable and robust bipedal walking.

The paper is structured as follows. In Section II, we first analyse the previous VPP method and propose a new method. Section III gives the main results of this paper, *i.e.*, planar bipedal walking simulation. Finally, we state concluding remarks in Section

II. Control for Upright Trunk

We seek for a control strategy for bipedal walking with upright trunk that is compatible with the compliant leg scheme, originated from spring-mass model. This type of model is called a bipedal trunk spring loaded inverted pendulum model (BTSLIP model [25]). An intriguing strategy named the VP concept and the VPP method [21] have inspired our method proposed in this section. We first review the VPP method and then proceed to a new method.

A. The VPP Model

The VPP model presented in [21] is illustrated in Figure 1. A planar bipedal walking model consists of a rigid trunk, of which center of mass (CoM) is located above hip, and two massless springy legs. This model is named the Bipedal Trunk Spring Loaded Inverted Pendulum (BTSLIP) model [25]. The springy legs are assumed to produce axial forces dependent on leg deflection from its rest length, and each leg is assumed to have hip torques that eventually generates tangential component of the GRF, perpendicular to its axial direction, between its point foot and the ground.

By introducing a variable β, a representative angle between the direction of the GRF and the leg axis, two components of the GRF (axial force F_r and tangential force F_t) are described as

$$\begin{cases} F_r = k(L_0 - L) \\ F_t = F_r \tan\beta, \end{cases} \tag{1}$$

where k is the stiffness of the leg and L_0 is the rest length of the spring. L is the length of the leg. In the VPP method, the hip torque is controlled to generate tangential force F_t in order to redirect the ground reaction force towards the VPP located above the CoM,

$$M_h = LF_t = LF_r \tan\beta,$$

where β is geometrically computed because the VPP is fixed on the trunk.

$$\tan\beta = \frac{r_h \sin\psi + r_{VPP}\sin(\psi - \gamma)}{L + r_h\cos\psi + r_{VPP}\cos(\psi-\gamma)}. \tag{2}$$

Here, r_h is the distance between CoM and hip, r_{VPP} is the distance between CoM and VPP, and γ is angle between torso longitudinal axis and a line connecting CoM and VPP. L and ψ are current leg length and angle, respectively. As originally proposed in [21], we regard $\gamma = 0$ throughout this paper. The insight behind the method is that the resultant GRF will *always* provide restoring moment about body tilting and the model can walk with upright trunk with this inherent mechanical property. Although a direct feedback of orientation of the trunk is not input to the hip torque controller, the trunk can maintain upright position with small oscillation as if a pendulum has a stable equilibrium point at its downright position. However, we have found that having a *single intersection point* for GRFs is not sufficient to always provide restoring moment to the body.

In Figure 2, we present all possible postures of the schematic model (trunk with a single compliant leg). The trunk may be upright or tilted in clockwise/counter-clockwise (CW/CCW) direction. At the same time, the foot of its stance leg (leg in touch with the ground) may be located right below or posterior/anterior the hip. Three possible postures of the trunk and three possible locations of foot relative to hip give eleven different postures to analyse. Mostly, as intended, the GRF pointing the VPP provides restoring moment, or at worst, zero moment. This allows the trunk be settle down in some region without specifying a desired posture. However, in some cases, the GRF pointing the VPP provides upsetting moment, which would cause the trunk to fall. The postures correspond to this case are depicted with red and shaded cells in the figure. Although this is an analysis to a static posture, we interpret that this property limits the performance of the model as will be shown in Section III.

In order to provide mathematical criterion, we introduce two variables $\tilde{\phi}$ and $\tilde{\beta}$, pitch orientation from upright posture and the angle between GRF and a virtual line connecting foot and CoM, respectively, as shown in Figure 3 (a). Note that the direction of the GRFs with respect to the CoM direction ($\tilde{\beta}$) is considered rather than β, because eventually this will determine the direction of the moment applied. Then, it can be shown that the cases which would destabilize the trunk, shown in Figure 2, can be represented by the following condition,

$$\tilde{\phi}\cdot\tilde{\beta} > 0. \tag{3}$$

For example, if we examine a posture in the left column and bottom row of the Figure 2, the trunk is tilted in clockwise direction and foot is posterior to the hip in both postures. However, if the controller tends to generate GRF towards the fixed VPP above the hip, in one model the resultant GRF would provide moment in counter-clockwise direction, which is a righting moment, whereas the moment in the other model

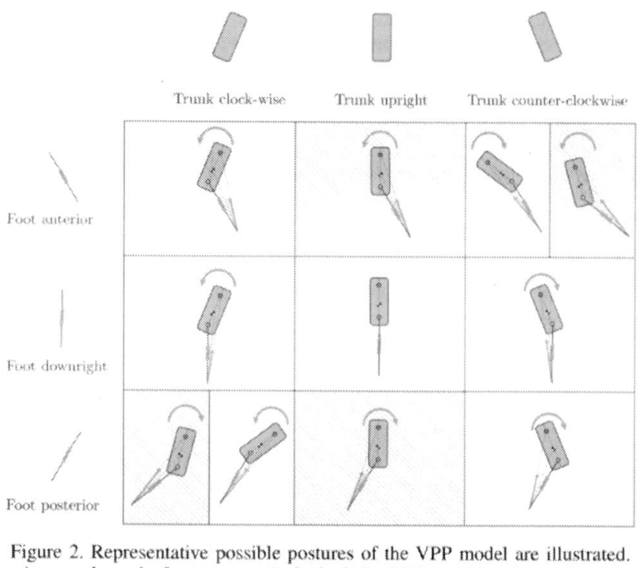

Figure 2. Representative possible postures of the VPP model are illustrated. Among these, in four postures(red, shaded), GRF provides the trunk with moments in destabilizing direction.

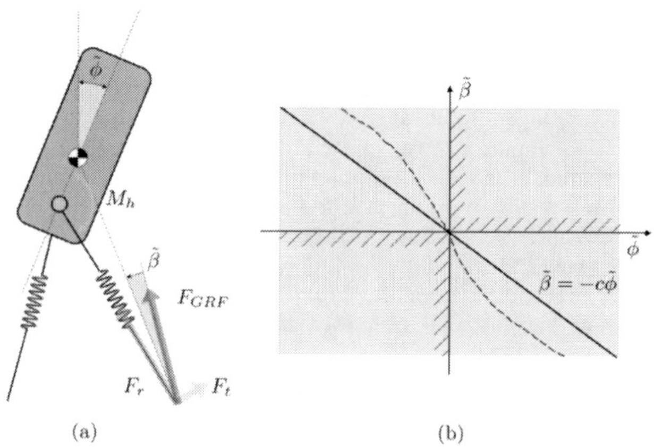

Figure 3. In order for analysis, a new variable $\tilde{\beta}$ and $\tilde{\phi}$ are introduced (a). In the domain of variables, the first and the third quadrant are not allowed (b). The controlled relation between $\tilde{\beta}$ and $\tilde{\phi}$ must lie within the second and the fourth quadrant.

in the shaded region will be in clock-wise direction, which results in a upsetting moment.

From this simple analysis, we end up with several remarks. First, a single fixed intersection point such as that in the VPP method is not sufficient for upright trunk. Actually, experimental findings indeed show that a single intersection point is not necessary for a VP system and cannot always be found [21]. Second, the *direction* of the GRF with respect to the CoM is what important factor to consider, rather than the *position* of the point where the GRF is redirected to, in order to approach the fascinating VP concept.

B. Proposed Control Strategy

Although the fixed VPP seems not sufficient, the general argument of the VP concept is still persuasive for us, in that, the direction of force generated at foot is important in upright trunk walking. Therefore, we keep the format of the controller (1) such that the hip torque redirect the force generated by the springy leg. It is also compatible with springy leg concept which seems important in dynamic walking. The difference is how to define the angle β.

Based on the above analysis, a proper GRF redirecting controller should aim $\tilde{\phi} \cdot \tilde{\beta} < 0$, which is represented by the region without shade in Figure 3 (a). We would like to argue that if the generated GRF by a suitable redirecting controller satisfies this condition, any form of control would work. The simplest form we can propose for a redirecting controller is the linear relationship as shown in Figure 3 (b).

$$\tilde{\beta} = -c\tilde{\phi}, \tag{4}$$

where c is a positive gain which should be properly designed.

Noting that the speed and the direction of motion of the planar robot model should also be considered in determining the direction of the GRFs, we end up with the following control form for force direction control.

$$\tilde{\beta} = -c\tilde{\phi} - d\dot{\tilde{\phi}}, \tag{5}$$

where d is another positive gain which should be properly designed. Corresponding hip torques will be computed to redirect axial leg force to desired direction with respect to CoM. The angle between the actual leg and the virtual line from foot to CoM can be computed from geometric information as well; denoting this angle as $\angle$, $\tan\beta = \tan(\tilde{\beta} + \angle)$ can be easily computed.

C. Feasible Direction of Foot-ground Interaction Force

As the direction of the GRF is a target control parameter, considering the constraints on the GRF becomes trivial in this framework. Typical constraints on the ground reaction force are friction cone and that the force is unilateral, i.e., it can only push the ground. These constraints put limit on determining $\tilde{\beta}$. In other words, the hip torques are uprighting the trunk as much as possible within feasible region.

III. SIMULATION RESULT

A. Model Description

In order to verify the proposed control method, we use dynamic simulation. The model configuration is illustrated in Figure 1 (a). The model parameters are listed in Table I.

The equations of motion of the model can be described as follows.

$$\begin{cases} m\ddot{x} = \sum_i F_x \\ m\ddot{y} = \sum_i F_y - mg \\ J\ddot{\phi} = \sum_i (\mathbf{r}_\mathrm{f} - \mathbf{r}_\mathrm{CoM}) \times \mathbf{F} \end{cases} \tag{6}$$

where $\mathbf{r}_\mathrm{CoM} = [x, y]^T$ is the CoM position, $\mathbf{r}_\mathrm{f}$ is the foot-in-contact position, ϕ is pitch angle in sagittal plane simulation.

TABLE I. MODEL PARAMETERS FOR THE SIMULATION

Parameter	Meaning	Value [unit]
m	total mass	80 [kg]
J	moment of inertia	4.58 [kg·m^2]
g	gravitational acceleration	9.81 [m/s^2]
k	leg stiffness	20,000 [N/m]
r_h	distance between CoM and hip	0.1 [m]

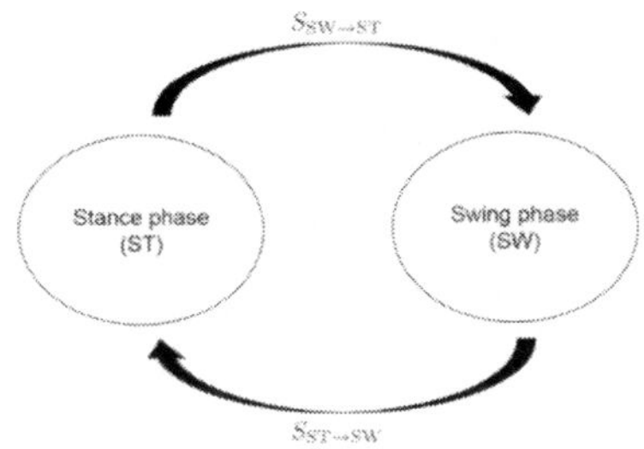

Figure 4. State transition of each leg.

$\mathbf{F} = [F_x, F_y]^T$ is the GRF at the foot in stance and can be described as

$$\begin{cases} F_x = F_r \cos\alpha + F_t \sin\alpha \\ F_y = F_r \sin\alpha - F_t \cos\alpha \end{cases} \tag{7}$$

where α is the angle between leg and the ground. $i\in$ [left, right] denotes leg in stance.

The model can have double support, single support, and possibly flight phase as shown in Figure 4. Transition between the phase and will not require additional computation nor changing the form of dynamical equations, because we do not consider impact dynamics when a swing leg touches down the ground when the leg is assumed massless. We only need to choose which leg provides forces to the body, *i.e.*, choose i properly. State transition of dynamical system is thus determined by the state transition of each leg, of which condition can be described as follows, where $\mathbf{x} = [x, y, \phi, \dot{x}, \dot{y}, \dot{\phi}]^T$ denote the state vector and $\mathbb{C}$ denote the admissible configuration space.

$$S_{\text{SW}\to\text{ST}} = \{\mathbf{x} \in \mathbb{C} | y_h - L_0 \sin\alpha_0 = 0\}$$
$$S_{\text{ST}\to\text{SW}} = \{\mathbf{x} \in \mathbb{C} | F_r = 0\}$$

In other words, swing to stance transition happens when the swing leg touches down the ground with the predefined angle of attack α_0, and the stance leg takes off the ground when ground reaction force becomes zero. Here, y_h is the vertical position of the hip.

B. Sagittal Plane Walking Simulation

The dynamics of the bipedal walking model with trunk and compliant legs is simulated for 20 seconds. Two methods, the VPP approach and the proposed control approach, are compared with the planar walking model in sagittal plane, of which control parameters are listed in Table II. In Figure 5 (a) and Figure 6 (a), the trajectories of the center of mass forward (x) and vertial (y) motion and pitch (ϕ) of the model are presented. Both methods have periodic solutions, and the simulation results are started from initial conditions a bit deviated from the periodic solution. With this initial condition, the proposed method quickly stabilize the model to its steady-state motion, whereas the model with the VPP method does not. The method cannot reject this errors. In the proposed method, pitch motion of the model is directly fed back to the controller and therefore the pitch stabilization is directly achieved, whereas in the VPP model, the pitch oscillation is maintained to some extent.

Figure 5 (b) and Figure 6 (b) present the models with the same initial conditions but with external force disturbance of

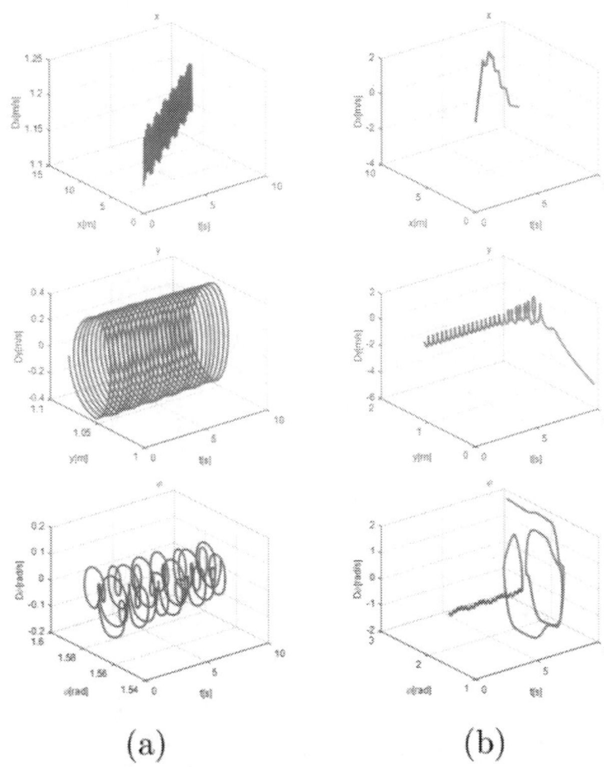

Figure 5. Simulation results with planar bipedal walking model with the VPP method on its sagittal plane. The response of the system without (a) and with (b) disturbance. The trajectories after the moment that force disturbance is applied are plotted with red.

$F_{\text{dist}} = [45, 0]^T$[N] that is applied at the right foot of the model during 0.2 seconds. This would affect both translational motion and rotational motion. Both models could reject small disturbances in the sense of not falling down, and this value is chosen to show the difference between the two. It is clear that the proposed method is more robust in the sense of not falling down than the VPP method. The pitch motion is immediately stabilized and at the same time, the translational motion is indirectly stabilized by the self-stabilizing property of mass-spring walking system [18]. However, in the VPP method, destabilized pitch motion induced gait instability.

IV. Future Work

We investigate the simple reduced-order models and develop the control method in order to build and control a real bipedal robotic platform. Regarding this, we present interesting future works of our great interest.

First of all, we consider investigating the role of foot and ankle is crucial in developing more comprehensive walking

TABLE II. CONTROL PARAMETERS FOR THE SIMULATION

Parameter	Meaning	Value [unit]
r_{VPP}	distance between VPP and CoM	0.1 [m]
α_0	fixed leg touchdown angle in sagittal plane	107 [deg]
c	position-proportional gain	5 [-]
d	velocity-proportional gain	1 [s]

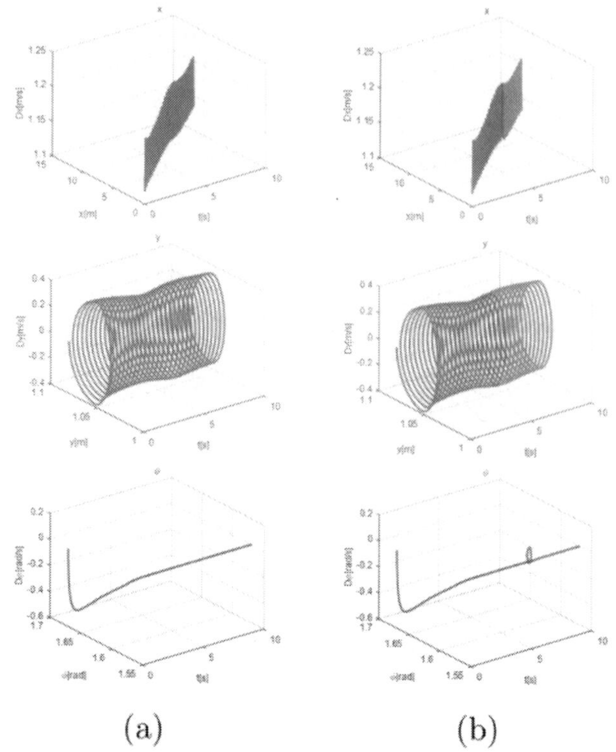

Figure 6. Simulation result with planar bipedal walking model with the proposed method on its sagittal plane. The response of the system without (a) and with (b) disturbance. The trajectories after the moment that force disturbance is applied are plotted with red.

model. In robotics, in order for the task of standing still, the foot and ankle seem crucial. On the other hand, in biomechanics, the role of foot and ankle have been studied in variety of perspective, including mechanical advantage of ankle push-off [26]. In [27], the authors have analyzed the role of ankle and foot in static posture, based on a similar trunk-upright control scheme. A similar study regarding dynamic behaviour would be interesting.

Second, as the model is based on a reduced-order model with massless legs, implementing the principles gained from the model onto more realistic articulated model is another important task. There are many available techniques developed in existing literatures, for example, readers are referred to [28]. We aim to apply the model to rigid-body articulated robotic model and develop a detailed control algorithm.

Third, we seek for developing a full 3-d robot in the near future, and therefore extending the model to 3-d would be important. we believe that the same control strategy would be valid in frontal plane (roll motion) balance, as the structure of the proposed strategy consisting of compliant legs and force redirecting hip torque is not restrained from sagittal plane walking. Once planar model in frontal plane is investigated, combining the sagittal and frontal plane control method in a single 3-D model would be possible.

V. CONCLUSION

In this paper, we proposed a novel method to stabilize trunk orientation of bipedal walking. The method is inspired from the VP concept and the VPP method. We focus on the fact that if the direction of the ground reaction force is computed based on rotational motion of the trunk and the magnitude of force which is computed based on axial compliance of the leg, it is possible to realize bipedal walking with dynamic characteristic of human walking. As for our future work, we aim to employ the method in controlling articulated robot simulation. Extending the simple model in 3-D is also of our great interest.

REFERENCES

[1] M. Vukobratović and B. Borovac, "Zero-moment pointthirty five years of its life," *International Journal of Humanoid Robotics*, vol. 1, no. 01, pp. 157–173, 2004.

[2] Y. S. et al., "The intelligent asimo: system overview and integration," in *IEEE/RSJ International Conference on Intelligent Robots and Systems*, vol. 3, 2002, pp. 2478–2483.

[3] Y. Choi, D. Kim, Y. Oh, and B. J. You, "Posture/walking control for humanoid robot based on kinematic resolution of com jacobian with embedded motion," *IEEE Transactions on Robotics*, vol. 23, no. 6, pp. 1285–1293, 2007.

[4] K. Kaneko, K. Harada, F. Kanehiro, G. Miyamori, and K. Akachi, "Humanoid robot hrp-3," in *IEEE/RSJ International Conference on Intelligent Robots and Systems*, 2008, pp. 2471–2478.

[5] E. R. Westervelt, J. W. Grizzle, and D. E. Koditschek, "Hybrid zero dynamics of planar biped walkers," *IEEE transactions on automatic control*, vol. 48, no. 1, pp. 42–56, 2003.

[6] E. R. Westervelt, J. W. Grizzle, C. Chevallereau, J. H. Choi, and B. Morris, *Feedback control of dynamic bipedal robot locomotion*. CRC press, 2007, vol. 28.

[7] K. Sreenath, H.-W. Park, I. Poulakakis, and J. W. Grizzle, "Embedding active force control within the compliant hybrid zero dynamics to achieve stable, fast running on mabel," *The International Journal of Robotics Research*, vol. 32, no. 3, pp. 324–345, 2013.

[8] I. R. Manchester, U. Mettin, F. Iida, and R. Tedrake, "Stable dynamic walking over uneven terrain," *The International Journal of Robotics Research*, vol. 30, no. 3, pp. 265–279, 2011.

[9] S. e. a. Rezazadeh, "Spring-mass walking with atrias in 3d: Robust gait control spanning zero to 4.3 kph on a heavily underactuated bipedal robot," in *ASME 2015 Dynamic Systems and Control Conference*. American Society of Mechanical Engineers, 2015, p. V001T04A003.

[10] R. J. Full and D. E. Koditschek, "Templates and anchors: neuromechanical hypotheses of legged locomotion on land," *Journal of Experimental Biology*, vol. 202, no. 23, pp. 3325–3332, 1999.

[11] D. G. Hobbelen and M. Wisse, "Controlling the walking speed in limit cycle walking," *The International Journal of Robotics Research*, vol. 27, no. 9, pp. 989–1005, 2008.

[12] D. J. Braun and M. Goldfarb, "A control approach for actuated dynamic walking in biped robots," *IEEE Transactions on Robotics*, vol. 25, no. 6, pp. 1292–1303, 2009.

[13] T. Geng and J. Q. Gan, "Planar biped walking with an equilibrium point controller and state machines," *IEEE/ASME Transactions on Mechatronics*, vol. 15, no. 2, pp. 253–260, 2010.

[14] R. Alexander, "Mechanics of bipedal locomotion," *Perspectives in experimental biology*, vol. 1, pp. 493–504, 1976.

[15] R. Blickhan, "The spring-mass model for running and hopping," *Journal of biomechanics*, vol. 22, no. 11, pp. 1217–1227, 1989.

[16] C. R. Lee and C. T. Farley, "Determinants of the center of mass trajectory in human walking and running," *Journal of experimental biology*, vol. 201, no. 21, pp. 2935–2944, 1998.

[17] M. G. Pandy, "Simple and complex models for studying muscle function in walking," *Philosophical Transactions of the Royal Society B: Biological Sciences*, vol. 358, no. 1437, pp. 1501–1509, 2003.

[18] H. Geyer, A. Seyfarth, and R. Blickhan, "Compliant leg behaviour explains basic dynamics of walking and running," *Proceedings of the Royal Society of London B: Biological Sciences*, vol. 273, no. 1603, pp. 2861–2867, 2006.

[19] M. H. Raibert, *Legged robots that balance*. MIT press, 1986.

[20] C. e. a. Hubicki, "Atrias: Design and validation of a tether-free 3d-capable spring-mass bipedal robot," *The International Journal of Robotics Research*, vol. 35, no. 12, pp. 1497–1521, 2016.

[21] H.-M. Maus, S. Lipfert, M. Gross, J. Rummel, and A. Seyfarth, "Upright human gait did not provide a major mechanical challenge for our ancestors," *Nature Communications*, vol. 1, p. 70, 2010.

[22] K. G. Gruben and W. L. Boehm, "Force direction pattern stabilizes sagittal plane mechanics of human walking," *Human movement science*, vol. 31, no. 3, pp. 649–659, 2012.

[23] M. A. e. a. Sharbafi, "Controllers for robust hopping with upright trunk based on the virtual pendulum concept," in *IEEE/RSJ International Conference on Intelligent Robots and Systems(IROS)*. IEEE, 2012, pp. 2222–2227.

[24] A. T. Peekema, "Template-based control of the bipedal robot atrias," Master's thesis, OSU, 2015.

[25] M. A. Sharbafi, C. Maufroy, M. N. Ahmadabadi, M. J. Yazdanpanah, and A. Seyfarth, "Robust hopping based on virtual pendulum posture control," *Bioinspiration & biomimetics*, vol. 8, no. 3, p. 036002, 2013.

[26] A. D. Kuo, "Choosing your steps carefully," *IEEE Robotics & Automation Magazine*, vol. 14, no. 2, pp. 18–29, 2007.

[27] K. G. Gruben and W. L. Boehm, "Ankle torque control that shifts the center of pressure from heel to toe contributes non-zero sagittal plane angular momentum during human walking," *Journal of biomechanics*, vol. 47, no. 6, pp. 1389–1394, 2014.

[28] G. Garofalo, C. Ott, and A. Albu-Schffer, "Walking control of fully actuated robots based on the bipedal slip model," in *2012 IEEE International Conference on Robotics and Automation*, May 2012, pp. 1456–1463.

Extended LALR(1) Parsing

Wuu Yang

Computer Science Department
National Chiao-Tung University
Taiwan, R.O.C.
Email: wuuyang@cs.nctu.edu.tw

***Abstract*—We identify a class of context-free grammars, called the *extended LALR(1)* (ELALR(1)), which is a superclass of LALR(1) and a subclass of LR(1). Our algorithm is essentially a smarter method for merging similar states in the LR(1) state machines. LALR(1) would merge *every* pair of similar states. In contrast, our algorithm merges a pair of similar states only if no (reduce-reduce) conflicts will be created. Thus, when no conflicts occur, our algorithm produces exactly the same state machines as the LALR(1) algorithm. However, when the LALR(1) algorithm reports conflicts, our algorithm may still produce a (larger) conflict-free state machine. In the extreme case when no states can be merged, our algorithm simply returns the original LR(1) machines. An important characteristic of the ELALR(1) algorithm is that there is no backtracking. On the other hand, the ELALR(1) algorithm does not guarantee the minimum state machines.**

Keywords–context-free grammar; grammar; extended LALR parser; LR parser; LALR parser; parsing

I. INTRODUCTION

Parsing is a basic step in every compiler and interpreter. LR parsers are powerful enough to handle almost all practical programming languages. The downside of LR parsers is the huge table size. This caused the development of several variants, such as LALR parsers, which requires significantly smaller tables at the expense of reduced capability. We identify a class of context-free grammars, called the *extended LALR (1)* (ELALR(1)), which is a superclass of LALR(1) and a subclass of LR(1) [1]. Figure 6 is an example of an ELALR(1) machine.

The core of the LR parsers is a finite state machine. The LALR(1) state machine may be obtained by merging *every* pair of similar states in the LR(1) machine [6]. In case (reduce-reduce) conflicts occur due to merging (note that only reduce-reduce conflicts may occur due to merging similar states) we will have to revert to the larger, original LR(1) machine. A practical advantage of LALR(1) grammars is the much smaller state machines than the original LR(1) machines. However, any conlficts will force the parser to use the larger LR(1) machine. The crux of our approach is to merge only pairs of similar states that do not cause conflicts.

A simple ELALR(1) grammar can be easily created by sequentially composing an LALR(1) grammar and an LR(1) grammar, as follows:

$P \to U; S$
$U \to \ldots$ (LALR(1))
$S \to \ldots$ (LR(1) but not LALR(1))

Assume the subset of production rules starting from the nonterminal U is completely independent of that starting from S. Further assume the U rules form an LALR(1) grammar and the S rules form a LR(1) but not LALR(1) grammar. The sequential composition of the U and S would form an ELALR(1) grammar. For parsing, we need to use the much larger LR(1) state machine.

In this paper, we propose a method that can somehow reduce the state machine of a LR(1)-but-non-LALR(1) grammar because certain parts of the grammar could be LALR(1) and hence these parts can be handled with the smaller LALR(1) state machine. The rest will be parsed with the stadard LR(1) machine.

Our idea is that we start from the LR(1) machine of the grammar and merge as many (similar) states as possible under the constraint that no conflict will be created due to merging. The resulting machine is called the ELALR(1) machine, which can be used in the standard shift/reduce LR parser.

Our algorithm never backtracks. Once the merging of a pair of similar states is committed, the pair of states will remain merged. The algorithm will never undo the merge later. The contribution of this paper is that we arrange the order of merging similar states so that no backtracking is needed. However, our algorithm does not guarantee a smallest ELALR(1) state machine.

LR(1) parsers are powerful enough to handle most practical programming languages [8]. The cannonical LR(1) parsers make use of big state machines. LALR(1) parsers [4] are deemed more practical in that much smaller state machines are used. There are several algorithms for computing the LALR machines and lookaheads efficiently [3][5][10]. None of these attempted to parse non-LALR grammars. The classical parser generator *yacc* [7] is based on the LALR(1) grammars. *Yacc* relies on ad hoc rules, such as the order of productions in the grammar, to resolve conflicts in order to apply an LALR parser to a non-LALR grammar. In contrast, this paper, which addresses ELALR(1) grammars, does not employ ad hoc rules. It is known that every language that admits an LR(k) parser

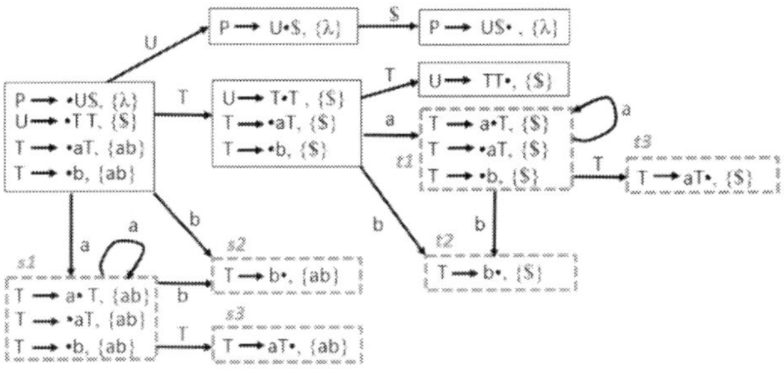

Fig. 1. The LR(1) machine of G_1.

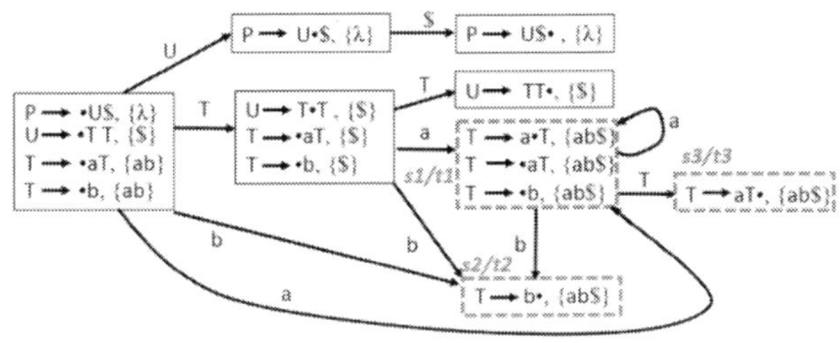

Fig. 2. The LALR(1) machine of G_1.

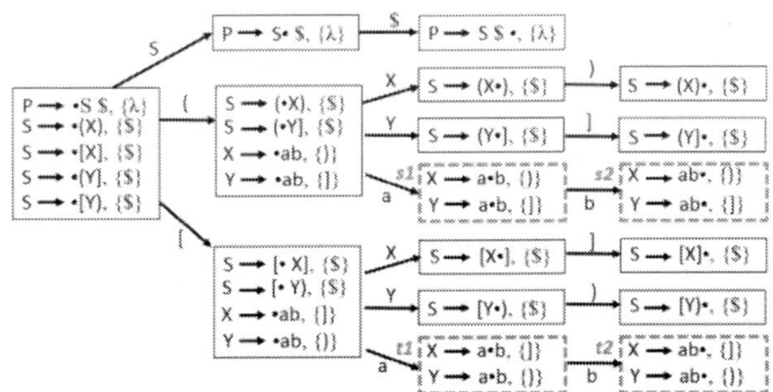

Fig. 3. The LR(1) machine of G_2.

also admits an LALR(1) parser [9]. In order to parse for a non-LALR(1) grammar, there used to be three approaches: (1) use the LR(1) parser; (2) add some ad hoc rules to the LALR(1) parser, similar to what yacc does; and (3) transform the grammar into LALR(1) and then generate a parser. The transformation approach may exponentially increase the number of productions [9] and the transformed grammar is usually unnatural. Our approach provides a fourth alternative: use the extended LALR(1) state machines.

The remainder of this paper is organized as follows. Section 2 will introduce the terminology and explain the extended LALR(1) grammars with examples. Our algorithm is presented in Section 3. Its correctness is also discussed there. Section 4 concludes this paper. In this paper, we are concerned only with one-token lookahead, that is, LR(1), LALR(1), and ELALR(1). We sometimes omit the "(1)" notation if no confusion occurs. However, our method may be extended to ELALR(k).

II. Background and Motivation

A grammar $G = (N, T, P, S)$ consists of a non-empty set of nonterminals N, a non-empty set of terminals T, a non-empty set of production rules P and a special nonterminal S, which is called the start symbol. We assume that $N \cap T = \emptyset$. A production rule has the form

$$A \to \gamma$$

where A is a nonterminal and γ is a (possibly empty) string of nonterminals and terminals. We use the production rules to derive a string of terminals from the start symbol.

LR parsing is based on a deterministic finite state machine, called *LR* machine. A state in the LR machine is a non-empty set of items. An item has the form $A \to \alpha \bullet \beta, la$, where $A \to \alpha\beta$ is one of the production rules, $\bullet$ indicates a position in the string $\alpha\beta$, and la (the *lookahead* set) is a set of terminals that could follow the nonterminal A in later derivation steps. Two states in the LR machine are *similar* if they have the same number of items and the corresponding items differ only in the lookahead sets. For example, states $s1$ and $t1$ in Figure 1, each of which contains three items, are similar states.

LALR(1) machines are obtained from LR(1) machines by merging *every* pair of similar states. For example, Figure 2 is the LALR(1) machine obtained from the LR(1) machine in Figure 1 by merging three pairs of similar states: $s1$ and $t1$; $s2$ and $t2$; and $s3$ and $t3$. (Remember two states are similar if they have the same items, except that the lookahdead sets might differ. To *merge two similar states*, we use the same items in the original states, except that the lookahead set of an item is the union of the lookahead sets of the two corresponding items in the original states.) The exact construction of LR and LALR machines from a context-free grammar is discussed in most compiler textbooks, such as [2][6].

Consider grammar G_1:

R1	$P \to U\$$
R2	$U \to TT$
R3	$T \to aT$
R4	$T \to b$

The LR(1) machine of G_1 is shown in Figure 1. States $s1$ and $t1$ are similar states. So are states $s2$ and $t2$ and states $s3$ and $t3$. The three pairs of states can be merged. The resulting machine is shown in Figure 2. Since there is no conflict in the resulting machine, G_1 is LALR(1).

Consider grammar G_2:

R5	$P \to S\$$
R6	$S \to (X)$
R7	$S \to [X]$
R8	$S \to (Y]$
R9	$S \to [Y)$
R10	$X \to ab$
R11	$Y \to ab$

The LR(1) machine of G_2 is shown in Figure 3. Since there is no conflict in Figure 3, grammar G_2 is LR(1).

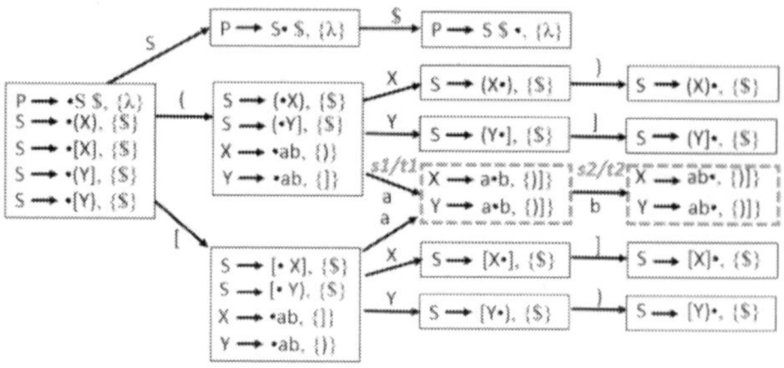

Fig. 4. The LALR(1) machine of G_2, which contains reduce-reduce conflicts.

There are two pairs of similar states in Figure 3: states $s1$ and $t1$; states $s2$ and $t2$. Figure 4 shows the resulting LALR(1) machine by merging the two pairs of similar states. Note that there are two reduce-reduce conflicts in state $s2/t2$ in Figure 4. Therefore, states $s2$ and $t2$ should not be merged. Furthermore, states $s1$ and $t1$ should not be merged either because LR machines are deterministic.

It is easy to combine G_1 and G_2 into a single grammar, in which some, but not all, pairs of similar states may be merged without creating conflicts. For instance, consider grammar G_3 below, which is a sequential combination of G_1 and G_2. Prodcution rules R1 and R6 are combined as a single new rule.

R1	$P \to US\$$
R2	$U \to TT$
R3	$T \to aT$
R4	$T \to b$
R6	$S \to (X)$
R7	$S \to [X]$
R8	$S \to (Y]$
R9	$S \to [Y)$
R10	$X \to ab$
R11	$Y \to ab$

Grammar G_3 is clearly not LALR(1). Hence the larger LR(1) machine must be used in parsing. However, it is still possible to reduce the size of LR machine for G_3. Figure 5 shows the LR(1) machine of G_3. There are five pairs of similar states: states $s1$ and $t1$; $s2$ and $t2$; $s3$ and $t3$; $s4$ and $t4$; and $s5$ and $t5$; However, states $s5$ and $t5$ cannot be merged due to a potential conflict. Furthermore, states $s4$ and $t4$ cannot be merged because LR machines must be deterministic. The other three pairs of similar states may be safely merged, creating a machine smaller than the standard LR(1) machine. The resulting machine is shown in Figure 6, which is called the *extended LALR(1) machine* of G_3.

Definition. A grammar is *ELALR(1)* if and only if at least a pair of similar states in its LR(1) machine may be merged without creating conflicts.

In other words, a grammar is ELALR(1) if and only if it has a conflict-free state machine that is smaller than the grammar's LR(1) machine.

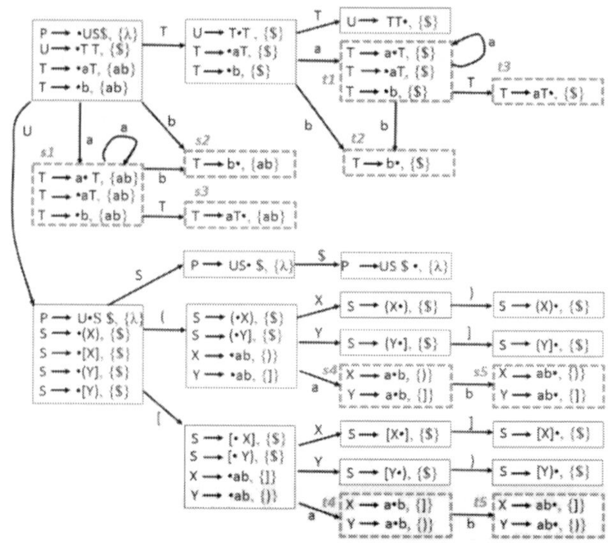

Fig. 5. The LR(1) machine of G_3.

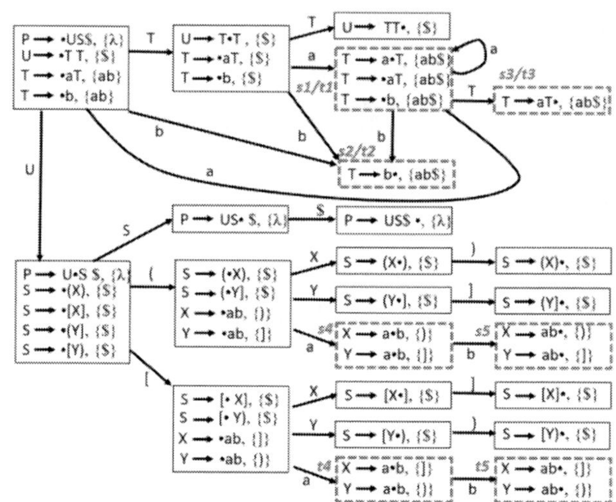

Fig. 6. The ELALR(1) machine of G_3.

In determining which pairs of similar states may be safely merged, trial-and-error is a straightforward method. However, we can do better.

We will start from a few observations and facts. First note that the LR(1) as well as the LALR(1) machines are all deterministic.

Theorem 1: Merging two similar states in LR(1) machines can possibly create reduce-reduce conflicts, but never shift-reduce conflicts.

For example, in Figure 4, there are reduce-reduce conflicts in the merged state $s2/t2$.

Lemma 2: Consider the fragment of an LR machine in Figure 7. If states $s1$ and $t1$ are similar, then (1) states $s1$ and $t1$ have the same number of successor states; and (2) their

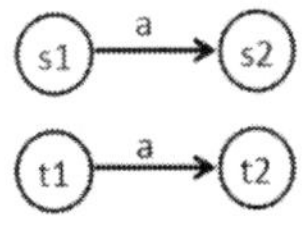

Fig. 7. A pair of similar states in an LR(1) machine. States $s1$ and $t1$ can be merged only if states $s2$ and $t2$ are merged. There will be an edge $(s1, t1) \rightarrow^{a} (s2, t2)$ in the similarity graph.

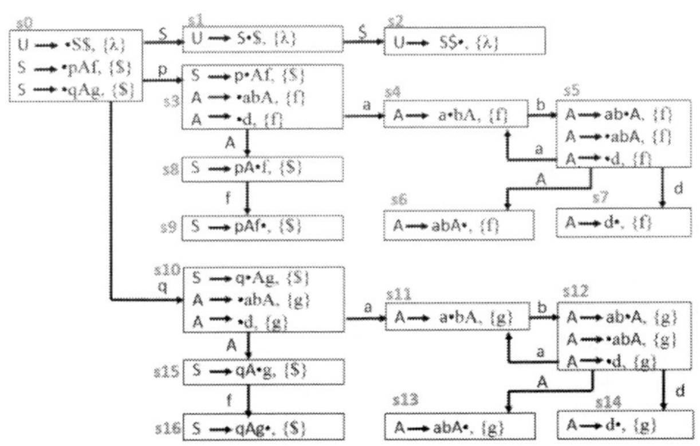

Fig. 8. The LR(1) machine for the example grammar.

corresponding successor states are also similar, *i.e.*, states $s2$ and $t2$ are also similar.

Proof. This is due to the construction of the LR machine. Q.E.D.

Lemma 3: Consider the fragment of an LR machine in Figure 7. Assume states $s1$ and $t1$ are similar (and hence states $s2$ and $t2$ are also similar). States $s1$ and $t1$ can be merged only if states $s2$ and $t2$ are merged.

Proof. This lemma is due to the fact that LR/LALR machines must be deterministic. Q.E.D.

Corollary 4: Consider The fragment of an LR machine in Figure 7. Assume states $s1$ and $t1$ are similar (and hence states $s2$ and $t2$ are also similar). If states $s2$ and $t2$ are not merged, then states $s1$ and $t1$ cannot be merged.

Due to Corollary 4, we should try to merge $s2$ and $t2$ *before* we try to merge $s1$ and $t1$. In general, when similar states in an LR(1) machine are merged, the order of merging had better be from leaves to root. However, the LR(1) machine may contain cycles and is not a tree in general.

Our algorithm, presented in the next section, will take care of these details. A directed cycle in a directed graph, such as states $s4$ and $s5$ in Figure 8, is called a *strongly connected component* (scc). According to Corollary 4, all states in an scc in the LR(1) machine must be merged with their respective similar states simultaneously or none should. In Figure 8, either both pairs of similar states $(s4, s11)$ and $(s5, s12)$ are merged or no pair should be merged. Due to this restriction, we use *aggregates*, which are sets of pairs of similar states, to represent two separate sccs that might be merged.

III. Algorithm

In this section, we explain our algorithm for constructing the finite state machine for extended LALR(1) grammars. We will use the following grammar G_4 to illustrate our algorithm. Figure 8 is the LR(1) machine for this grammar.

R1 $U \rightarrow S\$$
R2 $S \rightarrow pAf$
R3 $S \rightarrow qAg$
R4 $A \rightarrow abA$
R5 $A \rightarrow d$

We will start from an LR(1) grammar. Draw the LR(1) state machine of the grammar. Since the grammar is LR(1), there is no conflict in the LR(1) machine.

Then the strongly connected components in the LR(1) machine are identified. In Figure 8, states $s4$ and $s5$ form a strongly connected component (scc). So do states $s11$ and $s12$. Strongly connected components in the LR(1) machine can be traced to (direct or indirect) recursive production rules in the grammar. In Figure 8, the scc is due to the recursive rule $A \rightarrow abA$.

We then find all pairs of similar states. In Figure 8, there are four pairs of similar states: $(s4, s11)$, $(s5, s12)$, $(s6, s13)$, and $(s7, s14)$.

We then build the *similarity* graph. The similarity graph for the example grammar is shown in Figure 9(a). Initially, the similarity graph contains only vertices; edges are gradually inserted into the graph. Each vertex in the similarity graph denotes a pair of similar states taken from the LR(1) machine. During the construction of the similarity graph, we may add vertices of the form (s, s) (*i.e.*, a pair of identical states), which have no outgoing edges. For each pair of similar states (s_1, t_1), either (1) s_1 and t_1 are exactly the same state, or (2) neither has a successor state, or (3) they have the same number of successor states. Each successor state of s_1 corresponds to exactly one successor state of t_1. Note that the corresponding successors of s_1 and t_1 are s_2 and t_2 if the edges $s_1 \rightarrow^{u} s_2$ and $t_1 \rightarrow^{u} t_2$ carry the same label, which is u in this case.

In case (3), we add an edge from the vertex representing the pair (s_1, t_1) to the vertex representing the pair (s_2, t_2). This edge is denoted as $(s_1, t_1) \rightarrow^{u} (s_2, t_2)$ in the similarity graph, which indicates that s_1 and t_1 may be merged only if s_2 and t_2 are merged, according to Lemma 3. (Note that a pair of similar states could be written either as (s, t) or (t, s). In constructing the similarity graph, we had better fix the order of the pair of states. The first time the pair is encountered, the order of s and t is determined from the already constructed part of the similarity graph. When the pair is encountered again, we should use the order determined previously. Otherwise, a part of the similarity graph may be duplicated. Duplication only makes the algorithm spends more time but has no effect on the final result.)

Figure 9(a) is the similarity graph for the LR machine in Figure 8. Note that there may or may not be cycles in a

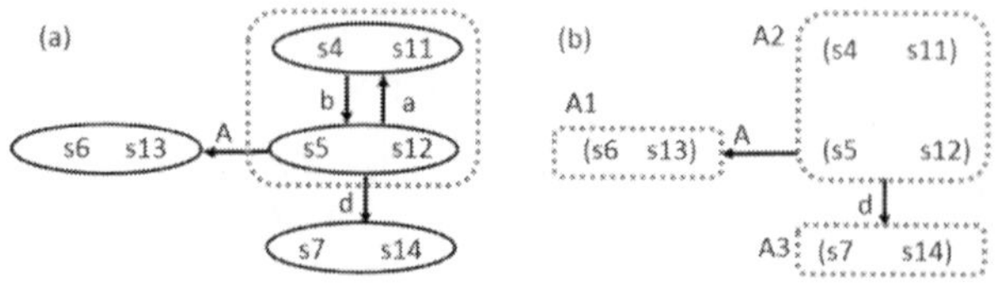

Fig. 9. (a) The similarity graph for Figure 8, in which each vertex represents a pair of similar states in the LR(1) machine. (b) The aggregation graph, in which each node (called an *aggregate*) represents a set of pairs of similar states. The aggregation graph must be acyclic.

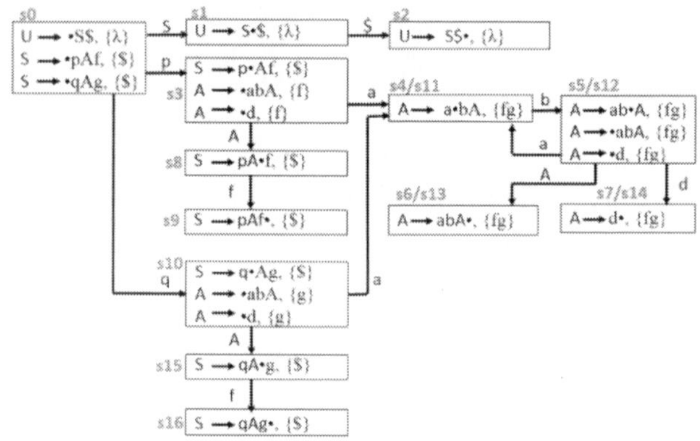

Fig. 10. The state machine after merging four pairs of states. This is actually the LALR(1) state machine.

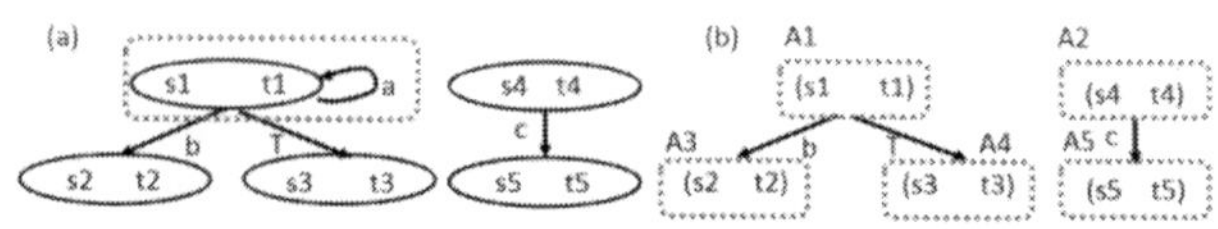

Fig. 11. The similarity graph and the aggregation graph for grammar G_3.

similarity graph. Since each vertex in the similarity graph represents a pair of states, we can switch the order of every pair of states, that is, from (s, t) to (t, s), resulting in an isomorphic graph.

Now consider the similarity graph. If vertices (*i.e.*, pairs of states), say $(p_1, q_1), (p_2, q_2), \ldots, (p_h, q_h)$, form a strongly connected component in the similarity graph (this implies that the states $p_1, p_2, \ldots, p_h$ form a strongly connected component in the LR(1) machine. So do the states $q_1, q_2, \ldots, q_h$), then mark these adjacent vertices as an *aggregate*. Finally, the pair of similar states which does not belong to any aggregates will form an aggregate by itself. We may say that the set of all pairs of similar states are partitioned into aggregates. In Figure 9(a), the two pairs of similar states $(s4, s11)$ and $(s5, s12)$ form an aggregate. Each of the remaining two pairs forms an aggregate by itself. These three aggregates, which are labeled *A1*, *A2*, and *A3*, constitute the *aggregation graph*, which is shown in Figure 9(b). Note that each pair of similar states (*i.e.*, a vertex) belongs to exactly one aggregate. We say one aggregate, say A_i, is a *successor* of another aggregate, say A_j, if there is an edge $A_j \rightarrow A_i$ in the aggregation graph. In Figure 9(b), $A1$ and $A3$ are successors of $A1$.

An aggregate is a set of pairs of similar states. These states are closely related to the strongly connected components in the LR(1) machine. According to Lemma 3, every pair of similar states in an aggregate must be merged if any pair of similar states in the same aggregate are merged or none will be merged.

Note that the resulting aggregation graph is acyclic. Thus, we can find a reverse topological order of the aggregates in the aggregation graph. For each aggregate A in the reverse topological order, first check if any of the successor aggregates of A is marked as *unmergable*. If so, then mark this aggregate A also as *unmergable*. Otherwise every pair of similar states in A are merged. If any conflicts occur due to the merge, then undo the merge and mark the aggregate A as *unmergable*. On the other hand, when no conflicts occur, this means that all the pairs of similar states in A can be safely merged. That is, the merge is comitted. We will proceed with the next aggregate in the reverse topological order.

In Figure 9(b), a reverse topological order is $A1$, $A3$, and $A2$. So we will merge the pair of similar states in aggregate $A1$ first. Then we attempt to merge the pair of similar states in aggregate $A3$. Finally we attempt to merge the two pairs of similar states in aggregate $A2$. Figures 10 shows the final state machine, which is actually the LALR(1) machine since this grammar is LALR(1).

If a grammar is LALR(1), that is, every pair of similar states can be merged without creating conflicts, our algorithm will eventually construct the LALR(1) machine. In the other extreme, if no similar states could be merged without creating conflicts, our algorithm will not merge any states and simply return the original LR(1) machine.

Example. The similarity graph and the aggregation graph for grammar G_3 are shown in Figure 11 (a) and (b), respectively. A topological order is $A3, A4, A1, A5, A2$. The pair of similar states $(s5, t5)$ cannot be merged due to a conflict. Consequently, the pair of similar states $(s4, t4)$ cannot be merged either. The resulting ELALR(1) state machine is shown in Figure 6.

Correctness of the algorithm. There are only finite pairs of similar states in an LR(1) state machine. The transitions among pairs of similar states are also finite. Hence, the similarity graph is finite and can be built in a finite amount of time. The aggregation graph is essentially a reduced similarity graph. Thus, it is also finite and can be built in a finite amount of time.

All the pairs of similar states in the LR(1) machine are partitioned into aggregates. Merging similar states is attempted step by step. In each step, all pairs of an aggregate are merged (if no conflicts occur) or ignored (otherwise). The aggregates are examined in a reverse topological order.

The starting point of our algorithm is the original LR(1) state machine, which is deterministic and satisfies the Viable-Prefix Lemma [6]. Let M be the state machine immediately

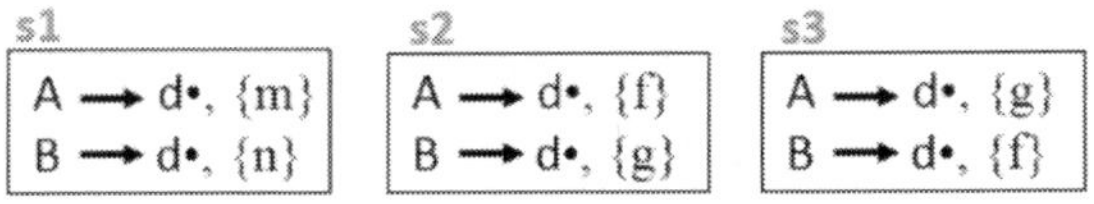

Fig. 12. Three similar states for grammar G_5.

before a step and M' be the one immediately after that step. We may make the following claim:

Claim. If M is deterministic and satisfies the Viable-Prefix Lemma, then M' is also deterministic and satisfies the Viable-Prefix Lemma.

Let AG be the aggregate considered in the current step. If no merging is done in the current step, $M' = M$. If some pairs of similar states are merged in the current step, due to the reverse topological order of merging, all pairs of similar states in all successor aggregates of AG in the aggregation graph have been merged. Therefore, M' is still deterministic. Furthermore, every path in M corresponds to exactly one path in M' and every path in M' is a path in M. If M satisfies the Viable-Prefix Lemma, so does M'.

Note that merging starts from an LR(1) machine, which is deterministic and satisfies the Viable-Prefix Lemma. We conclude that that the state machine eventually produced by our ELALR(1) algorithm is deterministic and satisfies the Viable-Prefix Lemma. Hence we may claim the correctness of our algorithm.

The ELALR(1) machines produced by our algorithm need not be minimum. Consider the following grammar G_5:

R1 $U \to S\$$
R2 $S \to pAf$
R3 $S \to pBg$
R4 $S \to qAg$
R5 $S \to qBf$
R6 $S \to rAm$
R7 $S \to rBn$
R8 $A \to d$
R9 $B \to d$

The LR(1) machine for G_5 will contain three similar states shown in Figure 12. States $s1$ and $s2$ may be safely merged. So do states $s1$ and $s3$. But states $s2$ and $s3$ cannot. It is hard to decide which pair of similar states should be merged in order to achieve the minimum ELALR(1) machine.

In our algorithm, $s1$ and $s2$ will be in one aggregate; $s1$ and $s3$ will be in another; and $s2$ and $s3$ will be in a third aggregate. Exactly which pair is merged depends on the reverse topological order in which the aggregates in the aggregation graph are visited.

For grammar G_5, the resulting state machine after merging states $s1$ and $s2$ has the same size as that after merging states $s1$ and $s3$. From this example, we know that there may not be a unique minimum ELALR(1) machine in general.

An obvious approach to produce a minimum ELALR(1) machine is to try all possible reverse topological orders of aggragates in the aggregation graph. To find the minimum state machines, a naïve algorithm may try all possibilities of merging similar states. However, our algorithm will try all reverse topological orders of aggregates instead of all combinations of pairs of similar states. Since there are fewer reverse topological orders of aggregates than combinations of pairs of similar states, our aggregate-based algorithm should be faster than the pair-of-states-based exhaustive search.

If trying all reverse topological orders is out of the question, we can choose a *plausible* topological order, as follows: We assign a *weight* to each aggregate in the aggragation graph. The weight of an aggregate A is the total number of pairs of similar states in all the aggregates that can reach A in the aggregation graph. For example, in Figure 9, the weights of $A1$ and $A3$ are 3 and the weight of $A2$ is 2. If there are more than one reverse topological order, the one in which un-related aggregates, such as $A1$ and $A3$ in Figure 9, are arranged in decreasing weights is chosen. This implies that we prefer to visit *heavier* aggregates first. This is based on the observation that more pairs of similar states depend on heavier aggregates.

IV. Conclusion

We identify the class of extended LALR grammars and the associated algorithm in this paper. ELALR is located between LR and LALR. Our algorithm is essentially a smarter method for merging similar states in the LR(1) machines. Our algorithm can be extended to ELALR(k), for any k, in a straightforward manner.

Acknowledgement

This work is supported, in part, by Ministry of Science and Technology, Taiwan, R.O.C., under contracts MOST 103-2221-E-009-105-MY3 and MOST 105-2221-E-009-078-MY3.

References

[1] A.V. Aho and S.C. Johnson, "LR Parsing," ACM Computing Surveys, vol. 6, no. 2, June 1974, pp. 99-124.
[2] A.V. Aho, M.S. Lam, R. Sethi, and J.D. Ullman, Compilers: Principles, Techniques, and Tools. (2nd Edition) Prentice Hall, New York, 2006.
[3] T. Anderson, J. Eve, and J. Horning, "Efficient LR(1) parsers," Acta Informatica, vol. 2, 1973, pp. 2-39.
[4] F.L. DeRemer, Practical translators for LR(k) languages. Project MAC Tech. Rep. TR-65, MIT, Cambridge, Mass., 1969.
[5] F.L. DeRemer and T. Pennello, "Efficient Computation of LALR(1) LookAhead Sets," ACM Trans. Programming Languages and Systems, vol. 4, no. 4, October 1982, pp. 615-649.
[6] C.N. Fischer, R.K. Cytron, and R.J. LeBlanc, Jr., Crafting A Compiler. Pearson, New York, 2010.
[7] S.C. Johnson, Yacc: Yet Another Compiler-Compiler. Bell Laboratories, Murray Hill, NJ, 1978.
[8] D. E. Knuth, "On the translation of languages from left to right," Information and Control, vol. 8, no. 6, July 1965, pp. 607-639. doi:10.1016/S0019-9958(65)90426-2.
[9] M.D. Mickunas, R.L. Lancaster, V.B. Schneider, "Transforming LR(k) Grammars to LR(1), SLR(1), and (1,1) Bounded Right-Context Grammars," Journal of the ACM, vol. 23, no. 3, July 1976, pp. 511-533. doi:10.1145/321958.321972
[10] D. Pager, "A practical general method for constructing LR(k) parsers," Acta Informatica, vol. 7, no. 3, 1977, pp. 249-268.

Empirical Investigation of Changes of Driving Behavior and Usability Evaluation Using an Advanced Driving Assistance System

Shota Matsubayashi, Kazuhisa Miwa
Graduate School of Information Science
Nagoya University
Aichi, Japan
email: matsubayashi@cog.human.nagoya-u.ac.jp;
email: miwa@is.nagoya-u.ac.jp

Takuma Yamaguchi
Institute of Innovation for Future Society (MIRAI)
Nagoya University
Aichi, Japan
email: t_yamaguchi@nuem.nagoya-u.ac.jp

Takafumi Kamiya, Tatsuya Suzuki
Graduate School of Engineering
Nagoya University
Aichi, Japan
email: ta_kamiya@nuem.nagoya-u.ac.jp;
email: t_suzuki@nuem.nagoya-u.ac.jp

Ryojun Ikeura, Soichiro Hayakawa
Graduate School of Engineering
Mie University
Mie, Japan
email: ikeura@ss.mach.mie-u.ac.jp;
email: hayakawa@ss.mach.mie-u.ac.jp

Takafumi Ito
DENSO CORPORATION
Aichi, Japan
email: takafumi_t_itou@denso.co.jp

Abstract—**It is known that the behavior of autonomous systems affects users' cognitive and behavioral aspects; however, further examination of sequential effects is required. We manipulated instructional information as cognitive guidance and the degree of behavioral intervention implemented by an advanced driving assistance system, and then assessed usability evaluation of the system and changes in user behavior. The results show that strict intervention reduces subjective evaluations, and the absence of instructional information hinders changes in user behavior.**

Keywords-usability evaluation; behavioral change; cognitive guidance; behavioral intervention; human-system cooperation; advanced driving assistance system.

I. Introduction

Recently, many autonomous systems have become popular. They perform various tasks autonomously and often take over user activities. However, due to complexity, users cannot delegate all the activities and are often required to share activities with systems cooperatively. In automated driving, four levels of driving from no automation to full automation are defined [1]. In these levels, drivers and the system must cooperate closely.

It is known that system intervention influences user behavior in many aspects. For example, a number of behavioral changes in driving are observed when an intelligent speed adaptation system is used. A previous study reported that driver behavior shifted to both safe and risky behaviors with various systems [2].

Why do users exhibit such risky behavior against guidance provided by such systems? Cognitive factors, such as user understanding of the systems, may cause these behaviors. A "black box problem" can arise when using highly intelligent autonomous systems. With the black box problem, users cannot recognize which systems operate internally and understand what those systems are intended to do [3]. Many experiments have verified this black box problem. After observing system errors but receiving no explanation about the errors, users tend to distrust systems, which reduces their reliability [4]. Adaptive cruise control systems that share the goal or provide assistance information are more trustworthy and acceptable than those that do not share [5].

Usability questionnaires have been used to measure how users evaluate systems. Recently, a new usability questionnaire was developed to evaluate autonomous systems that perform complex information processing. This questionnaire comprises six elements, i.e., effectiveness, efficiency, satisfaction, understandability, discomfort, and motivation. The latter three elements are assumed for autonomous systems [6].

Previous research has indicated that the behavior of autonomous systems influences users' cognitive and behavioral aspects. However, further inspection is required to examine sequential effects on users' cognitive and behavioral changes while performing tasks.

In the present study, we manipulated two factors that are expected to determine the automation levels of advanced driving assistance systems, and we investigated the effects on users' cognitive and behavioral aspects. The first manipulated factor refers to cognitive guidance that provides instructional information concerning driving safely. The second is the levels of automation, where the high level means strict intervention with user driving behavior and the low level means moderate intervention.

We address a method for the experiment in Section 2 and the results in Section 3. Discussion and conclusion follow in Sections 4 and 5.

II. Method

A. Apparatus

We used a driving simulator equipped with a driving assistance system in an experiment (Figure 1). The driver can operate the steering wheel, the accelerator, and the brake in a same manner as an actual car. This system detects driver blind spots that can cause accidents. Such risk identifications are made based on normative behavior of expert driving instructors. The following two driving assistance stages are employed [7] [8].

1) Cognitive guidance: This provides information about the surrounding environment and gives guidance to brake or turn.

2) Behavioral intervention: This intervenes in driver braking and steering behavior when cognitive guidance does not positively affect driver behavior.

The following information is provided when cognitive guidance and behavioral intervention are performed. Three stimuli are given: a beep and notification message (e.g., "Caution: A Parked Car") as auditory stimuli; a slowdown icon, an arrow pointing to the left/right, and an LED light on the steering wheel as visual stimuli; and steering wheel and accelerator vibration as tactile stimuli.

The extent of behavioral intervention (i.e., the power of braking and steering torque) depends on the status of the car and the safety region monitored by the system. Braking intervention decelerates the car to a fixed speed when crossing an intersection and passing a parked car or a pedestrian. Steering intervention autonomously operates a steering wheel, but this torque is sufficiently small; therefore, drivers can turn the steering wheel against the system's intervention. This intervention is performed when passing a parked car or a pedestrian, but not when crossing an intersection.

This driving assistance system provides information about potential risks and encourages drivers to change behavior if necessary. Assistance (i.e., cognitive guidance and behavioral intervention) is not provided when driving safely. From an educational prospective, if drivers understand the system's intent, they are expected to adopt safer driving behaviors.

B. Data

In the experiment, we collected the following data.

- *Usability evaluations:* A usability evaluation questionnaire measured six elements, i.e., effectiveness, efficiency, satisfaction, understandability, comfort, and motivation. Each element has three questions rated on a five-point scale.
- *Behavioral changes:* The driving behavior before and after run with the assistance system was measured to confirm its educational effect.

C. Procedure

We manipulated the following two factors of the system's behavior.

1) Cognitive guidance: Two cases were considered, i.e., whether or not the system provides instructual information.

2) Behavioral intervention: Two cases were considered, i.e., the system intervenes in driver behavior moderately (minimum system intervention) or strictly (active intervention).

Three experimental conditions were employed based on the above settings. A total of 89 participants were assigned to one of the three conditions.

- *Moderate assistance without cognitive guidance (MOD w/o GUD):* The system intervenes moderately without cognitive guidance.
- *Moderate assistance with cognitive guidance (MOD w/ GUD):* The system intervenes moderately with cognitive guidance.
- *Strict assistance with cognitive guidance (STR w/ GUD):* The system intervenes strictly with cognitive guidance.

Figure 1. Driving simulator used in the experiment (left). The system autonomously provides various information for cognitive guidance (right).

The length of the driving course used in the experiment was approximately 500 meters, and the same course was used in all trials. Participants were required to drive the course while passing a parked car, at an intersection without a traffic signal, and beside a pedestrian.

The flow of the experiment was as follows.

- *Practice run (two times):* To understand the driving simulator, participants were allowed to drive without assistance.
- *Pre-run (three times):* To measure the initial driving behavior without assistance, participants drove the course.
- *Practice run with assistance (two times):* To understand the assistance, participants were allowed to drive the course under one of the three conditions mentioned above.
- *Run with assistance (three times):* For training, participants drove the course in the same manner as the preceding practice run.
- *Usability evaluation:* Participants answered a questionnaire (18 questions).
- *Post-run (three times):* Participants drove the course in the same manner as the initial pre-run.

III. RESULTS

We excluded nine participants who experienced carsickness during the experiment. Therefore, 80 participants were analyzed. We conducted two examinations focusing on (1) the differences between MOD w/ GUD and MOD w/o GUD to investigate the effect of cognitive guidance, and (2) the differences between MOD w/ GUD and STR w/ GUD to investigate the effect of behavioral intervention.

A. Usability Evaluation

Figure 2 shows the usability evaluation for each condition. We conducted a between-participant ANOVA with one factor (condition: MOD w/o GUD, MOD w/ GUD, and STR w/ GUD) for the evaluation score for each of the six elements.

The results show significant main effects for efficiency, understandability, and comfort ($F(2, 77) = 6.81$, $p < .005$; $F(2, 77) = 4.85$, $p < .05$; $F(2, 77) = 3.22$, $p < .05$, respectively), and a marginal effect for motivation ($F(2, 77) = 3.03$, $p = .054$). No significant main effects were found for effectiveness and satisfaction ($F(2, 77) = 1.79$, *n.s.*; $F(2, 77) = 1.26$, *n.s.*, respectively). Ryan's analysis for efficiency, understandability, and comfort showed the scores in MOD w/ GUD were higher than those in STR w/ GUD ($t(50) = 3.47$, $p < .001$; $t(50) = 3.11$, $p < .005$; $t(50) = 2.54$, $p < .05$, respectively). There was no significant difference between MOD w/o GUD and MOD w/ GUD (all $ps > .10$).

As a result, we found that a system that intervenes strictly in user behavior reduces driver evaluation of efficiency, understandability, and comfort. However, there was no significant difference between the MOD w/ GUD and MOD w/o GUD conditions, indicating that cognitive guidance did not affect usability.

B. Behavioral Changes

Driving with the assistance system is expected to encourage drivers to adopt safer driving behaviors. We analyzed changes in driving behavior before and after using the assistance system. We used a 100-meter interval, including an intersection, for the former analysis, and a five-meter interval, including a parked car, for the latter analysis because the system was most likely to offer assistance in these intervals.

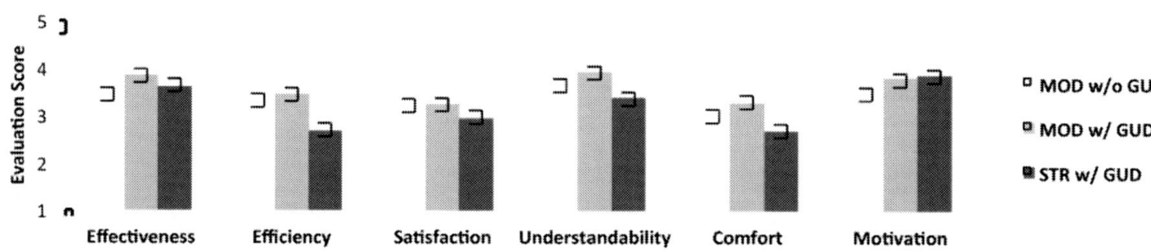

Figure 2. Mean of the usability evaluation of the driving assistance system. The error bar represents the standard error of the mean.

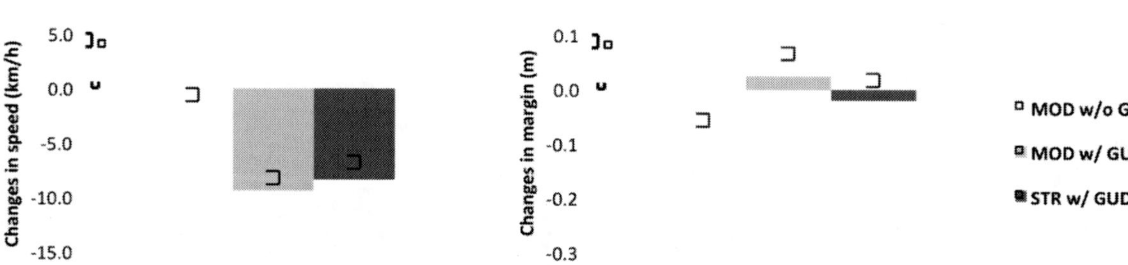

Figure 3. Changes in speed (left) and margin (right) between the pre-run and the post-run.

Figure 3 shows changes in average speed when crossing an intersection from the pre-run to post-run, and changes in average margin between the car and a parked car. A positive value indicates that the value for the post-run is higher than that of the pre-run. If drivers follow the guidance of the system, changes in speed are expected to be negative and those in margin are expected to be positive.

An ANOVA for changes in speed indicates a significant main effect ($F(2, 77) = 4.61$, $p < .05$). Ryan's analysis showed the changes in MOD w/ GUD are greater than that in in MOD w/o GUD ($t(52) = 2.78$, $p < .01$), but there is no significant difference between MOD w/ GUD and STR w/ GUD ($t(50) = 0.37$, *n.s.*). Similarly, the results for changes in margin showed a significant main effect ($F(2, 77) = 4.98$, $p < .01$). Ryan's analysis showed a significant difference between MOD w/o GUD and MOD w/ GUD ($t(52) = 3.05$, $p < .005$), but not between MOD w/ GUD and STR w/ GUD ($t(50) = 0.86$, *n.s.*).

The results reveals that behavioral intervention without instructional information decreases behavioral changes for both braking and steering operations compared to when intervention is performed with instructional information. A surprising result is that the margin in the post-run was significantly smaller than that in the pre-run in the MOD w/o GUD condition ($t(27) = 13.75$, $p < .001$), meaning that participants who were not provided instructional information adopted risker behavior against the behavioral guidance offered by the system. The experimental results also show that, despite strict assistance, behavioral improvements in both braking and steering operations for the STR w/ GUD condition were comparable to those for the MOD w/ GUD condition.

IV. Discussion

In this study, we manipulated instructional information provided by an assistance system as cognitive guidance and the degree of behavioral intervention. In an experiment, we verified that an advanced driving assistance system affects usability evaluations and behavioral changes.

The results showed the following findings. First, the degree of behavioral intervention has a significant effect on user subjective evaluations of the system; however, it does not affect behavioral changes significantly. The evaluation scores for efficiency, understandability, and comfort with the STR w/ GUD condition were substantially less than those for the MOD w/ GUD condition. This implies that strict intervention implemented by autonomous systems makes users uncomfortable and causes disinterest in understanding the system. In addition, we found no significant differences in behavioral changes between the MOD w/ GUD and STR w/ GUD conditions. It is assumed that users do not intend to accept all interventions provided by the system due to discomfort with the systems.

Second, the information provided by autonomous systems has a significant effect on users' behavioral changes but does not have significant effect on their subjective evaluations. The results showed no differences between the MOD w/o GUD and MOD w/ GUD conditions for all usability elements. It was surprising that cognitive guidance did not influence subjective evaluations of the system. Even in such a case, improvements to behavioral changes in the MOD w/o GUD condition were significantly smaller than those of the MOD w/ GUD condition. This indicates that the absence of instructional information provided by autonomous systems reduces educational effects and, in some cases, hinders user behavior improvements. It is likely that users cannot distinguish their own behavior and normative behavior guided by an assistance system if the system does not explicitly identify the differences.

For future research, we will consider how different environments affect drivers' usability and behavior, and what drivers understand about the assistance system.

V. Conclusion

We investigated how the behavior of autonomous systems affects users relative to cognitive and behavioral aspects. The results showed that the strict intervention reduces subjective evaluations, and the absence of instructional information hinders behavioral changes.

Acknowledgment

This research was supported by the Center of Innovation Program (Nagoya-COI) from Japan Science and Technology Agency, and by JSPS KAKENHI Grant Number JP16H02353.

References

[1] SAE International. *Taxonomy and Definitions for Terms Related to On-Road Motor Vehicle Automated Driving Systems*. [Online]. Available from: http://standards.sae.org/j3016_201609/ [retrived: April, 2017]

[2] S. L. Comte, "New systems: new behaviour?," Transportation Research Part F: Traffic Psychology and Behaviour, U.K., vol. 3, no. 2, pp. 95–111, June 2000.

[3] K. Miwa, "What We Should Know When Utilizing Automation Systems: Issues on Cognitive Disuse Atrophy," The Journal of Institute of Electronics, Information and Communication Engineers, Japan, vol. 97, no. 9, pp. 782–787, September 2014.

[4] M. T. Dzindolet, S. A.Peterson, R. A. Pomranky, L. G. Pierce, and H. P. Beck, "The role of trust in automation reliance," International Journal of Human Computer Studies, England, vol. 58, no. 6, pp. 697–718, June 2003.

[5] F. M. F. Verberne, J. Ham, and C. J. H. Midden, "Trust in Smart Systems: Sharing Driving Goals and Giving Information to Increase Trustworthiness and Acceptability of Smart Systems in Cars," Human Factors, United States, vol. 54, no. 5, pp. 799–810, October 2012.

[6] A. Maehigashi, K. Miwa, K. Kojima, and H. Terai, "Development of a Usability Questionnaire for Automation Systems," Lecture Notes in Computer Science, Germany, vol. 9731, pp. 340–349, June 2016.

[7] T. Yamaguchi et al., "Supervisory Cooperative Control and Its Verification," 2016 Society of Automoyive Engineers of Japan Annual Spring Congress (2016 JSAE), May 2016, no. 65-16S, pp. 1593–1598.

[8] T. Kamiya et al., "Experimental Verification for Cooperative Control by Supervisor," 2016 Society of Automoyive Engineers of Japan Annual Spring Congress (2016 JSAE), May 2016, no. 65-16S, pp. 1599–1604.

Neural Network Structure with Alternating Input Training Sets for Recognition of Marble Surfaces

Irina Topalova
Faculty of German Engineering Education and Industrial Management
Technical University of Sofia, Bulgaria
Sofia, Bulgaria
itopalova@abv.bg

Magdalina Uzunova
Department Mathematics
University of Architecture, Civil Engineering and Geodesy
UACEG
Sofia, Bulgaria
magi.uzunova@abv.bg

Abstract— **The automated recognition of marble slab surface textures is an important task in the contemporary marble tiles production. The simplicity of the applied methods corresponds with fast processing, which is important for real-time applications. In this research a supervised learning of a multi-layered neural network is proposed and tested. Aiming high recognition accuracy, combined with simple preprocessing, the neural network is trained with different alternating input training sets including combination of high correlated and de-correlated input data. The obtained good results in the recognition stage are represented and discussed, further research is proposed.**

Keywords-neural network; recognition; texture; preprocessing.

I. INTRODUCTION

The automated recognition of marble slab surfaces is a fudge factor for increasing the production efficiency. The prerequisite for that is to apply reduced hardware equipment and simple software methods to obtain fast processing in real-time work. Taking into account these requirements, the achieved recognition accuracy is very important especially in the case of similar marble surface textures. Finding the appropriate input data transformations would facilitate the next recognition step. Thus, the choice of simple texture parametrical descriptions and their interclass de-correlation in the preprocessing stage is an essential question. The next one is the right choice of an appropriate trained adaptive recognition structure.

In this research a simple hardware structure combined with a supervised learning of a multi-layered neural network (NN) is proposed and tested. Two different types of texture descriptions are used for training the network. Aiming high recognition accuracy, combined with simple preprocessing, the NN is trained with these alternating input training sets including combination of high correlated and de-correlated input data.

The obtained results, when training the network with a single type and with different types of alternating input training sets are represented. The obtained good results in the recognition stage even for similar textures are represented and discussed. Further research is proposed.

In Section II, the state of the art is represented, together with a discussion about disadvantages of the listed methods concerning the obtained results. In Section III, the selected preprocessing method is explained and the used system components are described. Section IV contains the experimental conditions and results, along with comparative discussions. In Section V, the conclusions and future work are defined.

II. RELATED WORKS

There are many related research proposals for recognition of similar, different shaded or hardly distinguishable marble textures. One of the often investigated proposals for extraction of texture feature descriptions is the statistical, instead of structural methods. In [1], the authors represent texture-based image classification using the gray-level co-occurrence matrices (GLCM) and self-organizing map (SOM) methods. They obtain 97.8 % accuracy and show the superiority of GLCM+SOM over the single and fused Support-Vector-Machine (SVM), over the Bayes classifiers using Bayes distance and Mahalanobis distance. To identify the textile texture defects, the authors in [2], propose also a method based on a GLCM feature extractor. The numerical simulation shows error recognition of 91%. The authors in [3], investigate marble slabs with small gradient of colors and hardly-distinguishable veins in the surface. They apply a faster version of a Co-occurrence matrix to form a feature vector of *mean, energy, entropy, contrast* and *homogeneity*, for each of the three color channels. Thus they constitute a NN input feature vector of 15 neurons and the designed network presents 15 neurons in the input layer. In this case the authors claim high-speed processing and recognition accuracy of 80-92.7%. Another known approach for texture segmentation and classification using NN as recognition structure, is the implementation of Wavelet transform over the image and feeding the network with a feature vector of Wavelet coefficients [4][5]. Training a hierarchical NN structure with texture histograms and their second derivative is also announced as giving good recognition accuracy [6]. Considering the explicated data, we could formulate some disadvantages of the approaches given above. The use of GLCM needs high computations and even faster version of a Co-occurrence matrix as given in [3], needs computations multiple times over the whole image for each of the three colors. The calculation of Wavelets is also a time-consuming operation. Using hierarchical NN structure, feeding different NNs [6], with different input feature vectors, would be more complicated, particularly for real-time applications in different hardware platforms. The obtained accuracy is not approaching 100%. Thus, the important source of optimizing the recognition method lies in the simplifying the preprocessing stage/the input feature vector and in finding a more efficient training method along with reducing the NN nodes.

III. Method and System Development

In this section, a motivation for choosing the proposed input training sets is given, along with description of the system components.

A. *Selecting a Preprocessing Method*

Complying with the finding that NN training would be more efficient, when applying different types of intra class input data [7][8], we choose to train a single MLP Back-propagation NN alternating with two types of input vectors. The first one is the calculated first derivative dH(g)/dg of the corresponding normalized grey level (g) texture histogram H(g). As we test marble tiles with similar textures, the obtained inter class vectors are high correlated, which will "embarrass" the NN class-separation capabilities. However, we use this training set because it reflects the vertical H(g) axis changes. To compensate the high inter class correlation, we investigated different types of simple mathematical transformations over the H(g), to find de-correlated input training vectors. In our case, U = Exp(k.H(g)) gave the best reduction of the inter class correlation coefficient and was chosen for second input training set. So, the NN is trained with these alternating input training sets including combination of high correlated and de-correlated input data.

B. *System Components*

The proposed test system includes one smart camera *NI 1742(300dpi)* with triggered infrared lighting, software *Vision Builder for Automated inspection AI'14 (VB for AI)* and *Neuro-System V5.0* - shown in Figure1. The images are taken at the same distance with the same spatial resolution. In off-line mode, the captured image contrast quality is improved in *VB for AI* applying simple lookup table, the corresponding preprocessing of the two types of training sets are calculated. In on-line/test mode the same operations are performed for each test sample, but the input data only "go" through the saved (after the training), weight matrix **W**. The results are given to *VB for AI* for visualization and preparation for extraction through standard interfaces.

IV. Experiments and Results

In this section, the details of the preprocessing stage are given, along with a description of the MLP NN training. Also, the choice of the NN parameters is explained. In the end of the section, the achieved results are shown and a comparative analysis is represented.

A. *Preprocessing Stage*

The experiments are carried out for three marble tiles/classes with similar textures given in Figure 2. The color images are transformed to grey level images applying the method (R+B+G)/3, which will reduce and average the color channel information. It is a loss of information, but it will simplify the further calculations. Calculating different color histograms or any color model parameters (as Hue color parameters), aiming to prepare different input vectors for MLP NN, would require a much more complex NN

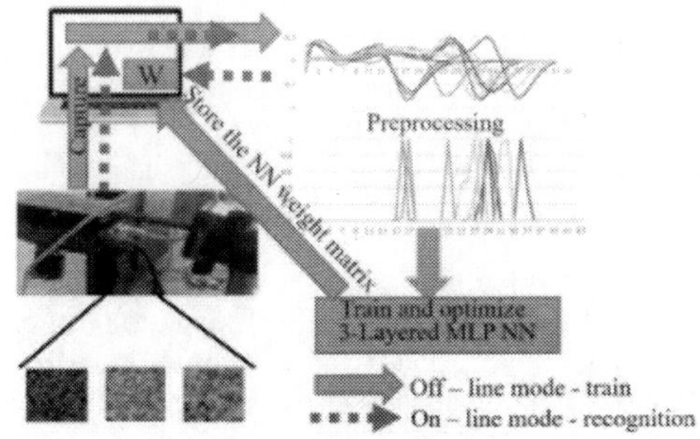

Figure 1. System components

structure. In our case, this loss of information is compensated by using de-correlated input data as Exp(k.H(g)). To evaluate the similarity between samples of

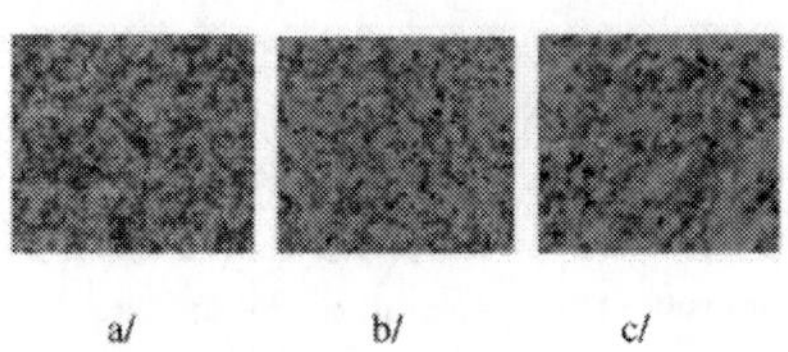

Figure 2. Grey level marble tiles – a/-class1, b/-class2, c/-class3

classes i, j for different input NN feature vector descriptions, the correlation coefficient r_{ij} is calculated according to [9]. Points 1 to 4 of X axis in Figure 3, show the correlation between some exemplars of classes 1 and 2, points 5 to 8 - the correlation between exemplars of classes 2 and 3, points 9 to 12 - the correlation between exemplars of classes 1 and 3. As the coefficient r_{ij} for H(g) varies in the range (-0.24;0.96), it shows very high similarity particularly between classes 2 and 3. That is the reason for searching additional transformations over H(g), to achieve low inter class correlation and better separation between the classes. Thus, the input training vectors will facilitate the NN generalizing capabilities. As the normalized $H(g)/H_{max}(g)$ variables are in the range (0;1), the function U= Exp(k.H(g)), where $k \in \mathbb{R}$, will be suitable, because the correlation coefficient is not invariant about this transformation. Good separable descriptions are obtained when choosing proper values for k (k=10, k=20, k=-10, etc.). With k=100, i.e., for U=Exp(100.H(g)), we achieve the best de-correlation results, shown in Figure 3., where r_{ij} varies in the range (-0.036;0.24). For the normalized H(g) values given in Figure 4, the calculated U are represented in Figure 5. As the function U has a smoothing effect over H(g), it also

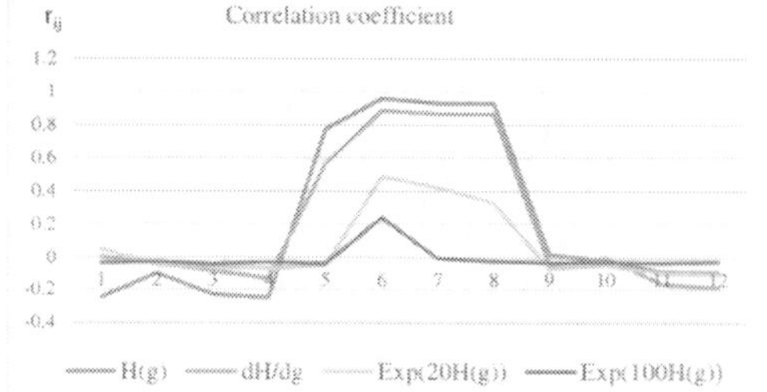

Figure 3. Correlation coefficient r_{ij} for different input training sets

reduces the sharpness of vertical changes in H(g). To conserve and even increase these informative areas we use dH(g)/dg as additional NN training set. It also gives better r_{ij} then H(g). The training set of dH(g)/dg is shown in Figure 6.

B. Train Method

The decision plane consists of a 3-layered MLP NN, trained with well-known Back-propagation algorithm [8]. The input layer has 45 sampled dH(g)/dg and U=Exp(100.H(g)) values over the histograms, calculated in

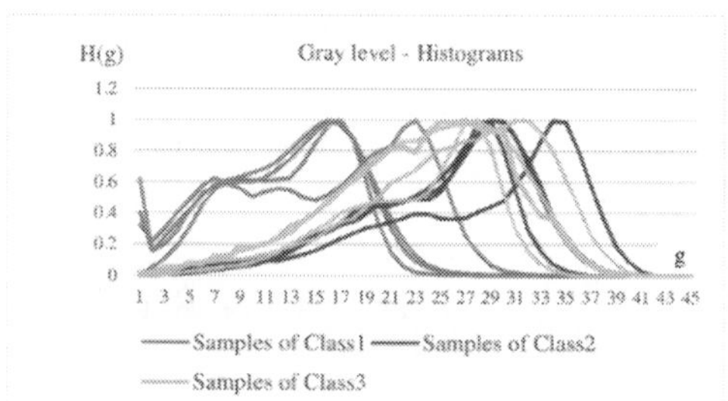

Figure 4. Normalized histogram values H(g) for samples of classes1, 2, 3

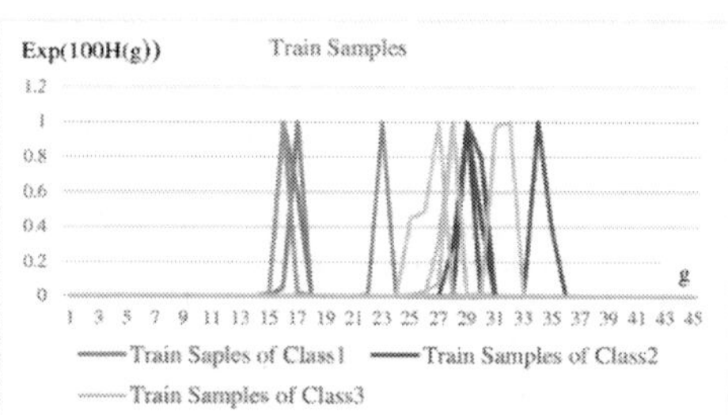

Figure 5. Train Exp(100.H(g)) values for the samples of classes1, 2, 3

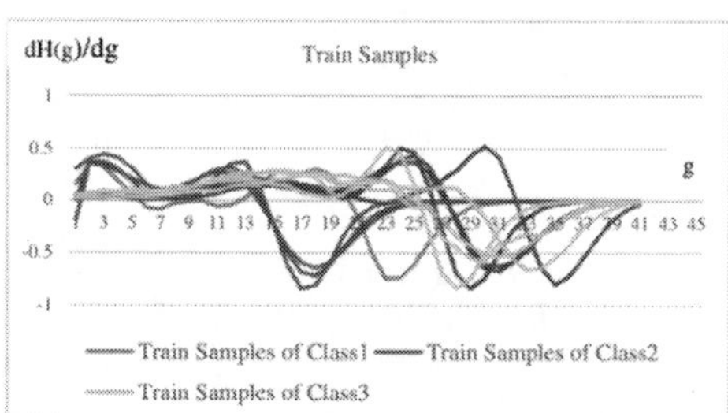

Figure 6. Train dH(g)/dg values for the samples of classes1,2 and 3

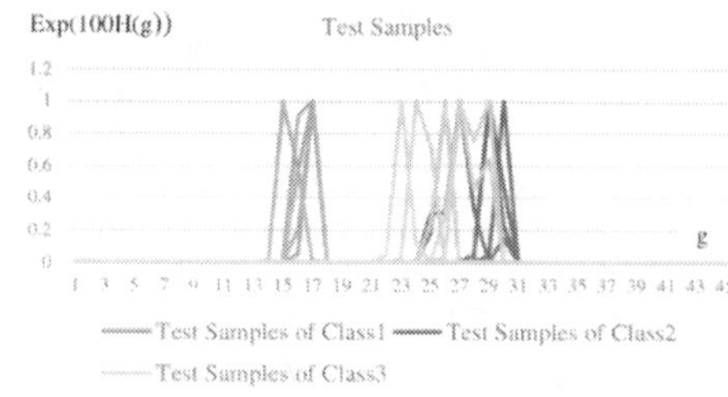

Figure 7. Test Exp(100.H(g)) values for the samples of classes1,2 and 3

VB for AI [10]. They are given alternative to the NN input layer nodes. By training of MLP NN we want to obtain "softer" transitions or larger regions, where the output stays near to "1" or "-1" (using tangent hyperbolic as activation function). The training in off-line was repeated to find the optimized MLP NN structure according to the method given in [5]. We obtained the best fitting structure with 18 hidden

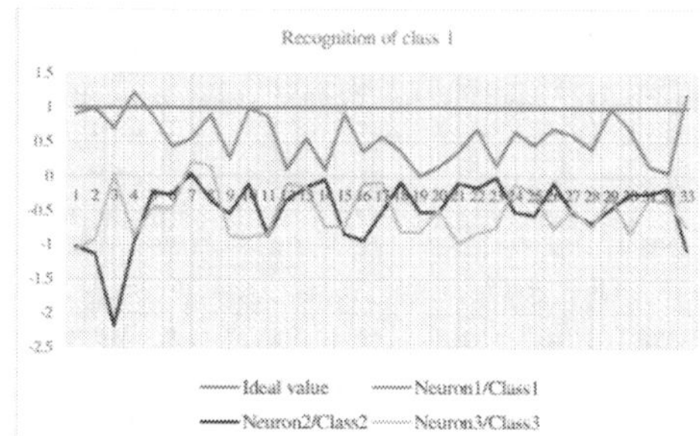

Figure 8. Output neuron values for recognition of class1 samples

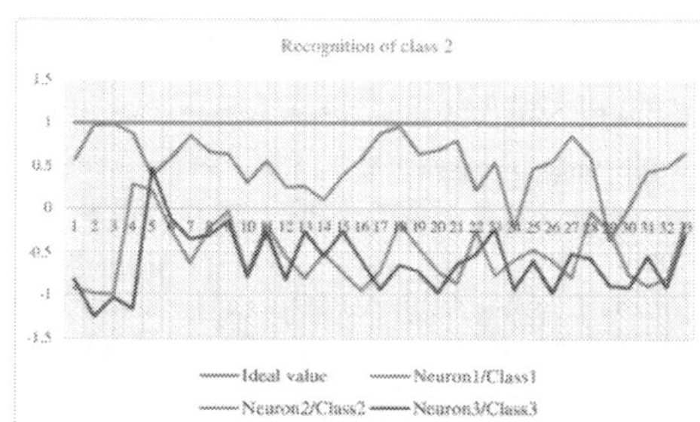

Figure 9. Output neuron values for recognition of class2 samples

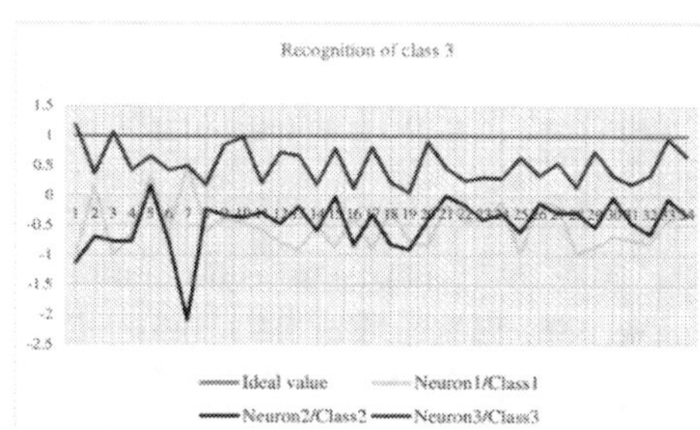

Figure 10. Output neuron values for recognition of class3 samples

TABLE I. RECOGNITION ACCURACY FOR ALL TESTED SAMPLES

Recognition Accuracy [%]	Recognized classes		
		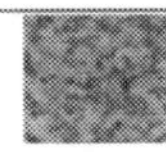	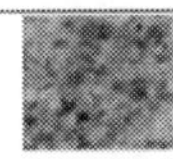
	Class1	*Class2*	*Class3*
Case 1-*dH/dg*	5/**84.8**%	7/ **78.8**%	8/ **75.7**%
Case 2-*Exp(100.H(g))*	3/ **90.9**%	5/ **84.8**%	6/ **81.8**%
Case 3-alternately (dH/dg; Exp(100.H(g))	0/ **100**%	2/ **94**%	1/ **97**%

layer neurons and 3 output neurons, corresponding to the three trained classes. Figures 4 through 7 represent respectively H(g), train dH(g)/dg, train Exp(100.H(g)) and test Exp(100.H(g)) values for four samples of each class. The achieved output neuron values when recognizing samples of class 1, 2 and 3 are shown in Figures 8, 9 and 10. The proportion of 60%-7%-33%: 60 train samples, 7 verification samples, 33 test samples of each class) between training, cross validating and testing set of the general sample number is used in the research [11]. The 60% of the samples for each class were randomly given to the MLP NN for training with 20 samples of each class. To some of the train exemplars Motion Blur or Gaussian Noise is added. Motion Blur is added to simulate the effect of smoothing and blurring the images, when they move on a conveyer belt. The value of 9Pix Motion Blur corresponds to an image resolution of 300 dpi or 118 Pix/cm, to 25 m/min linear velocity of the conveyer belt and to 1/500 sec camera exposure time. The same conditions but for 1/300 exposure time correspond to 15Pix Motion Blur and for 1/200 exposure time corresponds to 25 Pix Motion Blur. Gaussian Noise 2%, 3% or 9Pix Motion Blur to three of the train samples of each class was added. To five of the test samples for each class was added Gaussian Noise between 3 and 5% or Motion Blur between 10 and 15%.

The train process terminated when a Mean Square Error (MSE) of 0.01 was obtained. The recognition accuracy is calculated as (1 - Number of false recognized samples/Number of all test samples of each class) x 100 [%] and is given in Table I. The results are given for three different training modes: first case - train the NN only with dH(g)/dg; second case – train only with Exp(100.H(g)); third – train alternatively with both dH(g)/dg and Exp(100.H(g)). The best recognition accuracy between 94% and 100% is obtained in the third case. The output results are extracted through *VB for AI* in different conventional interface formats as Modbus, RS 232 and GigE Vision Standard. Table II shows the comparative results concerning recognition accuracy and real-time execution. They are related to the research given in [5][6] where the same images were tested, but applying pre-processing with Wavelets (DWT) and DCT over grey image histograms. Almost the same recognition accuracy was achieved as with DWT, but with a simplified

TABLE II. COMPARATIVE RESULTS FOR RECOGNITION ACCURACY AND REAL-TIME EXECUTION

Method	Number of hidden neurons	MSE [%]	Recognition accuracy [%]	Real-time execution [ms]
Histogram	50	0.16	85	578
DCT	50	0.01	95	638
DWT	25	0.16	100	649
Alternately (dH/dg; Exp(100.H(g))	18	0.01	97	247

NN structure (only 18 neurons in the hidden layer) because of simple pre-processing method providing at the same time de-correlation of the NN input train data. In the case of alternately training with dH/dg; Exp(100.H(g), the execution time is about three times reduced.

V. CONCLUSION

In this research, a simple method for recognition of similar marble tiles with high correlated histograms is proposed and tested for three texture classes. High recognition accuracy is obtained under very simple calculations in the preprocessing stage. Calculation of dH(g)/dg and Exp(100.H(g)) is a very simple single operation over H(g). Training the MLP NN with both – slightly de-correlated inter class data as dH(g)/dg, thus conserving the local changes of H(g) between neighbors g, and strong de-correlated data as Exp(100.H(g)) is a prerequisit to obtain very good recognition results. The choice of only one NN with a relatively small number of neurons, instead of a hierarchical NN structure and the simple processing, allows method implementation in real-time systems. In future work, the method will be tested for more classes with similar textures also for other type of textures, to generalize the results. It is also interesting to find analog transformations for good NN input data de-correlation.

REFERENCES

[1] C. W. D. Almeida, R.M.C.R. de Souza, and A. L. B. Candeias, "Texture Classification Based on a Co-Occurrence Matrix and Self-Organizing Map," IEEE International Conference on Systems Man & Cybernetics, University of Pernambuco, Recife, pp. 2487-2491, 2010.

[2] G. A. Azim, and S. Nasir, "Textile Defects Identification Based on NNs and Mutual Information," International Conference on Computer Applications Technology (ICCAT), Sousse Tunisia, pp. 1-8, 2013.

[3] J. M. C. de-V. Alajarin, T. Balibrea, and M. Luis, "Marble Slabs Quality Classifcation System using Texture Recognition and NNs Methodology," ESANN'1999 proceedings - European Symposium on Artificial NNs, Bruges, Belgium, pp. 75-80, 1999.

[4] D. Feng, Z. Yang, and X. Qiao, "Texture Image Segmentation Based on Improved Wavelet NN," LNCS, Springer, Heidelberg, vol. 4493, pp. 869–876, 2007.

[5] I. Topalova, "Automated Marble Plate Classification System Based on Different NN Input Training Sets and PLC Implementation," IJARAI – International Journal of Advanced Research in Artificial Intelligence, Volume1, Issue2, pp. 50-56, 2012.

[6] I. Topalova, "Recognition of Similar Wooden Surfaces with a Hierarchical NN Structure," SAI/ IJARAI – International Journal of Advanced Research in Artificial Intelligence, Volume 4, Issue10, pp. 35-39, 2015.

[7] B. Widrow and S. Stearns, "Adaptive Signal Processing," Prentice-Hall, Inc. Englewood Cliffs, N.J. 07632, pp.36-40, 2004.

[8] R. C. Gonzalez, and R. E Woods, "Digital Image Processing", 3rd Edition, Prentice Hall, India, 2008.

[9] Weisstein, Eric W. "Correlation Coefficient." From MathWorld, A Wolfram Web Resource. Available from: http://mathworld.wolfram.com/CorrelationCoefficient.html, 2017.

[10] Vision Builder AI, User Manuel, Copyright © 2013, pp. 45-58, 2013.

[11] Neuro Solutions, Copyright © 2014 by NeuroDimension, pp. 67-79, 2015.

Design and Development of the 24 GHz FMCW Radar Sensor for Blind Spot Detection and Lane Change Assistance Systems

Yeonghwan Ju, Sangdong Kim, Youngseok Jin, Jonghun Lee
Convergence Research Center for Future Automotive Technology
DGIST(Daegu Gyeongbuk Institute of Science & Technology)
Daegu, Korea
e-mail: {yhju, kimsd728, ysjin, jhlee} @dgist.ac.kr

Abstract— **In this paper, we designed and implemented the automotive radar based on Frequency Modulated Continuous Wave method for Lane Change Assist and Blind Spot Detection radar system. We also developed digital signal processing module and a 24 GHz FMCW radar RF module composed of a single transmitter, a single transmitting antenna array of five elements and three receivers to measure range, velocity and angle for LCA and BSD. In order to verify the developed radar system, we conducted experiments to measure the detection rate and the range accuracy in the anechoic chamber and real road environment. The experimental results show that the developed radar is feasible for use in BSD/LCA systems for automotive.**

Keywords- FMCW Radar; Automotive Radar; BSD; Bind Spot Detection; LCA; Lane Change Assistance.

I. INTRODUCTION

Recently, the smart car for autonomous driving has functions such as lane keeping support, lane change support, inter-vehicle distance control, etc. This function is based on radar and vision sensor. It is a precise distance measurement technology for various obstacles and moving objects is required. Lane change assist (LCA) and Blind spot detection (BSD) radars should be able to detect objects approaching at a medium distance as well as at the rear of the near side. Because the LCA/BSD system must be able to detect where the moving target is on the left and right lanes of the vehicle in the rear of the vehicle and to be able to detect whether there is a moving target in the blind zone area, the signal processing technique is needed [1]-[3].

Frequency modulated continuous Wave (FMCW) radar has been popularly used in automotive radar. It can detect range and velocity of the moving target, simultaneously. To overcome ambiguities, the fast ramp based FMCW radar has been proposed [4][5].

In this paper, we developed an integrated medium - range radar system with dual function for blind spot detection and lane change support. To verify the developed radar, we tested in the anechoic chamber of high frequency band.

This paper is organized as follows. The system design of the BSD/LCA radar is presented in Section II. To validate developed systems, experimental results are provided in Section III. Finally, a conclusion is drawn in Section IV.

II. BSD/LCA RADAR SYSTEM DEGIGN

We implemented the FMCW LCA/BSD radar systems at 24 GHz, which has two receiving antennas and analog-to-digital converter (ADC) channels. The transmitter contains a voltage controlled oscillator (VCO), a frequency synthesizer, and a 26 MHz oscillator. To generate the FMCW source, a frequency synthesizer controls the input voltage of the VCO. The source sweeps over the range of 24.0-24.25 GHz.

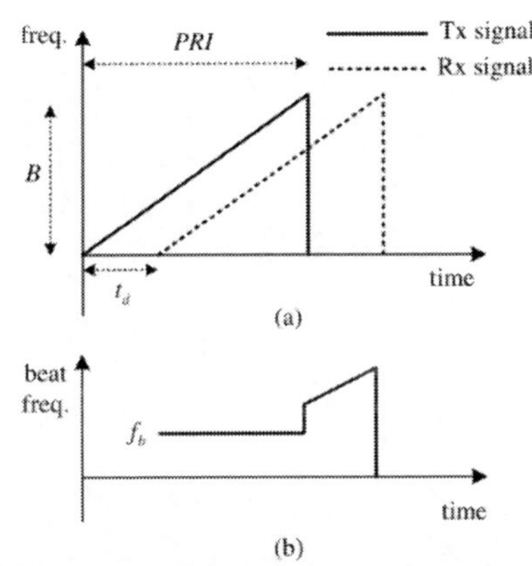

Figure 1. FMCW radar signal (a) the transmitted signal and received signal (b) beat signal.

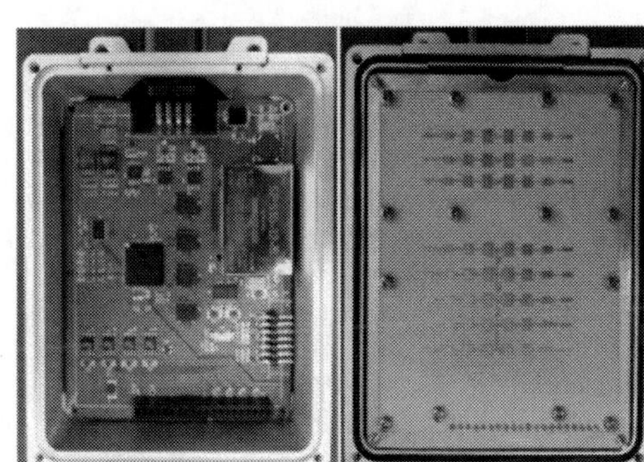

Figure 2. Signal processing module and transceiver of the Developed BSD/LCA radar system

Figure 1 shows frequencies as a function of time in the transmitted signals and received signals for a stationary target. The range beat frequency can be obtained by signal processing, and then the range of the target can be estimated using (1).

$$R = (C \cdot PRI \cdot f_b)/(2 \cdot B) \quad (1)$$

where, C is light speed, B is the modulation bandwidth, and t_d is the delay time between transmitted and received signals. The PRI is Pulse Repetition Interval, which is a chirp period.
The signal processing module and the transceiver are shown in Figure 2. The detection algorithm based on 2D fast fourier transform (FFT) using fast ramp was implemented in the signal processing module. Transceiver consists of a transmit antenna with five arrays, a receive antenna with three channels, which has three receiving antennas and four ADC channels.

III. Experimental Results

This section presents experimental results to demonstrate the performance of the developed BSD/LCA radar in the anechoic chamber and road environment.

We experimented in chamber with frequency band from 8GHz to 110GHz to obtain the accurate measurement results. As shown in Figure 3, the dimension is 10m (L) × 5m (W) × 4m (H).

Figure 3. Photo of the anechoic chamber

In our chamber environment, we performed range accuracy experiments with multiple targets. Figure 2 shows the signal processing module and the radio frequency (RF) transceiver module of the developed LCA / BSD radar.

BSD/LCA radar algorithm is implemented in TI DSP TMS320F28335 as shown Figure 2. The MS320F28335 processor is a low cost, high efficiency processor that operates at 150MHz and provides interfaces and signal processing libraries such as ADC, direct memory access (DMA), and control area network (CAN). The RF transceiver module consists of a transmit antenna with five arrays, a receive antenna with three channels, and an RF module.

To verify the effectiveness of the proposed method, we tested the detection performance of the developed radar system using the two-channel FMCW RF module shown in Figure 2.

TABLE I. RANGE ACCURACY

	Range (m)						
	0.5	1	1.5	2	2.5	3	3.4
Measured average range	0.47	0.94	1.41	1.88	2.34	2.81	3.28
Range accuracy	0.03	0.06	0.09	0.12	0.16	0.19	0.12
	Range (m)						
	10	20	30	40	50	60	70
Measured average range	10.53	20.60	30.68	40.74	50.81	59.97	71.41
Range accuracy	0.53	0.60	0.68	0.74	0.81	0.03	1.41

By using the chamber environment, we can avoid the negative effect of the unknown echoes on the algorithm performance. We performed the range estimation of the developed 24 GHz FMCW BSD/LCA radar sensor for single target, placed at different location in chamber room. We have captured the beat signal through Ethernet using radar signal processing module. Range accuracy was measured 1,000 times in the anechoic chamber. The target is located 0.5m to 3m in intervals of 0.5m. We measured the range changing the distance in 10m intervals from 10m to 70m to demonstrate the performance of the maximum detection range. Table 1 shows the measurement results of the range accuracy. The experimental results show that the measured average distance accuracy is about 0.11m at distance between 0.5 m and 3.4 m and about 0.69m at distance between 10m to 70m respectively.

(a)

(b)

Figure 4. Experiment environments (a) radar setup (b) snapshot of the scenario

Figure 4 shows the experimental environment for the verification of the algorithm of the developed BSD/LCA radar in this paper. Figure 4 (a) shows that the developed radar for the experiment on an actual road environment is mounted on an experimental vehicle bumper. Figure 4 (b) shows an experiment in which the radar detects a moving target. The measured results of the developed radar system are passed through CAN, and the results are sent to a PC through a CAN to LAN convertor. The final results were displayed using a monitoring program as shown Figure 5 and Figure 6.

Figure 5. Experimental results of the LCA zone on urban road environment

Figure 6. Experimental results of the BSD zone on urban road environment

The experiments were performed to verify the developed radar could simultaneously detect the BSD and LCA zones on urban road environment. The purpose of this experiment is to verify that the BSD/LCA radar system gives warnings when required as the target vehicle overtakes the radar vehicle on real road environment.

Figure 5 shows the experimental results of the LCA zone of the developed radar on real road environment. The measured detection results of the LCA zone shows that developed radar can detect the target vehicle approaching the radar vehicle at high speed as shown Figure 5. Figure 6 shows the measured detection results of the BSD zone of the developed radar on real road environment. The detection results of the BSD zone show that developed radar can detect the target vehicle in the BSD area within 5m as shown Figure 6. Figure 5 and 6 show the range, velocity, and angel of the radar output.

IV. Conclusions

In this paper, the LCA/BSD radar system was presented. We developed the radar system to obtain high accuracy range and velocity for LCA/BSD. The LCA/BSD radar algorithm is implemented on DSP chip of the developed signal processing module. We verified the radar sensor connected with a 24 GHz front-end-module transceiver to obtain accurate measurement results in anechoic chamber. And we demonstrated that the developed radar has target detection capabilities of BSD area (within 5m) and LCA area (maximum 70m) for BSD/LCA application. Convincing results confirm the feasibility of the complete system and are encouraging for further research activities.

Acknowledgment

This work was supported by the DGIST R&D Program of the Ministry of Science, ICT and Future Planning, Korea (17-IT-01).

References

[1] C. Fernandez, D. F. Llorca, M. A. Sotelo, I. G. Daza, A. M. Hellín and S. Álvarez, "Real-time visionbased blind spot warning system: Experiments with motorcycles in daytime/nighttime conditions," Int. J. Automotive Technology 14, 1, pp.113–122, 2013.

[2] G. Forkenbrock, R. L. Hoover, E. Gerdus, and T. R. Van Buskirk and M. Heitz, "Blind Spot Monitoring in Light Vehicles – System Performance," Technical Report of NHTSA (National Highway Traffic Safety Administration), U.S. Department of Transportation), 2014.

[3] S. Kim, "System design and simulation of multi-function automotive FMCW radar sensor," IEEE International Conference on. ICWITS and ACES, pp. 1-2, 2016.

[4] S. Miyahara, "New algorithm for multiple object detection in FM-CW radar," No. 2004-01-0177. SAE Technical Paper, 2004.

[5] V. Winkler, " Range Doppler detection for automotive FMCW radar," Proc. IEEE European Radar Conf., pp.166–169, 2007.

Simplified Fuzzy Dynamic Cognitive Maps Applied to the Maintenance Management of Electric Motors

Patrick P. Soares/ Lucas B. de Souza/ Márcio Mendonça
DAELE (Electric Department)
UTFPR-CP
Cornélio Procópio, Brazil
{p.prietosoares, lucasbotoni}@hotmail.com
mendonca@utfpr.edu.br

Ivan Rossato Chrun[1] / Michelle E. C. Rocha[2]
[1]CPGEI
[1]UTFPR-CT / [2]SEJU
[1,2]Curitiba, Brazil
{ivanchrun, melizacrocha}@gmail.com

Abstract— Systems and machines must operate under satisfactory conditions to attest to the quality of its production. Using Fuzzy Cognitive Maps based in concepts of the Reliability Centered Maintenance in order to obtain quantitative feedback to support the decision-making process and maintenance strategy, as proposed in this research, one can propose great reliability. This article presents Reliability Centered Maintenance (RCM) through a generic maintenance checklist for electric motors. Through fault and / or fault correction maintenance procedures, a simplified Cognitive Fuzzy Dynamic Map (sDFCM) that will present a quantitative diagnosis offering a computational tool to assist in maintenance management, providing upgrades to the system or machine can model it.

Keywords— Reliability Centered Maintenance, Management Maintenance, Electric Motors, Fuzzy Cognitive Maps, Quantitative Analysis.

I. Introduction

The rapid development of the industrial process, from the Industrial Revolution (seventeenth century), provoked within the industry, as a whole, the technological evolution. This fact has changed the importance of maintenance, aiming to provide greater quality and competitiveness for the manufacturing sector. This scenario indicates that more and more companies, to achieve what is called "World-Class Performance", are demanding great efforts to improve quality, productivity, and reduce costs, having a direct impact on effective maintenance [1].

Electric motors are extremely energy efficient. These devices, in a production system due to their importance, must have a maintenance schedule. Although engines have highly efficient parts, like any other equipment, are still susceptible to failure. When the fault happens, the drive can be sent to be rewound or a new engine is purchased to replace the faulty one. Failure of the electric motor may result in loss of capacity as well as excessive repair and maintenance costs.

By routinely performing corrective, preventive and predictive tasks, the life of an engine can be extended, and it is efficiency improved. Some companies describe their maintenance procedures so that each maintenance team follows the same methodology. On the other hand, in most countries of the world, electric motors consume up about 66% of the electricity generated. On average, the energy consumed by an induction motor during its life cycle is 60–100 times the initial cost of the motor [2].

For Tsang, the evolution of maintenance techniques and methods needs to prioritize current operational strategies, expectations of environmental preservation and security by society, technological changes, increasing environmental and organizational changes [3]. Thus, the main objective is to present the methodology MRC - Maintenance Reliability Centered regarding an analysis in electric motors. The specific objectives of this work are to present a brief rationale on Reliability Centered Maintenance, to suggest Fuzzy Cognitive Maps (FCM) to quantify maintenance reliability and provide maintenance reliability level feedback. However, the suggested FCM is still at the level of belief, that is, according to the view of experts or specialists. So, the need for maintenance management of this equipment becomes essential. Conceptually, maintenance is the activity that seeks to preserve the technical characteristics of an equipment at the level of its specified performance.

The maintenance of equipment and machinery must include technical knowledge and administrative procedures to maintain its characteristics of functionality, safety and environmental. Otherwise, the maintenance must allow the equipment to operate ensuring the continuous production of the company and / or industry, besides preventing failures that may partially or fully harm the production line involved.

The application of maintenance strategies focuses directly on the particularities of the aging stage of equipment and installations. According to the concept of maintenance and conservation of machines and equipment, it can be mentioned the Reliability Centered Maintenance (RCM) methodology, which is oriented to failures and defects of machines or systems. In short, RCM, in its classic form, is the application of a structured method to establish the best maintenance strategy for a given system or equipment. Thus, the concepts of failure and structured analysis will be used in the development of this research. Even though the proposed tool is in an initial stage, it can be extended and applied in others devices, such as electrical transformers with different powers and specifications.

The main goal of this work is to develop a methodology for the creation of maintenance indicators in industrial electric motors, which will be used to achieve strategic planning in favor of a continuous improvement in the productive process of goods and services. The specific goal of this work is to present a brief background on maintenance's aspects to suggest the Simplified Dynamic Fuzzy Cognitive Maps (sDFCM) to quantify the maintenance reliability level.

The structure of this paper is as it follows. Section 2 conceptualizes aspects of maintenance and industrial maintenance. Section 3 discusses the main aspects of FCM and sDFCM, and presents the approach towards maintenance management inspired on RCM applied in electric motors. Section 4 presents the simulated results, and Section 5 concludes the paper and suggests future works.

II. Maintenance Management Concepts

The management of maintenance systems is a complex activity, especially when there are several contracting companies acting as executors of planned and emergency activities. In particular, the maintenance of electrical motors, due to the need of uninterrupted work in factory floor [4].

In industrial plants, the stoppage for maintenance, in general, generates concern about the scheduling and production progress. The organization must be structured with the purpose of fulfilling the binding requirements, relating technics in the manufacturing process, the personnel involved with the product and maintenance of the machines used in the manufacturing process and the type of product to be manufactured.

The adaptation of all administrative practices with technical and supervisory actions, which happens through direct or indirect equipment processes, shall be aimed at ensuring the safety and efficiency of the functions and standards required in the manufacture or service supply in which the equipment was designed for.

Managing equipment requires a maintenance routine that must involve several actions that configure the best functioning and allow reliability in the process in which it is inserted, such as electrical motors in discharge conveyor. In this context, the development of a strategy that indicates reliability levels can be used to help in the management of the maintenance, identifying points of possible improvements in the quality, e.g. the technical knowledge of the manpower.

It is not the scope of this work to substantiate the types of maintenance. Only the concepts required for maintenance management inspired by the RCM technique by means of an sDFCM will be aproached.

The types of classic maintenance considered in the development of this work are:

- Corrective Maintenance: performed when a failure occurs over certain equipment. It can be planned when the equipment indicates symptoms that its operation is not under normal conditions, or that the cost-benefit relation to Preventive Maintenance is more interesting and profitable. It is also identified as unplanned, where an unexpected failure occurs and a rapid corrective action is required.
- Preventive Maintenance: indicated when it is necessary to replace parts or recover the equipment. This type of maintenance analyzes the best moment for the maintenance to happen in critical equipment, preventing the manifestation of failures.
- Predictive Maintenance: it requires a constant monitoring of the equipment through more sophisticated instruments, which allows equipment's maintenance before a break happens and it stops working. Some of the main methods used to monitor equipment, vibration analysis, thermography analysis, noise analysis, insulation resistance, rolling check among other potential problems.

The goal of this work is to develop a maintenance strategy inspired by the RCM through the occurrence of faults and defects, and predictive and preventive maintenance levels in industrial electric motors, aiming the construction of a tool to assist on decision-making process regarding failures and defects, especially failures. Thereby, it is important to define:

- Defect: an anomaly in equipment that can cause it to operate irregularly or below its rated capacity. If not corrected in time, it can evolve and cause the equipment to fail and be removed from service.
- Fault: an anomaly in equipment that necessarily requires the interruption of the equipment in operation, i.e. withdrawing it from service.

Failures and defects can be expanded in more complexity levels, but the purpose of this work is to develop a tool for diagnosis by the frequency of their occurrence and not intrinsic analysis of the causes. Thus, reliability can be defined as the ability of an item to perform a specified required function over a given time interval. Failures can be classified by their origin, speed and manifestation [5].

There are several maintenance management strategies in the literature [6], among them it is noteworthy citing the RCM. The RCM is a technique used to develop cost-effective maintenance plans and criteria so the operational capability of equipment is achieved, restored, or maintained. Its main objective is to reduce the maintenance cost by focusing on the most important functions of the system. There are several different formulations of RCM processes in the literature. The RCM analysis may be carried out as a sequence of activities or steps.

The use of a checklist is usual in maintenance management for standardization and recording the sequence of the actions to be performed. The execution frequency of the check list procedures is of paramount importance, since some inspected items require annual, monthly, weekly or even daily monitoring and should be defined by the area experts [7]. The priority regarding the activity developed in maintenance should also be determined. Priorities are stipulated according to the importance and nature of the machine. A priori, suggestions of the main actions are presented, in a summarized way, adopted by the authors or specialists. This work's proposal is to use the concepts discussed and associate them to a checklist applied to electric motors, as presented in Table 1.

It is expected that one of the contributions of this research is the modeling of a maintenance management strategy, even though it is necessary to define its frequency of execution using suitable models. Thus, the development of a cognitive model that represents the management inspired by the concepts of Reliability Centered Maintenance prioritizes the representation of the concepts of potential failure / defect and functional failure / defect.

TABLE I. CHECKLIST MAINTENANCE IN ELETRIC MOTORS

Item	Maintenance actions description
01	Engine board data in the environment.
02	Check vibrations and noises outside of standard.
03	Grease bearings.
04	Measure and record voltage and current between phases.
05	Check status of lubricant types.
06	Measure and record the insulation resistance.
07	Measure and record temperature of the bearings and the wound elements.
08	Check and correct the condition of the seals or ring.
09	Vibration monitoring.
10	Visual inspection.
11	Motor circuit analysis.
12	Grounding situation.
13	Machine Reliability Level.

III. DYNAMIC FUZZY COGNITIVE MAPS APPLIED TO MAINTENANCE QUALITY LEVEL

This research suggests the use of a sDFCM, a variation of the classic FCM, to assign maintenance quality levels. The initial version of sDFCM1 is implemented in this paper and its complete version (sDFCM1 and sDFCM2, in a future work) to assist decision making in the maintenance management area.

A Fuzzy Cognitive Map (FCM) is a Fuzzy Influence Graph which is a result from the works of some psychologists. "Cognitive Maps" has been first introduced to describe complex topological memorizing behaviors in the rats [8]. Since the pioneering work of Kosko [9], which extended Axelrod's Cognitive Maps [10] by the inclusion of Fuzzy Logic, several applications of FCM have emerged in the literature in several knowledge areas. Some applications of the FCM and its variations can be found in the literature in the areas of artificial life [11] [12], spot detection in images generated by the stereo camera system [13], mobile robotics [14], decision making in the medical field [15]. Besides, time series prediction [16], multi agent systems [17] [18], process control [19], maintenance management [20], swarm robotics [21], among others. Recently, some studies are using learning algorithms to adjust interaction weights among the factors to overcome drawbacks in FCM [22]. In this way, evolutions of the FCM has appeared, such as ED-FCM (Event Driven-Fuzzy Cognitive Maps) applied in autonomous mobile robotics [23], and DCN (Dynamic Cognitive Networks) on process control [24] [25]. In [18] a formal adaptation of the original FCM is presented, this new tool is designated as TAFCM (Timed Automata Fuzzy Cognitive Maps). These are just a few of several examples that can be found in the literature.

Thus, Gonzalo and collaborators recently suggested that the Fuzzy Cognitive Maps (FCMs) are powerful tools for modeling dynamic systems. FCMs describe expert knowledge of complex systems with high dimensions and a variety of factors. An increased interest about the theory and application of FCMs in complex systems also has been noted. In short, FCMs are powerful tools for modeling dynamic systems. Although FCM are considered as neural systems, there are major differences regarding other types of artificial neural networks (ANN) [26]. In this way, according [17], the fundamental difference between FCM and ANN is that all nodes of the FCM have a strong semantic.

In general, the FCMs can be developed in two different ways, in an automatic way, through historical data, or manually [27]. The FCM used in this research was developed manually, because the causal relationships weights were adjusted empirically, so that the desired output is a quantitative diagnosis through the qualitative opinion of the experts.

Further constructions details of the classical FCM with different mathematical formalisms, inferences types and applications can be found in [28]. Recently, in [29] presents different evolutions of the classic FCM model and its new applications. In this work, especially in chapter 10, an algorithm based on FCM Ontology [30] is presented as development steps of an FCM model, as shown in Table 2.

TABLE II. FCM ONTOLOGY

Steps	Description
1	Identification of elementary concepts, their roles (input, output, decision and level) and their interconnections, determining its causal nature (positive, negative, neutral)
2	Initial set-up of concepts and relationships. The initial state values of the map (nodes/edges) can be acquired from experts, historical data analysis and / or system simulation
3	Determination of ontological influence among concepts. Design of the different ontological views of the system
4	To each view of the system, design of fuzzy rule bases and time varying functions computing the values for the weights of the DFCM fuzzy and/or time-varying relations
5	Design of management level corresponding to the development of the rule base that are associated to and selection relations, and, implementation of algorithm to on-line learning such as reinforcement learning rules
6	Model Validation

The DFCM development has 7 steps; the sDFCM has summarized it down to 6 steps, excluding the step that addresses information processing and dynamic tuning of the causal relationships. Thus, the basic difference between the proposed version and the former one, in this research, is the application of machine learning algorithms for dynamic tuning of the DFCM is not necessary. More information on the development of DFCM can be found in [12], in which it also discusses aspects of DFCM stability, relevant to the development of the cognitive model, as the one used in this research.

Steps 1, 2 and 3 of this algorithm are like classic FCM development. Step 4 is related to the inclusion of fuzzy relations that model cause-effect relationships in the graph. The use of a fuzzy relation allows modeling a relationship with more than a concept as antecedent and/or consequents and therefore a non-monotonic inference engine is represented. This step is quite common in recent models using FCM [31]. In step 5 the rule base associated with the strategic decision level is included. Finally, step 6 corresponds to the model validation.

The FCM inference is made through concepts and their respective causal relationships. They are updated through iteration with the other concepts and with their own value. This is given by the matrix with the causal relations weights, and is represented by the weight sum, equation (1), similarly used in [27].. The values of the concepts evolve after the iterations, as shown by the function of equation (1) and (2) until they stabilize at a fixed point or in a limit cycle.

$$A_i = f(\sum_{\substack{j=1 \\ j \neq i}}^{n} (A_j \times W_{ji}) \quad (1)$$

where n is the number of nodes in the graph, Wji is the arc's weight that connects the concept Cj to Ci, Ai is the Ci concept value in the present iteration, and the f function (equation (2)) is a sigmoidal type function:

$$f(x) = \frac{1}{1 + e^{-\lambda x}} \quad (2)$$

The FCM, in some cases, may not stabilize and oscillate, or even exhibit chaotic behavior [32]. Generally, for well-behaved systems, it is observed that after a finite number of iterations, generally a low value, the FCM stabilizes, as shown in Fig. 3; for the FCM in this work it stabilize after 3 or 4 iterations. The concepts values reach a fixed equilibrium point or a limit cycle, presenting a small variation around a fixed value. In [26] it is analyzed the convergence of the FCM.

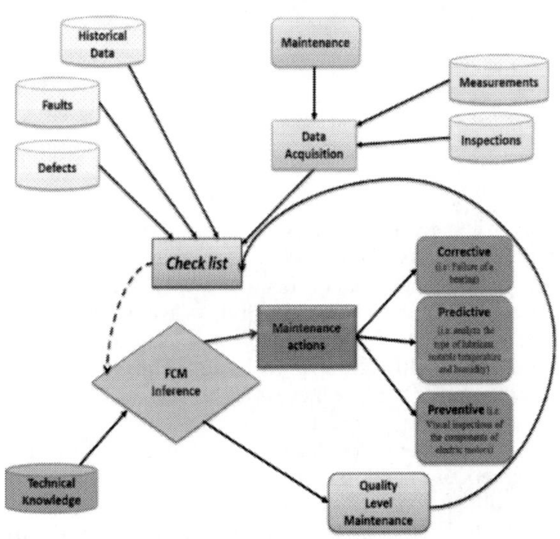

Figure 1. Maintenance management cognitive model.

Fig. 1 shows an overview of the decision-making sequence in which sDFCM is part of a maintenance strategy. It is observed that the FCM inference directly influences the decision-making, due to the reliability level found by the FCM. Also, according to Fig. 1, the check list processing determines the actions to be performed according to the maintenance information inputs. The initial propose of this research is to apply the same computational technique to different machines and / or equipment in the industry, such as electric motors and transformers. Thereby, it is intended to propose a generic soft-computing technique to contribute in the maintenance management area. It can be cited some papers that uses soft-computing techniques in maintenance management, ANN in [33] and in [20] it is used an FCM to assess the risks of maintenance outsourcing. Fuzzy Logic inference applied in maintenance management [34], and Mohammadreza's work [35] used Fuzzy Logic for strategy in maintenance management.

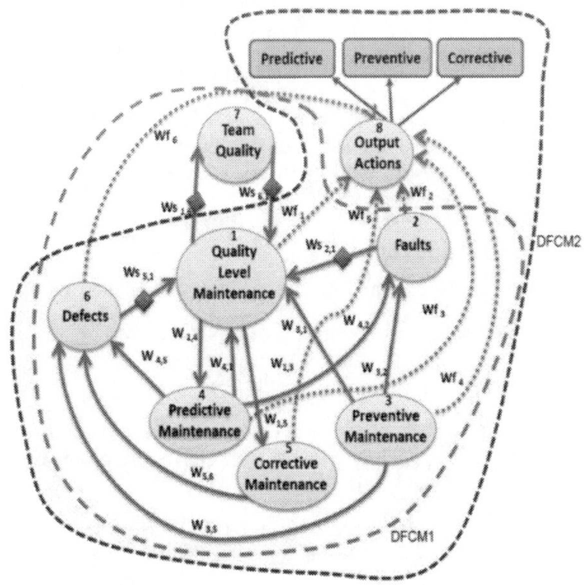

Figure 2. Complete sDFCM (sDFCM1 + sDFCM2)

An important aspect for this work is to characterize some of these properties come from measurements and are thus represented by real numbers. However, in many cases (such as this research), a large amount of information comes from expert estimates [36].

The complete sDFCM (Fig. 2) is divided in two parts to contemplate the cognitive model strategy presented in Fig. 1. The sDFCM1 (red dashed line) uses as input concepts the level of occurrence and quality of preventive and predictive maintenance. The established criteria are: when these levels are above 50% they have a positive influence in the reduction of the faults and defects, and consequently in the maintenance quality level; the maintenance quality level has a weak negative influence on the training and qualification of the team. Which suggests that when the maintenance level result is under the 50% criteria, it is needed a higher team qualification, and vice versa. The selection functions (represented by the red squares) are used for the inversion of the causality between the input concepts and the faults and defects occurrence associated with a rule or condition, in this case the threshold value of 50%. The discourse universe will be established by the maintenance policy.

The sDFCM2 (blue dashed line) completes the proposed strategy with maintenance suggestions according to the input intensities of related concepts and the maintenance quality level from sDFCM1. The connections are fuzzy values obtained through the inference by a set of fuzzy rules. As example, if the maintenance quality level is high and the defects levels are low, the sDFCM2 may suggest preventive maintenance. In short, sDFCM changes its structure according to variations of the input concepts. As result, after the cognitive model development, the W matrix in the original definition reported in [9] is now a time varying matrix which values are computed per the importance (level) of the modeled characteristic and the relationship types. Each weight in this matrix can be also modeled as a tuple:

$$(N, C_i, C_o, r, U, B_r) \tag{3}$$

Where:

- N identifies the layer or level where the relationships belongs, i.e., a pure causal relationship have N = 0, since it belongs the lowest layer level.
- Ci represents the input concepts composing the inference premise.
- Co represents the output concepts of the relationship.
- r is the type of relationship, which can be a causal relation, a time varying causal relation, a fuzzy relation or a selection relation.
- U describes the universe of discourse of the relationship, which can be a numeric value, an interval or a linguistic variable.
- Br is the index representing the rule base relevant to the relationship, thus pure causal or time varying causal relation has Br = 0.

IV. Initial sDFCM Results

This section will present and discuss the initial sDFCM1 results. It is noteworthy that the results reached a limit cycle, due to small variations in the output, as can be seen in Figs. 3 and 4. This paper is a work in progress, thus a comparison of this approach with other methodologies such as classic Fuzzy will be implemented and presented in future papers.

The initial version of the sDFCM was simulated in two scenarios, one with favorable conditions and the other with unfavorable conditions. Fig. 3 shows the initial results for the favorable conditions, when it is provided to the sDFCM1 considerably high levels of corrective and predictive maintenance, in which the system infer maintenance quality level over 89%. It suggests that team training need gets lower, and consequently, tends to lower faults and defects occurrences.

On the other hand, when it is provided an unfavorable condition to the sDFCM (Fig. 4), the maintenance quality level lowers considerably to around 55%. It suggests a greater need of team training and higher possibility of fault and defects occurrence.

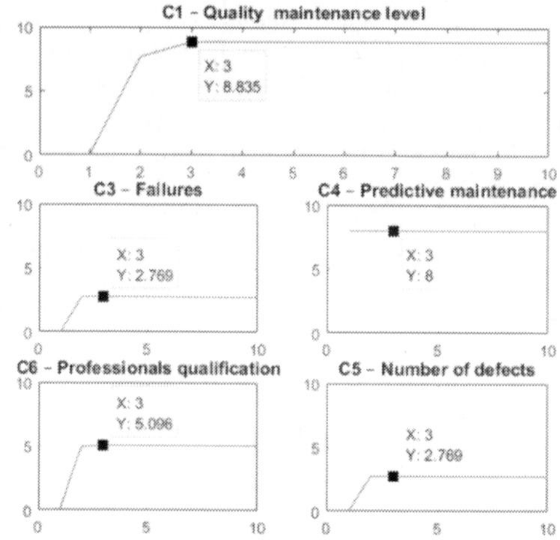

Figure 3. sDFCM initial results, favorable conditions.

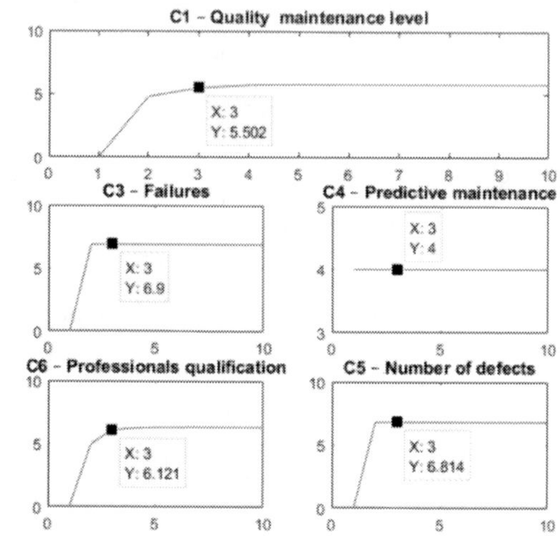

Figure 4. sDFCM initial results, unfavorable conditions.

V. Conclusions

According to the initial results, the sDFCM corresponded to the expectations of the work, assigning coherent quantitative values to the maintenance quality level in a favorable and unfavorable situation. The possibility levels of failures and defects occurrence were also coherent, as well the need for training and qualification of the team. Thus, to validate this tool, adjustments will be necessary in the model, which may occur according to different policies of each application.

It is expected to have contributed to maintenance management area and to Fuzzy Cognitive Maps models with a computational tool to provide a quantitative feedback for possible decision making through an initially qualitative knowledge-based model of the experts.

Future works will address a comparison of the computational complexity between sDFCM and DFCM, and the implementation of the sDFCM2. Finally, the application of the concepts presented in this research in a real case study to validate the sDFCM, as well the comparative with classic technique in the literature, such as classic Fuzzy.

REFERENCES

[1] Swanson L. Linking maintenance strategies to performance. Int. J. Production Economics 70. 2001

[2] M. Dems and K. Komeza, "The Influence of Electrical Sheet on the Core Losses at No-Load and Full-Load of Small Power Induction Motors," in *IEEE Transactions on Industrial Electronics*, vol. 64, no. 3, pp. 2433-2442, March 2017

[3] Tsang, A. H. C. Strategic dimensions of maintenance management. Journal of Quality in Maintenance Engineering, v. 8 n. 1, p.7-39, jan-abr, 2002.

[4] D. Sherwin, "A review of overall models for maintenance management", Journal of Quality in Maintenance Engineering, Vol. 6 No. 3, pp. 138-164. , 2000.

[5] SAE International. "SAE JA1012: A Guide to the Reliability-Centered Maintenance(RCM) Standard". Warrendale, USA, SAE Publication, 2002.

[6] A. M. Smith, "Reliability-Centered Maintenance," McGraw-Hill, New York, 1993.

[7] J. Moubray, "Reliability Centered Maintenance," Lutterworth, England, 2nd Edition, Aladon Ltd, 2000.

[8] E. Tolman, "Cognitive maps in rats and men," Psychological Review, vol. 55, no. 4, pp. 189–208, 1948.

[9] B. Kosko, "Fuzzy Cognitive Maps," Int.J. Man-Machine Studies, 1986.

[10] R. Axelrod, "Structure of Decision: The Cognitive Maps of Political Elites,". Princeton, NJ: Princeton Univ. Press., 1976.

[11] J. A. Dickerson and B. Kosko, "Virtual worlds as Fuzzy dynamical systems," In: SHEU, B. (Ed.) Technology for multimedia, New York: IEEE Press, 1996.

[12] L. V. R. Arruda, M. Mendonça, F. Neves, I. R. Chrun, and E. I. Papageorgiou, "Artificial life enviroment modeled by dynamic fuzzy cognitive maps," IEEE Transactions on Cognitive and Developmental Systems, 2016.

[13] G. Pajares and J. M. De La Cruz, "Fuzzy cognitive maps for stereovision matching," Pattern Recognition, vol. 39, no. 11, 2006.

[14] A. G. Pipe, "An architecture for building "potential field" cognitive maps in mobile robot navigation," Adaptive Behavior, v. 8, n. 2, p. 173-203, 2000.

[15] E. I. Papageorgiou, J. D. Roo, C. Huszka, and D. Colaert, "Formalization of treatment guidelines using Fuzzy Cognitive Mapping and semantic web tools,". Journal of Biomedical Informatics, vol. 45 no.1, pp. 45-60, 2012.

[16] W. Homenda, A. Jastrzebska, and W. Pedrycz, "Modeling time series with fuzzy cognitive maps," In Fuzzy Systems (FUZZ-IEEE), 2014 IEEE International Conference on, pp, 2055-2062, 6-11 July 2014.

[17] V. Rodin et al., "Multi-Agents System to Model Cell Signalling by Using Fuzzy Cognitive Maps. Application to Computer Simulation of Multiple Myeloma," 2009 Ninth IEEE International Conference on Bioinformatics and BioEngineering, Taichung, 2009.

[18] G. Acampora and V. Loia, "On the Temporal Granularity in Fuzzy Cognitive Maps," IEEE Transaction on Fuzzy Systems, vol. 19, no. 6, 2011.

[19] M. Mendonça, B. Angelico, L. V. R. Arruda, and F. Neves Jr. "A dynamic fuzzy cognitive map applied to chemical process supervision," Engineering Applications of Artificial Intelligence, v. 26, n. 4, p. 1199-1210, 2013.

[20] A. Jamshidi, "Dynamic risk modeling and assessing in maintenance outsourcing with FCM," Industrial Engineering and Systems Management (IESM), 2015 International Conference on, 2015.

[21] M. Mendonça, I. R. Chrun, F. Jr Neves and L. V. R. Arruda, "A cooperative architecture for swarm robotic based on dynamic fuzzy cognitive maps", Engineering Applications of Artificial Intelligence. Vol. 59. Pg 122-132, 2017.

[22] C. T. Chen and Y. T. Chiu, "A study of fuzzy cognitive map model with dynamic adjustment method for the interaction weights, " 2016 International Conference on Advanced Materials for Science and Engineering (ICAMSE), Tainan, Taiwan, 2016.

[23] M. Mendonça, L. V. R. Arruda, and F. Neves, "Autonomous navigation system using event driven-fuzzy cognitive maps," Springer Science+Business Media, 2011.

[24] Y. Miao, L. Zhi-Qiang, L. Shi, and C. K. Siew "Dynamical cognitive network-an extension of fuzzy cognitive map," Tools with Artificial Intelligence, Proceedings. 11th IEEE International Conference on, Chicago, IL, 1999.

[25] M. Mendonça, and L. V. R. Arruda, "A Contribution to the Intelligent Systems Development Using DCN," OmniScriptum GmbH & Co. KG., 2015.

[26] G. Nápoles, E. Papageorgiou, R. Bello, and K. Vanhoof, "On the onvergence of sigmoid fuzzy cognitive maps," Information Sciences, Elsevier, 2016.

[27] E. Yesil, C. Ozturk, M. F. Dodurka, and. A. Sakalli "Fuzzy cognitive maps learning using Artificial Bee Colony Optimization," Fuzzy Systems (FUZZ), IEEE International Conference on, Hyderabad, 2013.

[28] M. Glykas, "Fuzzy Cognitive Maps Advances in Theory, Methodologies," Tools and Applications. Greece Springer: 2010.

[29] E. I. Papageorgiou, "Fuzzy Cognitive Maps for Applied Sciences and Engineering From Fundamentals to Extensions and Learning Algorithms," Springer-Verlag Berlin Heidelberg, 2014.

[30] D. H. Lee and H. Lee, "Construction of holistic fuzzy cognitive maps using ontology matching method," Expert Systems with Applications, 2015.

[31] E. I. Papageorgiou "Learning algorithms for fuzzy cognitive maps: A review study,". IEEE Trans. Syst., Man Cybern. C Appl. Rev., 2012.

[32] C. D., Stylios, and P. P. Groumpos, "The challenge of modeling supervisory systems using fuzzy cognitive maps,". Journal of Intelligent Manufacturing, 1998.

[33] M. A. F., Finochio, J. J. Lopes, J. A. de França, J. C. Piai, and J. F. Mangili, "Neural networks applied to the design of dry-type transformers: an example to analyze the winding temperature and elevate the thermal quality," Int. Trans. Electr. Energ. Syst., 2016

[34] H. O. Henriques *et al.*, "Fuzzy Inference Method Applied to Georeferenced Maintenance Management," in *IEEE Latin America Transactions*, vol. 14, no. 9, pp. 4043-4047, Sept. 2016.

[35] E.Mohammadreza, S.S.Masoud, I.S.Javad. "Determining maintenance strategy by using Fuzzy Group MADM approach". European Online Journal of Natural and Social Sciences 2013; Vol.2, No.3 Special Issue on Accounting and Management

[36] V. Kreinovich, and C.D. Stylios. "Why Fuzzy Cognitive Maps are Efficient". International Journal Of Computers Communications & Control. Special Issue on Fuzzy Sets and Applications (Celebration of the 50th Anniversary of Fuzzy Sets). 10(6):825-833, December, 2015.

Dynamic Fuzzy Cognitive Maps Embedded and Classical Fuzzy Controllers Applied in Industrial Process

Lucas Botoni de Souza
Ruan Victor Pelloso Duarte Barros
Márcio Mendonça
DAELE (Electric Department)
UTFPR-CP - Cornélio Procópio, Brazil
lucasbotoni@hotmail.com
ruan_pelloso@yahoo.com.br
mendonca@utfpr.edu.br

Elpiniki I. Papageorgiou
Department of Computer Engineering
Technological Education Institute/ University of Applied Sciences of Central Greece
Lamia, Greece
epapageorgiou@teiste.gr

Abstract— **This research presents the application of intelligent techniques to control an industrial mixer. The controller design is based on Hebbian learning for evolution of Fuzzy Cognitive Maps. A Fuzzy Classic Controller and Artificial Neural Network was used to validate the simulation results. Experimental simulations and analysis in this control problem was made. In addition, the results were embedded using algorithms into the Arduino platform.**

Keywords-Dynamic Fuzzy Cognitive Maps; Hebbian Learning; Arduino Microcontroller; Process Control; Fuzzy Logic; Artificial Neural Network.

I. INTRODUCTION

In general, some of the difficulties found in acquiring knowledge in different areas of engineering (such as robotics, control or process control) are how to recognize the processes /systems; how to identify important variables and parameters. In addition, some questions are important: how to classify the type of physical problem; how to identify the family of mathematical models that can be associated; how to select the method and / or tool for the search and analysis of the model.

The final output of modern processes is significantly influenced by the selection of the set points of the process variables, as they fundamentally impact the product quality characteristics and the process performance metrics [1]. In this context, it is possible to define the main goal of this research: the development of techniques based on knowledge for the industrial mixer process control, a classic problem of Fuzzy Cognitive Maps area. It is worth mentioning this work is inspired by a previous work [2].

The article proposal is a different setup, especially the initial situation and a comparison with a new controller using Fuzzy-Logic with ANN (artificial neural network). The motivation of this research is developments in intelligent control area, expanding the adaptive concept and studying the feasibility of an autonomous control in practice.

Intelligent control techniques take control actions without depending on a complete or partial mathematical model. In these cases, human beings can deal with complicated processes based on inaccurate and/or approximate information. The strategy adopted by them is also of imprecise nature and usually capable of being expressed in linguistic terms. Thus, by means of Fuzzy Logic concepts, it is possible to model this type of information [3].

In general, Fuzzy Cognitive Map (FCM) is a tool for modeling the human knowledge. It can be obtained through linguistic terms, inherent to Fuzzy Systems, but with a structure like the Artificial Neural Networks (ANN), which facilitates data processing, and has capabilities for training and adaptation. FCM is a technique based on the knowledge that inherits characteristics of Cognitive Maps and Artificial Neural Networks [4]-[6], with applications in different areas of knowledge [7]-[14]. Besides the advantages and characteristics inherited from these primary techniques, FCM was originally proposed as a tool to build models or cognitive maps in various fields of knowledge. It makes the tool easier to abstract the information necessary for modeling complex systems, which are similar in the construction to the human reasoning. Dynamic Fuzzy Cognitive Maps (DFCM) should be developed to a model that can manage behaviors of non-linear time-dependent system and sometimes in real time. Classic FCM has drawback for time modeling [12]. In this way, examples of different variation of the classic or standard FCMs [4] can be found in the recent literature, e.g., [12]-[18].

This paper has two objectives. First objective is the development of two controllers using an acyclic DFCM with same knowledge as this of Fuzzy and Fuzzy Neural Controller, and with similar heuristic, thus producing comparable simulated results. Second goal is to show an embedded DFCM in the low-cost processing microcontroller Arduino with more noise and disturbances (valve locking) to test the adaptability of the DFCM. To reach the goals, we initially use the similar DFCM proposed initially in [13] to control an industrial mixing tank. As opposed to [13], we use the Hebbian algorithm to dynamically adapt the DFCM weights. In order to validate our DFCM controller, we compared its performance with a Fuzzy Logic Controller. This comparison is carried out with simulated data.

This work is developed as follows: Section 2 discusses the process development; Section 3 presents controllers development; Section 4 presents the DFCM development; Section 5 discusses results; Section 6 concludes and addresses future works.

II. DEVELOPMENT

To demonstrate the evolution of the proposed technique (DFCM) we will use a case study well known in the literature as seen in [2][5] and others. This case was selected to illustrate the need for refinement of a model based on FCM built exclusively with knowledge. The process shown in Fig. 1 consists of a tank with two inlet valves for different liquids, a mixer, an outlet valve for removal of the final product and a specific gravity meter that measures the specific gravity of the produced liquid. In this research, to illustrate and exemplify the operation of the industrial mixer, the liquids are water with specific gravity 1 and soybean oil with a specific gravity of about 0.9.

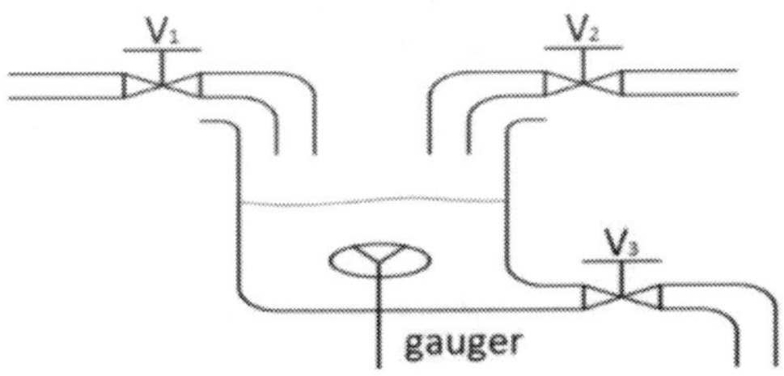

Figure 1. Mixer tank (Source: adapted from [20]).

Valves (V1) and (V2) insert two different liquids (specific gravities) in the tank. During the reaction of the two liquids, a new liquid characterized by its new specific gravity value is produced. At this time, the valve (V3) empties the tank in accordance with a campaign output flow, but the liquid mixture should match the specified levels of the volume and specific gravity.

Although relatively simple, this process is a Two Inputs Two Outputs (TITO) type with coupled variables. To establish the quality of the control system of the produced fluid, a weighting machine placed in the tank measures the (specific gravity) produced liquid. When the value of the measured variable G (liquid mass) reaches the range of values between the maximum and minimum [Gmin, Gmax] specified, the desired mixed liquid is ready. The removal of liquid is only possible when the volume (V) is in a specified range between the values [Vmin and Vmax]. The control consists to keep these two variables in their operating ranges, as:

$$V_{min} < V < V_{max} \quad (1)$$

$$G_{min} < G < G_{max} \quad (2)$$

In this study, it was tried to limit these values from approximately the range of 810 to 850 [mg] for the mass and approximately the range of 840 to 880 [ml] for the volume. The initial values for mass and volume are 800mg and 850ml respectively. According to Papageorgiou and collaborators [21], through the observation and analysis of the process, it is possible for experts to define a list of key concepts related to physical quantities involved. The concepts and cognitive model are:

- Concept 1 - State of the valve 1 (closed, open or partially open).
- Concept 2 - State of the valve 2 (closed, open or partially open).
- Concept 3 - State of the valve 3 (closed, open or partially open).
- Concept 4 - quantity of mixture (volume) in the tank, which depends on the operational state of the valves V1, V2 and V3.
- Concept 5 - value measured by the G sensor for the specific gravity of the liquid.

Considering the initial proposed evolution for FCM we use a DFCM to control the mixer which should maintain levels of volume and mass within specified limits.

The process model uses the mass conservation principle in incompressible fluid to derive a set of differential equations representing the process used to test the DFCM controller. As a result, the tank volume is the volume over the initial input flow of the inlet valves V1 and V2 minus the outflow valve V3, this valve V3 and the output campaign was introduced in this work to increase the complexity original process [20]. Similarly, the mass of the tank follows the same principle as shown below. The values used for m_{e1} and m_{e2} were 1.0 and 0.9, respectively.

$$V_{tank} = V_i + V_1 + V_2 - V_3 \quad (3)$$

$$Weight_{tank} = M_i + (V_1 m_{e1}) + (V_2 m_{e2}) - M_{out} \quad (4)$$

III. FUZZY CONTROLLER DEVELOPMENT

To establish a correlation and a future comparison between techniques, a Fuzzy Controller was also developed. The Fuzzy rules base uses the same heuristic control strategy and conditions.

Fuzzy logic has proved to can provide satisfactory non-linear controllers even when only the nominal plant model is available, or when plant parameters are not known with precision [22]-[24]. Fuzzy Control is a technique used for decades, especially in process controlling [5].

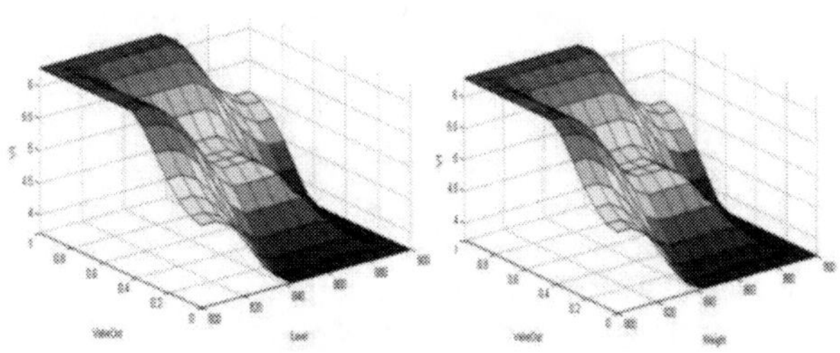

Figure 2. Fuzzy Controller Surfaces, V1 and V2.

It is a motivation to validate DFCM, so in this study it was used the same approach for two controllers, with two different formalisms. It is not in the scope to discuss the development of the Fuzzy Controller, but, some details of the structure are pertinent: functions are triangles and trapezoidal and 6 rules are considered in its base. The surface of this controller is showed in Fig. 2. Moreover, the rules are symmetric and similar by two output valves; in this specific case the surface of valve 2 is the same as in valve 1. The examples of base rules are:

1. If (Level is medium) or (Valve Out is medium) then (V1 is medium) and (V2 is medium).
2. If (Level is high) or (Valve Out is low) then (V1 is low) and (V2 is low).
3. If (Weight is medium) or (Valve Out is medium) then (V1 is medium) and (V2 is medium).

The rules and structure of the Fuzzy Controller used on its development was based on the DFCM heuristic.

Figure 3 show structure with same variables input and output like DFCM.

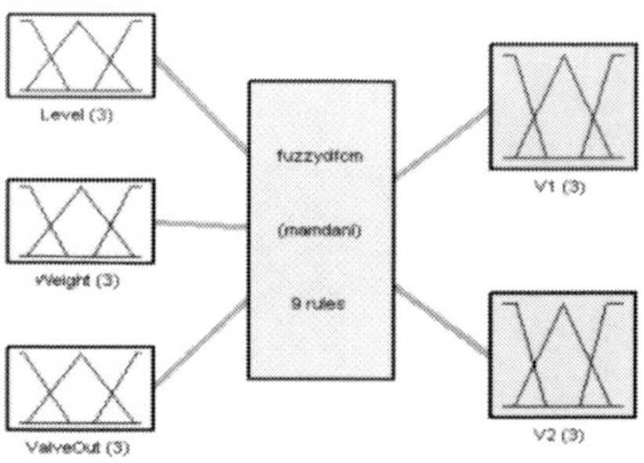

Figure 3. Fuzzy Structure.

A Fuzzy-ANN cascade controller had its ANN (multilayer perceptron) trained with the output data of the Fuzzy controller. The topology was empirically chosen by observing the learning time and output error. Therefore, 200 neurons were used on its hidden layer. Moreover, there were used 6000 points from inside the control region.

IV. DFCM DEVELOPMENT

The structure of the DFCM controller is similar to the developed Fuzzy controller, using same heuristics, e.g., if the output valve (V3, in accordance to Fig. 1) increases its flow, the inlet valves (V1 and V2) increase too. In other hand, in case volume and weight of the mixture increase, the inlet valves decrease. For example, the relationships W54 and W53, in the DFCM, are similar in effects or control actions of the Fuzzy controller's base rules.

The development of the DFCM is made through three distinct stages. First, the DFCM is developed as structure, concepts and causal relationships, similar to a classic FCM, where concepts and causal relationships are identified through sensors and actuators of the process. The concepts can be variables and/or control actions, as already mentioned.

The output valve is defined by a positive relationship, i.e., when the campaign increases, the output flow (V3) also increases, similarly, the input valves increase too; moreover, when the mixture volume and weight increase, V1 and V2 decrease. In both cases, the flow of the valves increases or decreases proportionally. The second development stage is the well-known Genetic Algorithm [25]. The Fig. 4 shows the schematic graph of a DFCM controller.

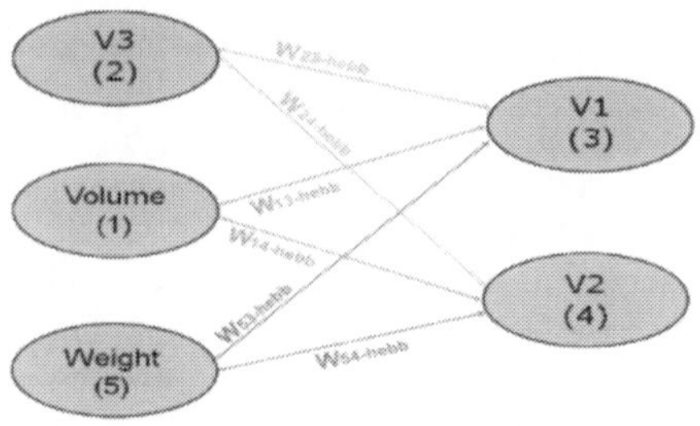

Figure 4. DFCM Controller

In this research, the initial values of causal relationships are determined through genetic algorithms. The genetic algorithm used is a conventional one, with a population of 20 individuals, simple crossing and approximately 1% of mutation. The chromosomes were generated by real numbers with all the DFCM weights, individuals were random and the initial method of classification was the tournament method with 3 individuals.

Finally, the fitness function for simplicity considers the overall error of the two desired outputs with 60 generations of the Genetic Algorithm proposed; it stabilizes and reaches the initial solution for the opening of the valves, approximately 42%.

Table 1 shows initial values of the DFCM weighs. Different proposals and variations of this method applied in tuning FCM can be found [16].

TABLE I. INITIALS CASUAL RELATIONSHIP WEIGHTS

W23	*W24*	*W13*	*W14*	*W53*	*W54*
-0.23	-0.26	-0.26	-0.26	0.23	0.15

The third stage of the DFCM development concerns the tuning or refinement of the model for dynamic response of the controller. In this case, when a change of output set-point in the campaign occurs, the weights of the causal relationships are dynamically tuned. To perform this, function a new kind of concept and relation was included in the cognitive model.

To dynamically adapt the DFCM weights we used the Hebbian learning algorithm for FCM that is an adaptation of the classic Hebbian method [4]. Different proposals and variations of this method applied in tuning or in learning for FCM are known in the literature, for example [15]. In this paper, the method is used to update the intensity of causal relationships in a deterministic way according to the variation or error in the intensity of the concept or input process variable, equations 5 and 6 show this. Specifically, the application of Hebbian learning algorithm provides control actions as follows: if the weight or volume of the liquid mixture increases, the inlet valves have a causal relationship negatively intensified and tend to close more quickly. In addition, if the volume or weight mixture decreases, the inlet valves have a causal relationship positively intensified. The mathematical equation is presented in (5).

$$W_i(k) = W_{ij}(k-1) \pm \gamma \Delta A_i \quad (5)$$

Where: ΔAi is the concept variation resulting from causal relationship, and it is given by ΔAi = Ai (k)-Ai (k-1), γ is the learning rate at iteration k.

This version of the Hebbian algorithm is an evolution of the two proposals of Matsumoto and collaborators [26].

Causal relationships that have negative causality has negative sign and similarly to positive causal relationships. The equations applied in this work are adapted of the Hebb original version.

$$W_i(k) = k_p * (W_{ij}(k-1) - \gamma * \Delta A_i) \quad (6)$$

Where: γ=1, and **kp** is different for every weight pairs. It has their assigned values empirically by observing the dynamics of process performance, recursive method, **kp** =40 for (W14; W23), **kp** =18 for (W13; W24) and kp =2.35 for (W53; W54), with normalized values.
The DFCM inference is like Classic FCM [4], and the inference equations are shown below (equation 7 and 8).

$$A_i = f\left(\sum_{\substack{j=1 \\ j\neq i}}^{n}(A_j \cdot W_{ji})\right) + A_i^{previous} \quad (7)$$

$$f(x) = \frac{1}{1+e^{-\lambda x}} \quad (8)$$

Fig. 5 shows the results of Hebbian Learning Algorithm for FCM considering the variations ΔAi of the concepts concerning volume, weight, outlet valve state, and the weights of the causal relationship in the process. This figure also shows the evolution of the weights of the causal relationships during the process into a range of [-1, 1].

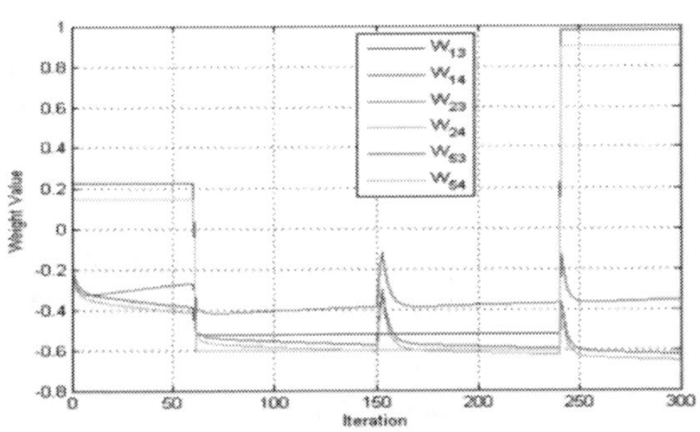

Figure 5. Evolution of the weights in the Hebbian Learning

V. SIMULATED EXPERIMENTAL RESULTS

The results of DFCM are shown in Fig. 6, which shows the behavior of the controlled variables within the predetermined range of the volume and weight of the mixture. It is noteworthy that the controller keeps the variables in the control range and pursues a trajectory according to a campaign, where the output flow is also predetermined. In this initial experiment, a campaign with a sequence of values ranging from 7, 5 and 11 ml/min can be a set-point output flow (outlet valve). Similarly, the results of the Fuzzy Controller are shown in Fig. 7. It is observed that the behavior of DFCM and Fuzzy controllers were similar when the tank is empty, with a slightly advantage for the Fuzzy controller that reached the desired result after 230 steps, while the DFCM needed 250 steps with the adaptation off.

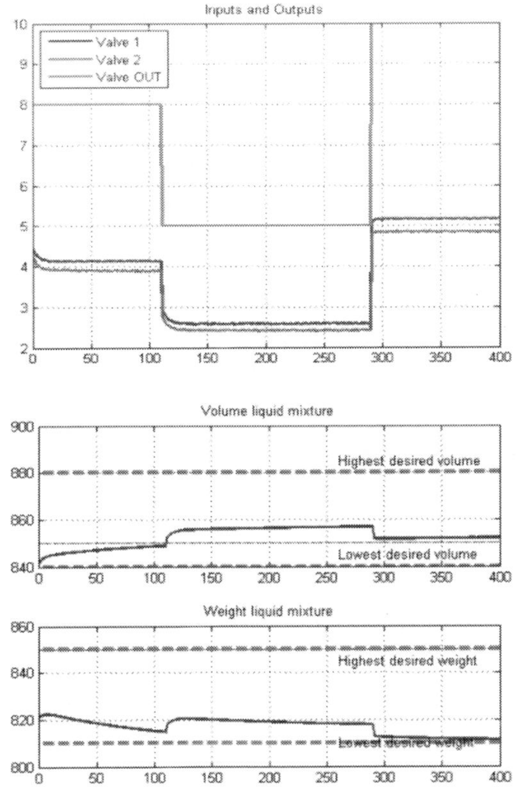

Figure 6. Valver and Results of the DFCM Controller

Table 2 shows that the simulated numeric results of the DFCM controller had a similar performance compared to the conventional Fuzzy Logic Controller, and DFCM embedded in Arduino with small difference in same conditions, with simulated small noise.

TABLE II. QUANTITATIVE RESULTS

	DFCM	*DFCM-Arduino*	*Fuzzy Logic*	*Fuzzy-ANN*
	Max-Min	**Max-Min**	**Max-Min**	**Max-Min**
Volume Mix (ml)	13.6	16.9	31.2	51.9
Weight Mix (mg)	17.1	14.1	27.5	31.2

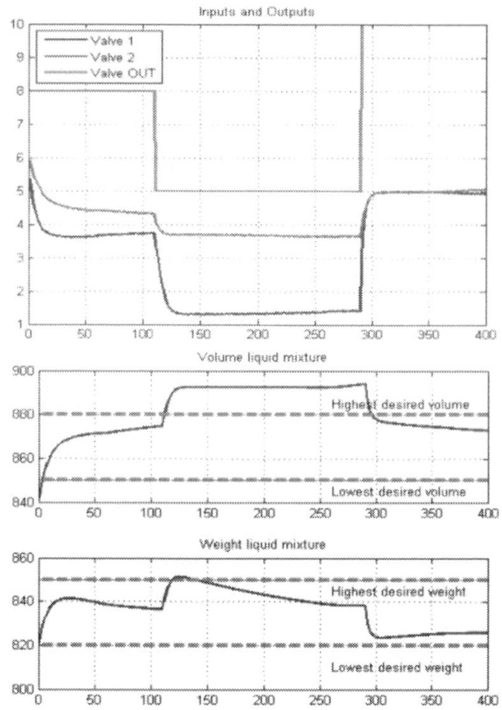

Figure 7. Valves and Results of the Fuzzy Controller

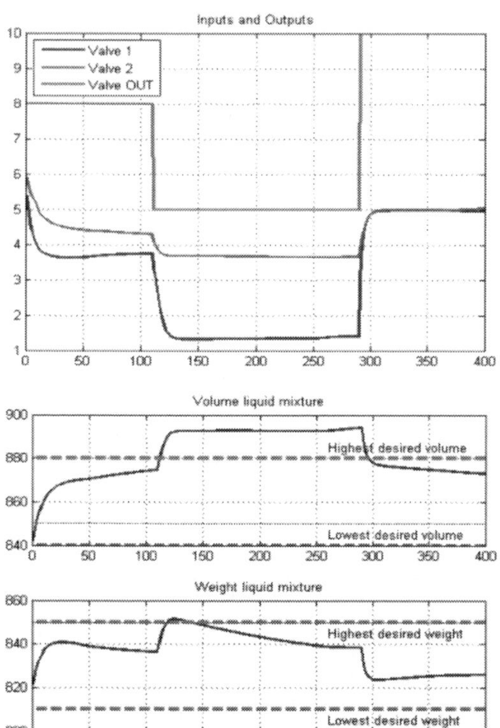

Figure 8. Valves and Results of the Fuzzy-ANN Controller

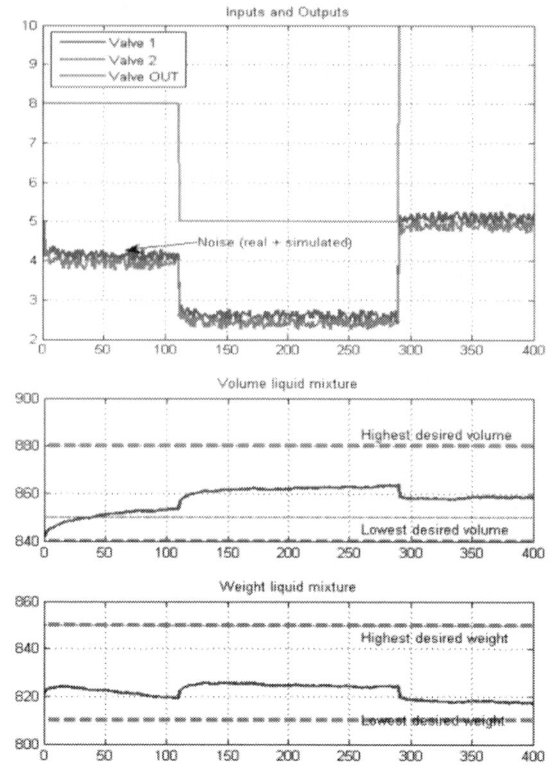

Figure 9. Valves and Results of the Arduino embedded DFCM

In order to extend the applicability of this work, the developed DFCM controller is embedded into an Arduino platform which ensures the portability of the FCM generated code. Arduino is an open-source electronic prototyping platform. Arduino was chosen because it is a cheap controller, and mainly because of its low processing capacity, to emphasize the low computational complexity of FCM [16].

The equations for volume and weight are calculated by Matlab, simulating the process. Through a serial communication established with Arduino, Matlab sends the current values of volume, weight and output valve to Arduino that receives these data, calculates the values of the concept 1 (valve 1) and concept 2 (valve 2) and then returns these data to Matlab. After this, new values of volume and weight are recalculated. Details on how this technique can be used are presented in Matlab Tutorial, Matlab and Arduino codes, by accessing the link [27]. The cycle of communication between Arduino to Matlab can be checked in [26].

Fig. 9 shows the results obtained with the Arduino platform providing data of the actuators, Valve 1 and Valve 2, with Matlab performing data acquisition. The algorithm switches the sets of causal relations that operate similarly to a DFCM simulated with noise and disturb in the valve 1. The noise in Fig. 9 is the sum of the real noise, observed in data transference between Arduino and Matlab, and a simulated white noise. Equation (9) shows the composition of the experiment noise.

$$Noise_{Experiment} = Noise_{Simulated} + Noise_{Arduino-Matlab} \quad (9)$$

VI. Conclusion

The contribution of this study focuses on the introduction of Fuzzy Cognitive Maps in the embedded control area. In simulated data, the results are similar for the three controllers, with a small advantage for DFCM with or without Arduino, observed that DFCM controller is adaptive. The results obtained from both controllers were quite the same. However, the Fuzzy-ANN did not have any significant improvement, there was a slightly reduction of the noise which can be a major factor on industrial plants.

From the data obtained from Arduino microcontroller, based on the variations of the DFCM embedded in the platform, it is observed that the controlled variables were in well-behaved ranges, which suggests that the DFCM codes have low computational complexity due to the simplicity of its inference mathematical processing.

Thus, we can emphasize the portability and the possibility of developing DFCM controllers on low cost platforms. In short, this work showed that DFCM can be embedded in low cost microcontrollers.

Future studies will quantify the computational complexity of the DFCM, for a more general conclusion, results with real prototype. Finally, other controllers with dynamic adaptation, like adaptively fuzzy controllers, ANFIS can be used for the comparison.

References

[1] Marchal, P. C.; García, J. G.; Ortega, J. G. "Application of Fuzzy Cognitive Maps and Run-to-Run Control to a Decision Support System for Global Set-Point Determination," in IEEE Transactions on Systems, Man, and Cybernetics: Systems , vol.PP, no.99, pp.1-12, 2017.

[2] Mendonça, M.; Neves Jr, F.; Arruda, L. V. R.; Papageorgiou, E.; Chrun, I. Embedded Dynamic Fuzzy Cognitive Maps for Controller in Industrial Mixer. In: 8th International KES Conference on Intelligent Decision Technologies KES-IDT-16, 2016, Tenerife. KES-IDT-16, 2016. P. 1-10.

[3] Zadeh, L. A. An introduction to Fuzzy logic applications in intelligent systems. Boston: Kluwer Academic Publisher, 1992.

[4] Kosko, B. Fuzzy cognitive maps. International Journal Man-Machine Studies, v. 24, n. 1, p.65-75, 1986.

[5] Glykas M. Fuzzy Cognitive Maps: Advances in Theory, Methodologies, Tools and Applications. Springer-Velarg Berlin Heidelberg, 2010.

[6] Kosko, B. Neural networks and fuzzy systems: a dynamical systems approach to machine intelligence. New York: Prentice Hall, 1992.

[7] Lee, K. C.; Lee, S. A cognitive map simulation approach to adjusting the design factors of the electronic commerce web sites. Expert Systems with Applications, v. 24, n. 1, p. 1-11, 2003.

[8] Papageorgiou, E.; Stylios, C.; Groumpos, P. Novel for supporting medical decision making of different data types based on Fuzzy Cognitive Map Framework. Proceedings of the 29th annual international conference of the IEEE embs cité internationale, Lyon, France August, p. 23-26, 2007.

[9] Papageorgiou, E.; Stylios, C.; Groumpos, P. A. Combined Fuzzy cognitive map and decision trees model for medical decision making. Annual International Conference of the IEEE Engineering in Medicine and Biology Society. IEEE Engineering in Medicine and Biology Society, v. 1, p. 6117-6120, 2006.

[10] Huang, Y. C.; Wang, X. Z. Application of Fuzzy causal networks to waste water treatment plants. Chemical Engineering Science, v. 54, n. 13/14, p. 2731-2738, 1999.

[11] Dickerson, J. A.; Kosko, B. Virtual Worlds as Fuzzy cognitive maps. Presence, v. 3, n. 2, p. 173-189, 1994.

[12] Papageorgiou, E. I. (2014). Fuzzy Cognitive Maps for Applied Sciences and Engineering from Fundamentals to Extensions and Learning Algorithms. Springer.

[13] Mendonça, M.; Angélico, B.; Arruda, L.V.R.; Neves, F. A dynamic fuzzy cognitive map applied to chemical process supervision. Engineering Applications of Artificial Intelligence, v. 26, p. 1199-1210, 2013.

[14] Mendonça, M.; Chrun, I. R. ; Neves, F. Jr; Arruda, nd L. V. R. "A cooperative architecture for swarm robotic based on dynamic fuzzy cognitive maps", Engineering Applications of Artificial Intelligence. Vol. 59. Pg 122-132, 2017.

[15] Miao, Y.; Liu, Z. Q.; Siew, C. K..; Miao, C. Y. Transformation of cognitive maps. IEEE Transactions on Fuzzy Systems, v. 18, n. 1, p. 114-124, 2010.

[16] Papageorgiou, E. Learning Algorithms for Fuzzy Cognitive Maps. IEEE Transactions on Systems and Cybernetics. Part C: Applications and Reviews, v. 42, p. 150-163. 2012.

[17] Mendonça, M., Arruda, L. V. R., A Contribution to the Intelligent Systems Development Using DCN, OmniScriptum GmbH & Co. KG, 2015

[18] Miao, Y.; Liu, Z. Q.; Siew, C. K.; Miao, C. Y. Dynamical cognitive network - an Extension of fuzzy cognitive. IEEE Trans. on Fuzzy Systems, Vol. 9, no. 5, pp. 760-770, 2001.

[19] Axelrod, R. Structure of decision: the cognitive maps of political elites. New Jersey: Prince-ton University Press, 1976.

[20] Stylios C. D.; Groumpos P. P.; Georgopoulos V. C. An Fuzzy Cognitive Maps Approach to Process Control Systems J. Advanced Computational Intelligence, n. 5, p. 1-9, 1999.

[21] Papageorgiou, E. I.; Parsopoulos, K. E.; Stylios, C. S.; Groumpos, P. P.; Vrahatis, M. N. Fuzzy cognitive maps learning using particle swarm optimization. Journal of Intelligent Information Systems , v. 25, p. 95–121, 2005.

[22] Ross, T. J. Fuzzy logic, with Engineering Aplications, 2nd Ed., England, John Whiley & Sons, 2004.

[23] Konar, A., "Computacional intelligence, Principles, Techniques and Applications", New York, Springer, 2005.

[24] Farinwata, S. S.; Filev, D.; Langari, R. (editors), *"Fuzzy Control, Synthesis and Analysis"*, West Sussex, England, John Wiley & Sons, 2000.

[25] Goldberg, D. E. Genetic algorithmos in search optimization and machine learning. Mass: Addison-Wesley, 1989.

[26] Matsumoto, D. E.; Mendonça, M.; Arruda, L. V. R. and Papageorgiou, E. "Embedded Dynamic fuzzy cognitive maps applied to the control of industrial mixer". Simpósio Brasileiro de Automação Inteligente – XI SBAI. 2013.

[27] <http://epapageorgiou.com/index.php/fcm-research-group> Access date: 10/02/17.

Fuzzy Cognitive Maps and Weighted Classic Fuzzy Applied on Student Satisfaction Level

Lucas Botoni de Souza
Ruan Victor Pelloso Duarte Barros
Patrick Prieto Soares
DAELE (Electric Department)
UTFPR-CP
Cornélio Procópio, Brazil
lucasbotoni@hotmail.com
ruan_pelloso@yahoo.com.br
p.prietosoares@hotmail.com

Jeferson Gonçalves Ferreira
UTFPR-CP
Cornélio Procópio, Brazil
goncalves_jeferson@outlook.com
Márcio Mendonça
DAELE (Eletric Department)
UTFPR-CP
Cornélio Procópio, Brazil
mendonca@utfpr.edu.br

***Abstract*—This research aims to develop a Fuzzy Cognitive Map (FCM) and Weighted Classic Fuzzy (WCF) for the satisfaction level of students at Federal Technological University of Parana, Campus Cornélio Procópio (UTFPR-CP). The FCM combines aspects of other intelligent techniques. This tool has inference capacity through concepts and causal relations among them (the influence level among the variables of the model). Its development begins with the determination of the possible areas that would affect or fit as indicators for satisfaction level in UTFPR-CP. Through online forms, it was possible to quantify the influence of the following initially detected areas: professor training, structures of laboratories and classrooms, habitation, library and cleaning. In general, educational institutions do not have tools to provide a critical analysis of its quality. This work proposes a tool for improving the institution in a few years. Thus, with the development of the FCM model, it was possible to identify the positive and negative points that affect the satisfaction level in UTFPR-CP. Finally, to validate the results a WCF was used with same structure and heuristic for comparison with FCM.**

Keywords- Fuzzy Cognitive Maps; Quantitative Analysis; Level of Satisfaction; Operational Research; Weighted Classic Fuzzy.

I. INTRODUCTION

In Brazil, educational statistics show that only 9% of young between 18-24 years enrolled in higher education at the beginning of this decade. As motivation of this work, it is observed that in Brazil there is an evaluation policy, SINAES (in Portuguese, Sistema Nacional de Avaliação do Ensino Superior), National System for the Evaluation of Higher Education, which since 2004 allowed the participation of students in the evaluation of their university and graduation courses. It should be emphasized that the increasing number of opportunities itself does not guarantee the permanence of young people in higher education [1]. It is necessary to invest in the conditions that the student enters in the university, trying to understand their needs, difficulties and satisfaction.

Currently, the evaluation of higher education, especially in the engineering area, is an important part of the evaluation of the existing educational system, which plays a key role in strengthening the management of higher education [2]. In that way, one can observe the capacity of evaluation for educational standard. So, the purpose of education is to help students create a modern consciousness to improve the capacity for innovation and criticism by various means, such as university, business and government [3].

It is important to remember that despite the large expansion, many institutional managers do not give importance to students' opinions to identify their level of satisfaction. In the case of public institutions, one has the impression that this aspect does not deserve attention, because it is a service provision. It should also be remembered that public institutions are paid through public resources, which makes it obligatory for the citizen attended by them to be heard and helped in their needs.

Developing and testing methods and techniques that can assess reliability and results of student satisfaction levels is an indispensable task and a powerful tool for academic and financial management. Nevertheless, a statistical analysis cannot be done with the purpose of assessing higher scores of academic productions of researchers. Such data should be part of the management agenda of institutions that should listen to students, teachers and the community.

The preceding paragraphs define the purpose and justification of this work, which is corroborated with the construction of a computational intelligence tool that, based on qualitative information, can quantitatively diagnose and identify critical points. Moreover, Decision Support Systems can provide assistance during the process of decision making. FCMs have been used successfully to develop Decision Support Systems (DSS). The important advantage of FCMs is that they can handle even incomplete or conflicting information. This is essential, where experts should take many factors under consideration before they can reach a decision [4].

Among all computational intelligence techniques, Artificial Neural Networks exceeds by its ability to process massive data at the same time [5], or by acquiring knowledge from one or more experts using Fuzzy systems. About the Fuzzy Logic, it can be mentioned its ability to reason based on uncertain data through rules and membership functions [6].

In Fuzzy systems, Fuzzy Cognitive Maps can be highlighted by how it abstracts knowledge, mainly, when structured in graphs [7]. Cognitive maps are the origin of FCM, and they were first proposed by Axelrod [8] to represent words, ideas, tasks or different items connected and radially organized around a central concept. Graphs are diagrams representing connections among concepts from a certain theme. Those elements are intuitively arranged accordingly to its importance in a structured way.

In Franco and Montibeller's work [9], the goal is not to reach a consensus, but that the participants agree about the problem formulation. Throughout this process, the handler has the important duty of supporting the participants on exploring their thoughts on the problem and expressing their perspective.

As mentioned above, in a specific manner, this paper is focused on estimating the satisfaction level of the university student body, and, also on identifying critical points or factors that can be improved in order to achieve better results, in this paper the university [10].

This work is developed as follows: Section 2 discusses the fundamentals of computational intelligence systems and discusses Fuzzy systems applied in correlated areas. Section 3 presents background FCM. In Section 4 is presented and discussed the results. Section 5 concludes, addresses future works and finalize the paper.

II. Fuzzy System Applicated on Education

Similar works can be found in literature, like the work proposed in [10], which presents a FCM practical use on modelling educational success critical factors for Control Engineering through case study at Istanbul Technical University (ITU). A survey is applied on eight academics and, through the results, eight FCMs are extracted and later aggregated in a resulting FCM. Concepts like academic and personal profile and teacher's excessive work load are used as input concepts, and the output concept is the Control Engineering program success.

One can also cite the work of Gao et al. [2], which uses a Fuzzy Logic method to improve the engineering courses tendencies, having great importance in an engineering professional education evaluation to reach a global dimension.

The work in [11] proposes the Fuzzy Analytical Hierarchy Process (FAHP) to evaluate a case study at Nanyang Institute of Technology, with the objective of offering theoretic and practical orientation for the development of innovative education. In this work, it's proposed an indices' table for the evaluation of teaching quality and innovation, which includes four dimensions: government, society, university and student. In each one of these dimensions are sub-concepts included and specified. For the government dimension: fund entry, management organization, politics and measurements; the university dimension includes: concept and planning, curriculum system, professors staff, cultural environment and base installation; the society dimension consist of: social reputation and environment, company groups; lastly, in the student dimension: research fulfillment and capacity, entrepreneurship and practical activities. The work shown in [12] uses a Fuzzy Neural Network-based model to estimate the contribution of different educational levels of human capital (abilities and expertise). Through Fuzzy Neural Network (FNN) mapping, four contribution levels of education in human capital are estimated in China's three regions, each one with different knowledge areas and technology levels. They are: illiteracy and primary, fundamental, graduation and postgraduate.

The work seen in [13] uses a FNN in students' emotion recognition, and it's applied in smart educational systems that use facial recognition systems for pre-programmed teaching strategy adjustment or adaptation in the proposed intelligent system. The emotion recognition technique uses three characteristics from the students' images: facial area, distance between eyelids, and mouth's corner.

At last, the work in [14] uses a FNN to map human capital levels in the university through two methods. According to the authors, the human capital concept in the university refers to workman knowledge and abilities, which is formed by the educational investment, professional formation, health and migration. More specifically, one can cite the Mendonça and collaborators work [15], which employs a Classic FCM to determinate the student´s satisfaction level in the university.

III. Fuzzy Cognitive Maps, Background and Development

This section presents a FCM background and development diagnostic using FCM and classic Fuzzy.

A. FCM Background

Since Kosko's pioneer work [15], which extended Axelrod's cognitive maps [8] for the inclusion of Fuzzy Logic, countless FCM applications are reported in literature in several areas of knowledge. There are applications in artificial life [16]-[17], social systems [18], modelling and decision making in corporate and e-commerce environments [19], image point detection in stereo camera systems [20] and decision making in medical area [21]. The works [22]-[23] apply FCM evolutions in autonomous mobile robotics and process control, respectively Event Driven – Fuzzy Cognitive Maps (ED-FCM) and Dynamic Cognitive Networks (DCN).

In [24] a formal adaptation of the FCM is presented: this new tool is designed as TAFCM (Timed Automata Fuzzy Cognitive Maps). In addition, [17] presents a DFCM (Dynamic Fuzzy Cognitive Maps), an FCM evolution. It is observed that these works also present semantic variations of the original proposal, adapting the FCM structure according to the treated problem.

This work manually develops the FCM, because the desired output is a diagnostic. Thus, causal relations cannot be adjusted by genetic algorithms, for example, because every causal relation has a semantic meaning. The values were defined by checking the student's opinion. In another way, as in robotics and control applications, the FCM controllers must achieve objectives, as in the specific case of valve actuation, used in the Mendonça's and collaborators works [22]-[23]. The cognitive maps technique is widely used in structuring complex problems in groups.

To model the problem and obtain qualitative results, it was decided to use the Classic FCM, which had its structure modeled by concept definitions and causal relations, in order to establish influence between them. Thus, specialists' knowledge was applied in the proposed FCM elaboration, which has as function to evaluate the student satisfaction level of the Cornélio Procópio campus of Federal Technical University of Paraná (UTFPR-CP).

In general, it can be defined that FCM combines Artificial Neural Network (ANN) aspects [5], Fuzzy Logic [6], Semantic Nets [25], among other computational intelligence techniques. In this context, it can be conceptualized that FCM is a knowledge-based causality methodology to model complex-decision systems [15]. A FCM describes an unknown system behavior in concept terms, which represents an entity, state, variable or system characteristic [26]. A Classic FCM example is a graph and a synaptic weights matrix, which can be found in [27].

The FCM concepts can be updated through iteration with the other concepts and their own value. This is given by matrix (3), with the causal relations weights, and is represented by the sum's weight. The concepts values evolve after several iterations, as shown in equation (1), until they stabilize at a fixed point or limit cycle [28].

$$A_i = f(\sum_{\substack{j=1 \\ j\neq i}}^{n}(A_j \times W_{ji}) + A_i^{previous} \quad (1)$$

Since **k** is the iteration counter, **n** is the number of graph nodes, $\mathbf{W_{ij}}$ are the weight of the arc which connects concept $\mathbf{C_j}$ to concept $\mathbf{C_i}$. $\mathbf{A_i^{previous}}$ are the concept value $\mathbf{C_i}$ in the actual iteration (previous), and **f** function (equation 2) is a sigmoid:

$$f(x) = \frac{1}{1+e^{-\lambda x}} \quad (2)$$

In some cases, the FCM may not stabilize and oscillate, or even show chaotic behavior [27]. Generally, for well-behaved systems, it is observed that after a finite number of iterations, the concepts values reach an equilibrium point or a limit cycle. This can be observed in Fig. 4, in which after 4 iterations the previously modelled concept final values stay fixed. Recently, the FCM convergence is investigated by [38].

B. FCM Development

This paper is models a classic FCM, similar to Kosko's, by identifying the relevant variables of the proposed problem, and the causal relations are obtained through a survey on electric engineering students.

The initial development phase is the identification and construction of the cognitive model using expertise knowledge and the causal relations obtained from student's opinion. Then, the FCM inference equations (2) and (3) are applied. The next phase consists of obtaining the quantitative values of the "satisfaction level of the student body" (main goal of this research), and the values of the other concepts. And finally, validating those results with the opinion of those interviewed. To simplify, all concepts started with score zero, for later evaluation of the FCM inference.

There are many aspects that may have an effect on the satisfaction level. In this paper, eight aspects were chosen and the causal relations among them were defined through a quiz. A sample of students gave a score from zero to ten for each of the concepts connection that could actuate on the satisfaction level of the students of UTFPR-CP (Federal University of Technology – Paraná, Cornélio Procópio Campus), mainly from the electric engineering and control and automation engineering.

Since the 1960s, many researches attempted to identify the students' satisfaction levels. It's important to mention that satisfaction itself is a concept of difficult analysis for being relative to each student perspective. The vast diversity of models, scales and methods to asses this concept proves that complexity. One of the most used methods is the *College Student Satisfaction Questionnaire* [29]. More researches made in Brazil on this topic can be seen in [30] and [31]. Altogether, this paper tries to capture how the students perceive the course and the education conditions propitiated by the institutions, that way being of major interest of manager and teachers.

According to the general statistic theory [32], in the literature an analysis was made with a sample of 30 students, from the data acquired, it was obtained a 90% of reliability and a margin of error of 6.8%, representing a group about 500 students [15]. Considering the Control and Automation Engineering course still has no graduates and have approximately 200 students, this same analysis can be applied, thus, 35 students are used in this research.

The results and structure does not intend to classify nor

qualify the institution or course. However, because of its exploratory nature, this paper can be used to give a quantitative evaluation of the satisfaction level, work and/or study in the Campus. Another aspect of this approach is identifying possible improvement points on the variables of the cognitive model.

Fig. 3 shows the final model with the structure and its causal relation. It's noteworthy that the model applied is the same classic from [15] and so, does not consider time, in other words, all concepts take place simultaneously. In this context, there are improvements on FCM that deals with this "disadvantage", for example: E-FCM (*Extended*-FCM) on [33], RB-FCM (*Rule Based*-FCM) on [34] and DCN (*Dynamic Cognitive Networks*) on [35]. There is a recent review of the last 10 years about other improvement applications and training of FCMs. The concepts chosen for the FCM model are shown on table I:

TABLE I. FCM CONCEPTS RELATIONS

C1:	Student Satisfaction Level
C2:	Professor's Capacitation/Performance
C3:	Pedagogic Structure - Library
C4:	Habitation
C5:	University Restaurant Quality
C6:	Cleaning - Accessibility
C7:	Leisure and Sports Activities

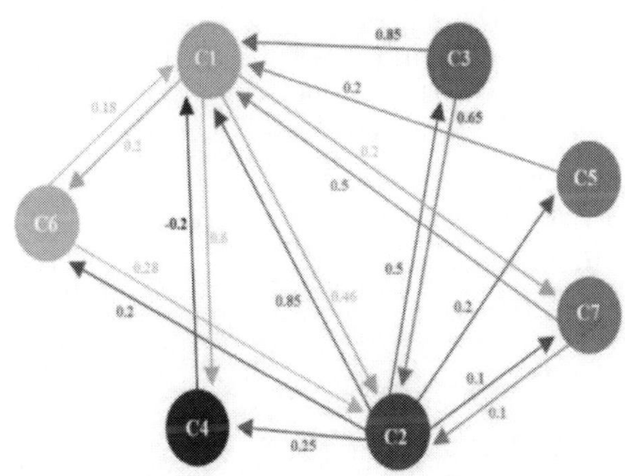

Figure 1. Student satisfaction level FCM

Fig. 1 shows all variable involved on obtaining the satisfaction level of the students. The equation (4) shows the cause and effect relation among the concepts. Thereby, according to the intensity of the causality among the concepts, the final values are changed, especially the C1 – output concept of the satisfaction level.

$$W = \begin{vmatrix} 0 & 0.46 & 0 & 0.6 & 0 & 0.20 & 0.20 \\ 0.85 & 0 & 0.5 & 0.25 & -0.20 & 0.20 & 0.1 \\ 0.85 & 0.65 & 0 & 0 & 0 & 0 & 0 \\ -0.20 & 0 & 0 & 0 & 0 & 0 & 0 \\ 0.20 & 0 & 0 & 0 & 0 & 0 & 0 \\ 0.18 & 0.28 & 0 & 0 & 0 & 0 & 0 \\ 0.50 & 0.10 & 0 & 0 & 0 & 0 & 0 \end{vmatrix} \quad (4)$$

In order to validate the FCM proposed and establish a possible comparison with the same heuristic, it was opted to use in this research a classic inference system through a Fuzzy system, but it's not in the scope of this paper to demonstrate its development details; more information of can be seen in [36].

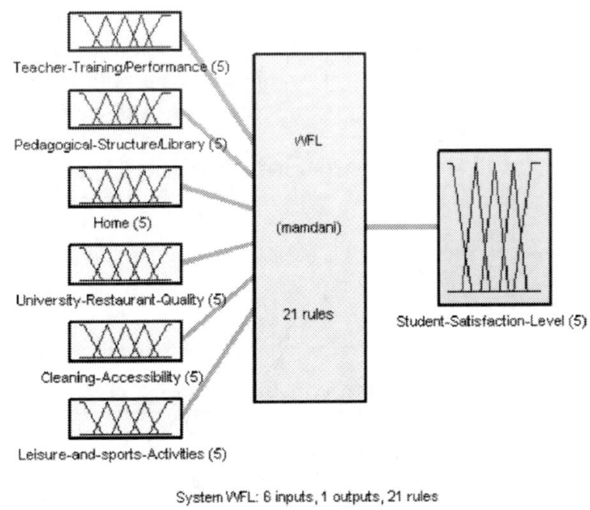

Figure 2. Fuzzy structure

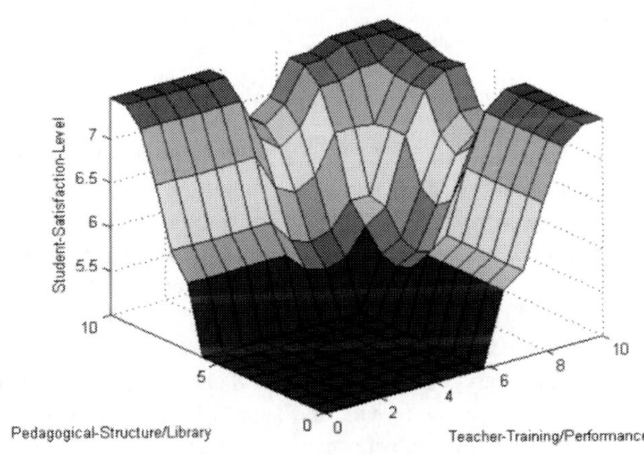

Figure 3. Fuzzy example surface

Fuzzy systems are universal approximators, with applications in many areas, as seen on [6] and [37]. It was opted to use a Weighted Classic Fuzzy with weights given to each rule in order to vary their influence on the Fuzzy inference, and a similar structure of FCM.

The Fuzzy inference method chose was Mandani's with 6 input and 1 output concept. Each variable had 5 membership functions, triangular and trapezoidal ones, and a total of 21 rules were used, for the simplicity of the developed Fuzzy system according to the FCM values. The Fig. 2 shows the structure and figure 3 shows an example of its surface.

IV. Results and Discussion

After modeling the concepts, especially the numerical values of the causal relations voted by the students, the model is calculated by equations (3) and (4) and it evolves to the final values, which are the objective of the work. It is observed that the initial values of the concepts were considered zero.

The Fig.4 shows the results and evolution of each of the concepts modeled in a scale from zero to ten, with emphasis on the output concept (level of satisfaction in UTFPR-CP).

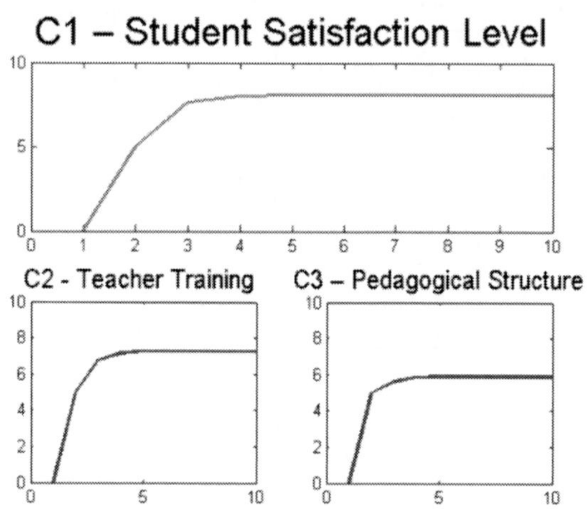

Figure 3. Results by Fuzzy Cognitive Maps

It is observed in this FCM that it stably evolved reaching a critical point (a short variation around the final result). It can also be observed that there were some critical points in the research and construction of the model, such as the parking conditions in places near the University, Quality of the university restaurant in relation to the small physical space for the demand of students causing delays in the classes after lunches and breaks, and others. This is due to its rapid growth in the last ten years and should be reviewed by its managers with government officials for future improvements. However, the final grade of this research was relatively good, close to eight, with possibilities for improvement with treatment of the critical points identified in this research.

Since this work addresses a situation of static or time invariant diagnosis, it does not make sense to present an evolution curve of the fuzzy system, only the output with the inputs based on the values of the weights of the FCM causal relations. Thus, the output of the WCF was approximately 79%. It is emphasized that the classic version of FCM has the drawback of not modeling dynamical systems, because the causal relations are constant [7].

The results are initial, therefore researches that take into account students' perceptions, identifying their satisfaction, are important tools that have the potential to diagnose problems and propose solutions ranging from structural aspects, such as the availability of current titles in the library, to pedagogical aspects. In this context, and according to the obtained results, it can be affirmed that the satisfaction level of UTFPR-CP students had a significant final mark of approval, among the items chosen using FCM and Classic Fuzzy.

V. Conclusion and Future Works

The results obtained from both proposals were similar with approximately 80% of the level of student satisfaction. The result was satisfactory and expected due to the relation with the Brazilian Ministry of Education's evaluation of UTFPR engineering courses that obtained four stars in a domain of discourse from zero to five. To corroborate the final result found, a sample of 45 students was consulted to assign a final grade to UTFPR and the result found was approximately 8.45 on a scale from zero to ten.

The techniques used the same logic or heuristic in their respective structures, and the objectives were reached by the results obtained from qualitative data of a research done with a sample of the university students. Future works addresses new checking in other UTFPR courses, apply in other universities or institutes. And finally, compare this approach with other intelligent techniques, such as ANFIS.

References

[1] Sistema Nacional de Avaliação da Educação Superior (Sinaes). http://bit.ly/2ml4ILG access date: 10/02/2017

[2] Gao Y., Yang, Jiwei and Liu F. The Research on the Comprehensive Assessment of Higher Engineering Education Based on Fuzzy Comprehensive Evaluation Method, in Future Information Technology and Management Engineering, 2009. FITME '09. Second International Conference on, pp.124-127, 13-14 Dec. 2009.

[3] Pingwen L.Management Analysis & Diagnose",Fujian: Press of Xiamen University, pp. 310-335, 2004.

[4] E. Bourgani, G. Manis, C. D. Stylios and V. C. Georgopoulos, "Timed-Fuzzy Cognitive Maps: An overview," 2016 IEEE International Conference on Systems, Man, and Cybernetics (SMC), Budapest, 2016, pp. 004483-004488.

[5] Haykin, S. Neural Networks and Learning Machines (3rd Edition), McMaster University, Pearson Prentice Hall, 2008.

[6] Pedrycz, W. and Gomide. F. An Introduction to Fuzzy Sets: Analysis and Design, MIT Press, 1998.

[7] Kosko. B. Fuzzy Cognitive Maps. Int.J. Man-Machine Studies, vol. 24, pp. 65–75, 1986.

[8] Axelrod R., Structure of Decision: The Cognitive Maps of Political, Elites. Princeton, NJ: Princeton Univ. Press, 1976.

[9] Franco, L. A. and Montibeller, G. Facilitated modeling in operational research. European Journal of Operational Research, vol. 205, no. 3, pp. 489-500, 2010.

[10] Yesil, E.: Ozturk, C.; Dodurka, M.F.and Sahin, A., "Control engineering education critical success factors modeling via Fuzzy

Cognitive Maps," in Information Technology Based Higher Education and Training (ITHET), 2013 International Conference on, pp.1-8, 10-12 Oct. 2013

[11] Hezhan, Y. Application of Fuzzy Analytical Hierarchy Process in innovation education quality evaluation of higher education institution, in Information Management, Innovation Management and Industrial Engineering (ICIII), 2012 International Conference on, vol.1, pp.438-441, 20-21 Oct. 2012.

[12] Yu, S. and Zhu, K. Fuzzy Neural Network Applications on Estimating the Contribution of Different Education Levels on Human Capital of China, in Service Systems and Service Management, 2007 International Conference on, pp.1-4, 9-11 June 2007.

[13] Xiang, P. Research on the Emotion Recognition Based on the Fuzzy Neural Network in the Intelligence Education System, in Digital Manufacturing and Automation (ICDMA), 2011 Second International Conference on, pp.1030-1033, 5-7 Aug. 2011

[14] Yu, S. and Zhu, K. Fuzzy Neural Network Applications on Estimating the Contribution of Different Education Levels on Human Capital of China," in Service Systems and Service Management, 2007 International Conference on, pp.1-4, 9-11 June 2007.

[15] Mendonca, M.; Chrun, I. R.; Finocchio, M. A. F. and de Mello, E. E.; "Fuzzy Cognitive Maps Applied to Student Satisfaction Level in an University," in *IEEE Latin America Transactions*, vol. 13, no. 12, pp. 3922-3927, Dec. 2015

[16] Dickerson, J. A. and Kosko, B. Virtual worlds as Fuzzy dynamical systems. In: SHEU, B. (Ed.) Technology for multimedia. New York: IEEE Press, 1996

[17] L. V. Arruda; M. Mendonca; F. Neves-Jr; I. Chrun; E. PAPAGEORGIOU, "Artificial Life Environment Modeled by Dynamic Fuzzy Cognitive Maps," in *IEEE Transactions on Cognitive and Developmental Systems*, vol.PP, no.99, pp.1-

[18] Taber, R. Fuzzy cognitive maps model social systems. AI Expert, v. 9, p. 18-23, 1994.

[19] Lee, K. C. and Lee, S. A cognitive map simulation approach to adjusting the design factors of the electronic commerce web sites. Expert Systems with Applications, v. 24, n. 1, p. 1-11, jan. 2003.

[20] Pajares, G. and De La Cruz, J. M. Fuzzy cognitive maps for stereovision matching Pattern Recognition, vol. 39, no. 11, pp. 2101-2114, Nov. 2006.

[21] Papageorgiou, E.; Stylios, C. and Groumpos, P. Novel for supporting medical decision making of different data types based on Fuzzy Cognitive Map Framework. PROCEEDINGS OF THE 29TH Annual International Conference of the Ieee Embs Cité Internationale, Lyon, France August 23-26, 2007

[22] Mendonça, M.; Arruda, L.; Neves, F. Autonomous navigation system using event driven-fuzzy cognitive maps. Springer Science+Business Media. Outubro, 2011.

[23] Mendonça, M.; Angélico, B. A.; Arruda, L. V. R. and Neves, F. Jr. A Subsumption Architecture to Develop Dynamic Cognitive Network-Based Models with Autonomous Navigation Application. Journal of Control, Automation and Electrical Systems, vol. 1, pp. 3–14, 2013.

[24] Acampora, G.; and Loia, V. On the Temporal Granularity in Fuzzy Cognitive Maps. IEEE Transaction on Fuzzy Systems, vol. 19, no. 6, 2011.

[25] Russell S. J., and Norvig P., Artificial intelligence: a modern approach. Englewood Cliffs: Prentice Hall. 1995.

[26] Kosko, B. Neural networks and Fuzzy systems: a dynamical systems approach to machine intelligence. New York: Prentice Hall, 1992.

[27] Stylios, C. D.; Georgopoulos, V. C. and Groumpos, P. P. The use of Fuzzy cognitive maps in modeling systems. In: 5th IEEE Mediterranean Conference on Control and Systems, Paphos, Cyprus, 21-23 July 1997.

[28] Stylios, C. D. and Groumpos, P. P. The challenge of modeling supervisory systems using fuzzy cognitive maps. Journal of Intelligent Manufacturing, vol. 9, pp. 339-345, 1998.

[29] Betz, E. L.; Menne, J. W.; Starr, A. M. and Klingensmith, J. E. A. Dimensional Analysis of College Student Satisfaction. Measurement and Evaluation in Guidance, vol. 4, no. 2, pp. 99-106, 1971.

[30] Walter, S. A., Tontini, G. and Domingues M. Identificação de Oportunidades de Melhoria em IES Através do Uso Conjunto do Modelo Kano e Matriz de Importância x Desempenho. Available in: https://repositorio.ufsc.br/xmlui/bitstream/handle/123456789/97432/Silvana%20Anita%20Walter.pdf?sequence=3&isAllowed=y access date: 15/02/2017

[31] Schleich, A. L. R., Polydoro, S. A. and Santos, A. A. Scale of satisfaction with academic experience of students of higher education. Avaliação Psicológica, vol. 5, no. 1, pp. 11-20, (2006). Available in: <http://pepsic.bvsalud.org/scielo.php?script=sci_arttext&pid=S1677-04712006000100003&lng=pt&tlng=pt> access date: 23/02/2017

[32] Larsen, Richard J.; Marx, Morris L. Introduction to Mathematical Statistics and Its Applications. 5. ed. Florida: Pearson Higher Ed Usa, 2013. 744 p.

[33] Hagiwara, M. Extended Fuzzy cognitive maps. In: Proceedings of IEEE international conference on fuzzy system, New York, 1992. pp. 795–801.

[34] Carvalho, J. P. and Tomé, J. A. Rule based Fuzzy cognitive maps-qualitative systems dynamics. In: Proceedings 19th international conference of the North America. Fuzzy information fuzzy processing society, pp. 407–411, 2000.

[35] Miao, Y. C.; Miao, Y.; Tao, X.; Shen, Z. and Liu, Z. Transformation of cognitive maps. IEEE Transactions on Fuzzy Systems, vol. 18, no. 1, pp. 114–124, Feb. 2010.

[36] Zadeh, L. Fuzzy Sets - Information and Control, vol. 8, pp 338-353, 1965.

[37] Psssino, M. K.; Yourkovich, S. Fuzzy Control. Menlo Park: Addison-Wesley, 1997.

[38] Nápoles, G.; Papageorgiou, E.; Bello, R. and Vanhoof, K. "On the onvergence of sigmoid fuzzy cognitive maps," Information Sciences, Elsevier, 2016.

Empirical Comparison of Fuzzy Cognitive Maps and Dynamic Rule-based Fuzzy Cognitive Maps

Asmaa Mourhir
Computer Science Department
Al Akhawayn University in Ifrane
Ifrane, Morocco
email: a.mourhir@aui.ma

Elpiniki I. Papageorgiou
Computer Engineering Department
Technological Education Institute (TEI) of Sterea Ellada,
Lamia, Greece
email: epapageorgiou@teiste.gr

Abstract— **Among the soft computing techniques that can be used effectively to model decision tasks in autonomous robotics are Fuzzy Cognitive Maps. Dynamic Rule-based Fuzzy Cognitive Maps (DRBFCMs) are a Fuzzy Cognitive Map variant that allows modeling of dynamic causal maps, where influence weights are determined dynamically at simulation time using Fuzzy Inference Systems, in order to adapt to new conditions. We aim in this work to compare and contrast DRBFCM to a conventional Fuzzy Cognitive Map in application of cotton yield in precision farming. The cotton yield model shows the relationships between soil properties like pH, K, P, Mg, N, Ca, Na and cotton yield. DRBFCM was evaluated for 360 cases measured for three years (2001, 2003 and 2006) in a 5 ha experimental cotton field. The results revealed an accuracy of predictions of 85.55%, 87.22% and 73.33%, against 73.80%, 67.20% and 69.65% for the conventional FCM model, and against 75.55%, 68.86% and 71.32% for the FCM model with the Nonlinear Hebbian Learning algorithm, for the years 2001, 2003 and 2006 respectively. DRBFCM proved, in this case study, to predict more accurately the yield while being faithful to the real world model.**

Keywords— fuzzy cognitive maps; fuzzy inference systems; dynamic rule-based fuzzy cognitive maps; cotton yield prediction

I. Introduction

A Fuzzy Cognitive Map (FCM) is a soft computing technique and semi-quantitative technique that can be used as an intuitive elicitation tool to transfer individuals' tacit knowledge into a causal network. FCMs can be used effectively as an approach to bridge the gap between the design of causal loops and their effective use in any decision making process. FCM's graph structure facilitates causal reasoning to study systems' dynamics in complex problems. FCMs also inherently support vagueness and ambiguities, and causal reasoning in FCMs allows handling of feedback loops. Moreover, FCM models produced by different individuals or groups can be combined to produce a larger and more reliable knowledge base, which can help solving knowledge inconsistencies by generating aggregated system complexities, using multiple participants or experts. FCM simulations can model the evolution of scenarios over time, and produce projections by evolving forward and letting concepts interact with one another.

FCMs have been applied successfully in many scientific fields, including autonomous robotics. For example the authors in [1] used FCM causal inference as a mechanism to derive required control values from the FCM's motion concepts and their interaction. The authors in [2] used a new FCM variant, named Event Driven-Fuzzy Cognitive Maps (ED-FCM), to model decision tasks in autonomous navigation. The authors in [3] [4] proposed Hybrid-Dynamic Fuzzy Cognitive Maps (HD-FCM) which incorporate different types of concepts and causal relations able to circumvent the main drawbacks of FCM modeling. In a recent work [5], the authors propose Dynamic Fuzzy Cognitive Maps (DFCM), with a multi-agent approach to develop an autonomous navigation system that has skills for learning, self-adaptation, behavior management and cooperative data sharing. A general review on FCMs' research during the last decade can be found in [6].

Many implementations of FCMs exist in the literature, but most of them focus on depicting causalities between system variables, rather than cause and effect relationships, and FCM inference allows drawing conclusions about what is caused and what is not caused, which is a major limitation in dynamic systems where reasoning is characterized by magnitudes of change and effects. Another shortcoming with FCMs is that the links' weights are forced into a static value in the range [-1, 1]. In dynamic systems, the weight should be a function of other factors' influences, which allows modeling of non-monotonic, nonlinear and dynamic relationships; in fact the effect of a variable X on Y should depend on the value of X. Moreover, variables in real models map to a universe of discourse within their minimum and maximum state limits; however, in FCM models, a threshold function normalizes all values between 0 and 1.

A Dynamic Rule-based Fuzzy Cognitive Map (DRBFCM) is a FCM extension that allows reasoning in terms of deterministic magnitudes of effects. A major difference between DRBFCM and a conventional FCM model is that the weights are not fixed prior to running simulations, but are rather adapted dynamically during every step of a simulation, by using Fuzzy Inference Systems (FISs) [7].

In this work, we will validate DRBFCM numerically, and compare the accuracy of its predictions to a conventional FCM model in application of cotton yield in precision farming, by building on the work of Papageorgiou et al. [8].

The cotton yield model shows the relationships between soil properties, like Nitrogen (N), Phosphorus (P), Potassium (K), Sodium (Na), Clay (Cl), Sand (S), Calcium (Ca), Magnesium (Mg), pH, Electrical Conductivity (EC), Organic Matter (OM), and Cotton Yield (Y). DRBFCM is evaluated for 360 cases measured for three years (2001, 2003 and 2006) in a 5 ha experimental cotton yield.

The paper is organized as follows. Section II presents a general background about FCM models, FCM models with Fuzzy Weights, and DRBFCM models. In Section III, we describe the cotton yield DRBFCM model, and we discuss the results of predicting cotton yield and compare them to the conventional FCM model. We highlight some conclusions and directions for future work in Section IV.

II. MATERIALS AND METHODS

In this section, we introduce the FCM soft computing technique, we also give background about the DRBFCM extension that leverages Fuzzy Logic inference to compute the system variables' states, using quantified perturbations produced by FISs.

A. *Fuzzy Cognitive Maps*

At the structural level, a FCM is a directed graph where nodes represent system concepts or variables, and links represent perceived causal relationships (caused or not) between concepts. According to Kosko [9], all the values are fuzzy; each edge between two concepts C_i and C_j is associated with a weight w_{ij}, which varies from -1 to 1. There are three different types of possible causalities between two concepts C_i and C_j:

- A positive weight reflects an excitation relation.
- A negative weight designates an inhibition relation.
- A weight of zero indicates that C_i and C_j do not exert any influence on each other's.

These causal links (also called FCM connections) and their respective weights can be encoded into an NxN (N being the number of concepts) matrix, which is referred to as the Connection or Weight Matrix E.

FCM's graph structure facilitates causal reasoning; it is a decision support system where calculations can be made to perform an assessment of the consequences of a specific system state. FCM forward inference is very close to Artificial Neural Network (ANN) mechanisms, Kosko calculates each subsequent value of the causal state using previous state and weight matrix multiplication [9]. The concepts take values, which are also called *activation levels,* between 0 and 1, where zero means the concept being deactivated or not important, and 1 being activated or important. The State Vector of activations evolves in time according to the influences between concepts. By feeding the FCM with an initial stimulus $S^{(t)}$ (state vector at time (t)), it can model the evolution of a scenario over time by evolving forward and letting concepts interact with one another.

The next state of the system $S^{(t+1)}$ is produced by multiplying previous state vector $S^{(t)}$ by the graph's weight adjacency matrix E. In auto-associative ANNs, neurons are considered to have a memory with a self-feedback link weight of 1.

The next state value of each concept C_i is hence elaborated, during simulation, by retrieving its value at the previous iteration, and adding it to the propagated weighted values of all concepts C_j that have a direct influence on the concept according to (1).

$$C_i^{(k+1)} = F\left(C_i^{(k)} + \sum C_j^{(k)} * w_{ji}\right) \quad (1)$$

where $C_i^{(k+1)}$ is the activation value of concept C_i at iteration k+1, $C_i^{(k)}$ is the value of node C_i at iteration k, w_{ji} is the weight of the cause-effect link between C_j and C_i, and F is a threshold function like sigmoid used to normalize the values within the range [0, 1] as shown by (2) [10].

$$S(x) = \frac{1}{(1 + e^{(-x)})} \quad (2)$$

In order to generate projections based on a given simulated scenario, a series of vector-matrix multiplications is performed, until a fixed point attractor; that is the vector-matrix multiplication yields an equilibrium state, where the same vector is repeated over a number of iterations [9].

B. *FCM Approach with Fuzzy Weights*

A variant of FCMs was proposed by Papageorgiou et al. [8]; it consists in generating weights using fuzzy linguistic terms, extracted from rules collected from domain experts. The approach consists in pooling domain knowledge from experts in the form of Fuzzy Rules [11] from experts for each interconnection of the FCM model. Thus, a number of linguistic weights are obtained for each interconnection by considering the consequent of the rule only, ignoring hence the antecedent part [8].

In order to build the FCM weight matrix, the linguistic weights, obtained from all experts, are combined using Fuzzy Logic operators [12]. For every link connecting two concepts, the linguistic terms are aggregated by typically using the fuzzy *Union* operator [11]. The membership function of the Union of two Fuzzy Sets *A* and *B*, defined over the set *X*, with membership functions μ_A and μ_B respectively is defined by a *T-conorm* mapping. One of the most common used mappings is the *maximum* as shown by (3):

$$\mu_{A \cup B}(x) = \max\left[\mu_A(x), \mu_B(x)\right] \quad (3)$$

Then, a defuzzification method is employed to calculate a single numerical weight value of the link. Several methods have been used in practice for defuzzification, the most popular method is the "centroid" method [11], which calculates the center of gravity of the aggregated fuzzy set as shown by (4):

$$CoG = \int \mu_A(x)x\,dx \div \int \mu_A(x)\,dx \quad (4)$$

Thus, a numerical weight (w_{ij}) is calculated for the link between every pair of concepts C_i and C_j, prior to starting simulations. To demonstrate how the linguistic terms are aggregated, let us consider the relation between K (Potassium) and Y (cotton yield) using expert knowledge:

1st Expert

```
"IF K IS med THEN Y IS med. Infer: influence IS med"
```

2nd Expert

```
"IF K IS med THEN Y IS high. Infer: influence IS high"
```

3rd Expert:

```
"IF K IS high THEN Y IS very high. Infer: influence IS very high"
```

The linguistic influence terms ('med', 'high' and 'very high') are summed and an overall weight is produced, transforming hence the influence into the numerical constant weight $W_{K\text{-}Y} = 0.65$. The process of aggregation and defuzzification for this example is shown by Figure 1.

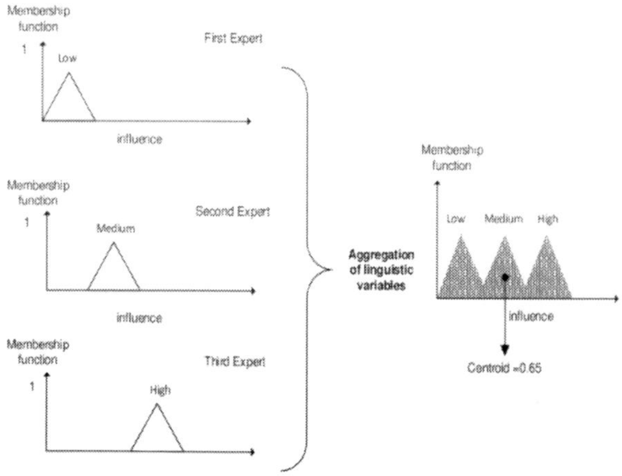

Figure 1. Aggregation and defuzzification of the three linguistic variables.

In [8], FCMs were also enriched with the unsupervised Nonlinear Hebbian Learning (NHL) algorithm. The technique was used to overcome inadequate knowledge of experts or non-acceptable FCM simulation results. The weight adaptation procedure is based on the Hebbian Learning rule proposed in [13]. The nonlinear Hebbian-type rule for ANNs learning has been adapted and modified for FCM models as proposed by the authors in [14].

C. Dynamic Rule-based Fuzzy Cognitive Maps

In this work, we build on the work of Mourhir et al. that proposes DRBFCM as an alternative to System Dynamics, using FCMs and Rule-based Systems [7]. DRBFCM models have three main properties. First, the fuzzy set theory adds true fuzziness to DRBFCM, and resolves ambiguities and subjectivity usually faced in complex real world problems [12]. Another main property is that the weights represent deterministic real values and not fuzzy binaries. The most fundamental property of a DRBFCM model is the ability to depict dynamic causalities between concepts, the influence induced on a given concept is not static, but depends on the initial state of influencing nodes. DRBFCM can adapt the weights dynamically by describing causal relationships using FISs.

In DRBFCM, concepts represent causes or effects that collectively characterize a system state at a given time. Each concept, analyzed by experts in the model, is divided into a number of intervals to determine linguistically descriptions corresponding to threshold intervals, or possible states it can exist in using membership functions [11].

A general Fuzzy variable called "Variation" is used consistently to represent the influence between concepts. The variation variable has the fuzzy sets like positively or negatively 'low', 'medium', 'high' or 'very high'. DRBFCM model structure is shown by Figure 2.

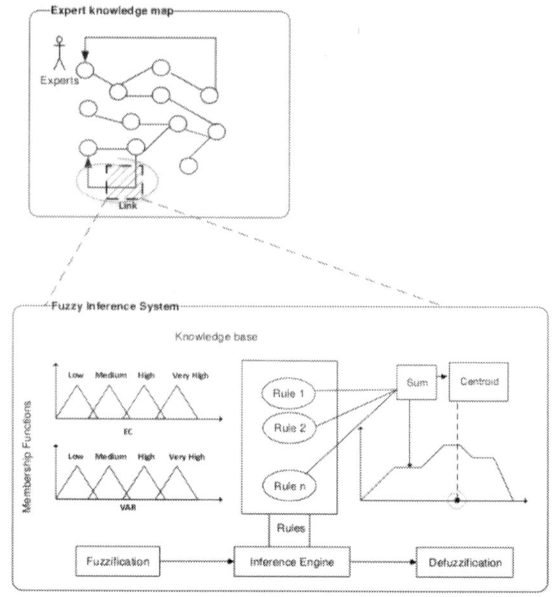

Figure 2. DRBFCM model structure.

The concepts' set of linguistic terms is used to describe the causal relationships and links between input concepts and outputs using fuzzy "if-then" rules. A link between two concepts C_i and C_j, depicted by a connection in a DRBFCM model is represented by a FIS [11]. Each FIS is described using the Fuzzy Control Language (FCL) [15]. In FCL, a FIS inference system is usually composed of one or more Function Blocks (FB). In DRBFCM models, each FB has one input variable, and an output variable as well as a Rule Block (RB). The rule block is composed of a set of rules, as well as the *aggregation*, *activation* and *accumulation* methods [11]. In DRBFCM, the rules have a single antecedent related to a concept state a or concept's variation, and output the variation strength which represents a perturbation in the target concept:

IF C_i is A THEN Variation is V_{ij} ON C_j

IF Variation is V_i IN C_i THEN Variation is V_{ij} ON C_j

Since FCL supports only rules that map input concept states to output concepts states, the authors modified the FCL grammar to cope with rules describing concept variations by adding two clauses to the condition part and the conclusion part: (i) an in_clause: IN^ ID in the subcondition, that is used to specify the causal variation, where "IN" is a keyword and ID is the cause variable, and (ii) an on_clause: ON^ ID in the subconclusion, that is used to specify the effect variation, where "ON" is a keyword and ID is the effect variable.

Inference is carried according to an algorithm for combining effects on a given concept and dealing with feedback. In a given scenario, the concepts are activated with their real deterministic values.

To run a simulation, the DRBFCM model is fed with the initial stimulus for a given scenario, and while the system does not converge or does not reach a minimum number of iterations, the inference algorithm is executed to update the activation value of each concept.

To update the state value of a given concept, all the incoming connections on that concept are retrieved, and then the variation induced by every incoming connection is evaluated. Since every connection between two concepts is a FIS, fuzzy inference is used to compute the output variation. DRBFCM models make use of the Mamdani's fuzzy inference process [16]. The implication method used is the "Min", the aggregation method is "Max", and the defuzzification method used to quantify the variation is Centroid [11]. Once the different variations are obtained, the state of the concept is updated by using the sate vector and weight matrix multiplication. Concepts are considered to have memory with a self-feedback link weight equal to 1, so the activation value of the concept is updated by recalling its old value, and adding it to the summation of weighted input activations.

Since DRBFCM models operate on real deterministic values, concepts are considered to have a maximum and a minimum state value. So when these are exceeded, the concept value is set to the maximum or the minimum value.

III. Numerical Comparison of FCM and DRBFCM Models in a Cotton Yield Application

In this section, we compare and contrast DRBFCM to a conventional cotton yield FCM model, developed by Papageorgiou et al. [8] in a precision farming application.

A. *DRBFCM Cotton Yield Model*

We developed the cotton yield model, following the DRBFCM approach described in the previous section. However, in our work, although we use crisp real values to determine the influence, we stimulated the FCM model using normalized values in order to generate results that can be contrasted and compared consistently to the approach proposed by the authors in [8]. The initial values of concepts are transformed into the range [0,1] using a linear transformation based on the universe of discourse of fuzzy variables as shown by (5).

$$C_{j normalized} = \frac{C_j - C_{jmin}}{C_{jmax} - C_{jmin}} \quad (5)$$

Moreover, since there are no feedback loops in the cotton yield model, we simplified the inference algorithm by generating the weight matrix once for every record. Hence, simulations are carried according to the algorithm of Figure 3. The knowledge and data were obtained from the work of Papageorgiou et al. [8] to predict cotton yield data. Three experts contributed to the development of the cotton yield map, one experienced cotton farmer, and two experienced soil scientists, one from Technological Educational Institute of Larissa, Greece, and the other from the Laboratory of Regional Soil Analysis and Agricultural Applications of Larissa, Greece [8].

The experts stated that there are elven soil parameters that can be used to determine cotton yield (t/ha) in precision farming, which are: Soil shallow Electrical Conductivity (mS/m), Magnesium (ppm), Calcium (ppm), Sodium (ppm), Potassium (ppm), Phosphorus (ppm), Nitrogen (ppm), Organic Matter (%), pH, Sand (%) and Clay (%).

The experts described the soil parameters and their threshold values using membership functions as depicted in Table I. The experts were also requested to define the degree of influence exerted by one concept on another, using "if-then" rules, representing the causal relationships between soil parameters and the cotton yield.

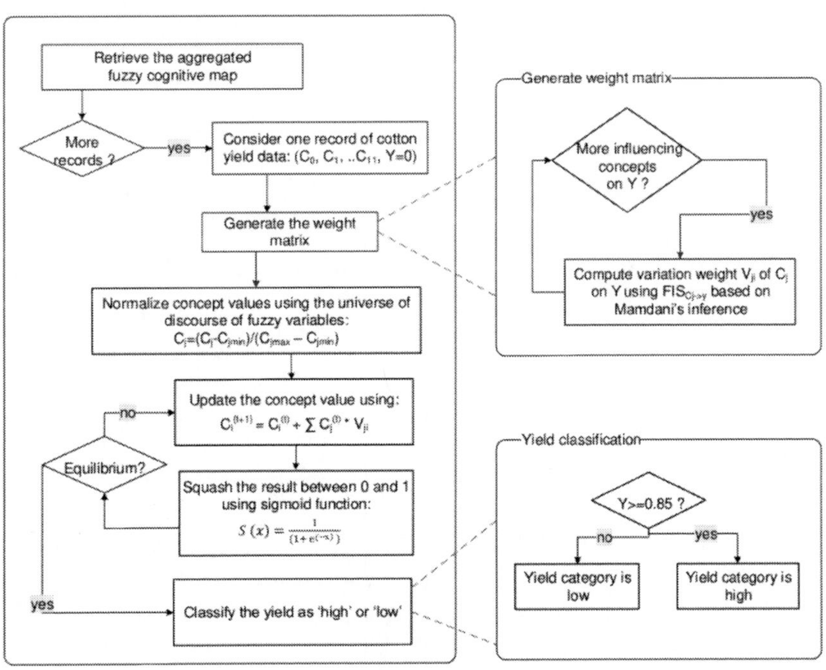

Figure 3. Cotton yield inference algorithm.

The list of fuzzy rules aggregated from the three experts is shown in Table II, where "VAR" is the variation fuzzy variable.

TABLE I. CONCEPTS' MEMBERSHIP FUNCTION PARAMETERS.

Concept	Membership functions
C1: Shallow EC (EC)	VL := TRAPE 0 0 7.5 15; L := TRIAN 10 18 25; M := TRIAN 25 28 35; H := TRIAN 30 38 45; VH := TRAPE 40 45 100 100;
C2: Magnesium (Mg)	VL := TRAPE 0 0 60 120; L := TRIAN 60 140 240; M := TRIAN 160 290 360; H := TRIAN 300 500 1400; VH := TRAPE 700 950 1400 1400;
C3: Calcium (Ca)	VL := TRAPE 0 0 455 1000; L := TRIAN 545 1273 2000; M := TRIAN 1363 2455 3000; H := TRIAN 2637 3909 5000; VH :=TRAPE 4000 4380 5000 5000;
C4: Sodium (Na)	VL := TRAPE 0 0 26 59; L := TRIAN 32 70 123; M := TRIAN 80 140 200; H := TRIAN 156 250 600; VH := TRAPE 350 450 600 600;
C5: Potassium (K)	VL := TRAPE 0 0 24 65; L := TRIAN 30 81 135; M := TRIAN 88 152 230; H := TRIAN 190 275 600; VH := TRAPE 300 470 600 600;
C6:Phosphorous (P)	VL := TRAPE 0 0 5 10; L := TRIAN 5 12.5 20; M := TRIAN 12.5 22 31.5; H := TRIAN 25 38 50; VH := TRAPE 40 45 50 60;
C7:Nitrogen (N)	VL := TRAPE 0 0 3 8; L := TRIAN 5 8 17.5; M := TRIAN 12 20 27.5; H := TRIAN 22 32 45; VH := TRAPE 35 40 45 45;
C8:Organic Matter (OM)	L := TRAPE 0 0 0.6 1.1; M := TRIAN 0.5 1.5 2.5; H := TRAPE 1.8 2.1 3 3;
C9: pH	VL := TRAPE 0 0 4 5; SL := TRIAN 5 6 7; L := TRIAN 4 5 6; M := TRIAN 6 7 8; SH := TRIAN 7 8 9; H := TRIAN 8 9 10; VH := TRAPE 9 10 11 11;
C10: Sand (S)	L := TRAPE 0 0 15 30; M := TRIAN 20 45 70; H := TRIAN 60 75 90; VH := TRAPE 80 90 100 100;
C11: Clay (Cl)	L := TRAPE 0 0 12.5 20; M := TRIAN 10 22.5 35; H := TRAPE 30 37.7 60 60;

TABLE II. COTTON YIELD FUZZY RULES.

Concept	If-then rules
C1: Shallow EC (EC)	IF EC IS VL THEN VAR IS PVL ON Y; IF EC IS M THEN VAR IS PL ON Y; IF EC IS H THEN VAR IS PM ON Y; IF EC IS H THEN VAR IS PH ON Y; IF EC IS VH THEN VAR IS PH ON Y; IF EC IS L THEN VAR IS PVL ON Y;
C2: Magnesium (Mg)	IF Mg IS VL THEN VAR IS NL ON Y; IF Mg IS L THEN VAR IS NL ON Y; IF Mg IS M THEN VAR IS NM ON Y; IF Mg IS H THEN VAR IS NM ON Y; IF Mg IS VH THEN VAR IS NM ON Y;
C3: Calcium (Ca)	IF Ca IS VL THEN VAR IS PM ON Y; IF Ca IS L THEN VAR IS PL ON Y; IF Ca IS M THEN VAR IS PM ON Y; IF Ca IS H THEN VAR IS PM ON Y; IF Ca IS VH THEN VAR IS PM ON Y; IF Ca IS VH THEN VAR IS PL ON Y;
C4: Sodium (Na)	IF Na IS VL THEN VAR IS NVH ON Y; IF Na IS VL THEN VAR IS NH ON Y; IF Na IS L THEN VAR IS NM ON Y; IF Na IS M THEN VAR IS NL ON Y; IF Na IS H THEN VAR IS NH ON Y; IF Na IS VH THEN VAR IS NH ON Y; IF Na IS VH THEN VAR IS NVH ON Y;
C5: Potassium (K)	IF K IS VL THEN VAR IS PVL ON Y; IF K IS L THEN VAR IS PVL ON Y; IF K IS M THEN VAR IS PM ON Y; IF K IS H THEN VAR IS PM ON Y; IF K IS VH THEN VAR IS PM ON Y; IF K IS VH THEN VAR IS PH ON Y;
C6:Phosphorous (P)	IF P IS VL THEN VAR IS PM ON Y; IF P IS L THEN VAR IS PM ON Y; IF P IS M THEN VAR IS PM ON Y; IF P IS H THEN VAR IS PM ON Y; IF P IS VH THEN VAR IS PM ON Y;
C7:Nitrogen (N)	IF N IS VL THEN VAR IS PVL ON Y; IF N IS L THEN VAR IS PL ON Y; IF N IS M THEN VAR IS PL ON Y; IF N IS H THEN VAR IS PL ON Y; IF N IS VH THEN VAR IS PM ON Y; IF N IS VH THEN VAR IS PL ON Y;
C8:Organic matter (OM)	IF OM IS L THEN VAR IS PL ON Y; IF OM IS M THEN VAR IS PL ON Y; IF OM IS H THEN VAR IS PM ON Y;
C9: pH	IF Ph IS VL THEN VAR IS PVL ON Y; IF Ph IS L THEN VAR IS PVL ON Y; IF Ph IS SL THEN VAR IS PVL ON Y; IF Ph IS M THEN VAR IS PVL ON Y; IF Ph IS SH THEN VAR IS PVL ON Y; IF Ph IS H THEN VAR IS PVL ON Y; IF Ph IS H THEN VAR IS PL ON Y; IF Ph IS VH THEN VAR IS PM ON Y;
C10: Sand (S)	IF S IS L THEN VAR IS NM ON Y; IF S IS M THEN VAR IS NM ON Y; IF S IS H THEN VAR IS NM ON Y; IF S IS VH THEN VAR IS NH ON Y;
C11: Clay (Cl)	IF Cl IS L THEN VAR IS PM ON Y; IF Cl IS M THEN VAR IS PM ON Y; IF Cl IS H THEN VAR IS PM ON Y;

The degree of variation induced by one concept on another one is elaborated through the fuzzy variable "Var" of Figure 4, with the following fuzzy sets ("VVH: very very high", "VH: very high", "H: high", "M: medium", "L: low", "VL: very low", "VVL: very very low"). The influence can be positive or negative.

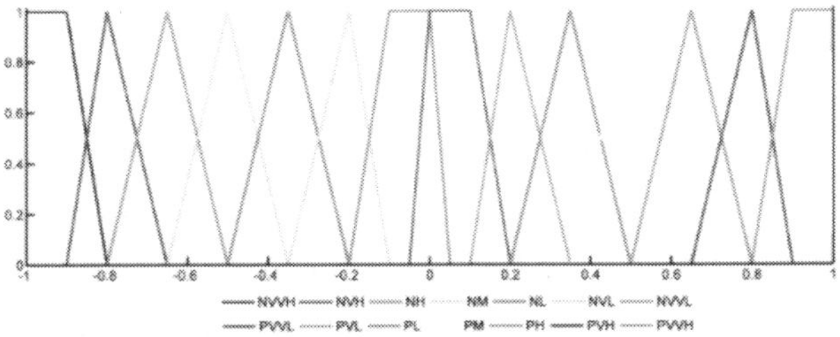

Figure 4. Variation fuzzy variable.

B. Results and Discussion

The used data consists of 360 entries measured for the years 2001, 2003 and 2006, as collected in a 5 ha field at Myrina, Karditsa prefecture, Central Greece. The FCM model has been developed based on raster data GIS approach, i.e., the data are stored in a two-dimensional matrix that represents the spatial distribution of every factor in the field. Each cell of the matrix corresponds to an area of 10 x 10 m, which is the spatial resolution of the yield data model. Measurements were collected in soil depth 0–30 cm.

FCM simulations were run on cotton yield data till the model reached convergence. In order to discriminate between the different yield categories, we used the threshold of 0.85 as in [8]. If the estimated yield value is less than 0.85, which means that the yield production is less than the 85% of desired cotton production, then yield is categorized as ''low''. If the estimated yield value is higher than 0.85, then yield is considered as ''high''.

It can be seen from Table III that the predictions made by DRBFCM are actually better than the ones obtained by Papageorgiou et al. [8], even when the NHL algorithm is used. The results of DRBFCM inference revealed an accuracy of predictions of 85.55%, 87.22% and 73.33%, against 73.80%, 67.20% and 69.65% for the conventional FCM model, and against 75.55%, 68.86% and 71.32% for the FCM model with the NHL algorithm, during the years of 2001, 2003 and 2006, respectively.

TABLE III. PREDICTION ACCURACY RESULTS

Year	**2001**	**2003**	**2006**
Conventional FCM accuracy	73.80%	67.20%	69.65%
FCM with NHL algorithm	75.55%	68.86%	71.32%
DRBFCM accuracy	85.55%	87.22%	73.33%

The DRBFCM modeling approach can hence enhance the results obtained by FCM modeling, while taking into consideration the ambiguities intrinsic to this type of applications. From the results of this case study, it can be also concluded that the simulations have proven DRBFCM to be more faithful with regards to the real world model structure. Indeed, in the traditional FCM, parts of the gathered rules are omitted. The antecedent of a rule would just be ignored, and the only thing that is used to draw a conclusion about the influence is the consequence: is the influence "high", "medium" or "low"? Only those are used to generate weights. This results in building a complex dynamic model with nonlinear relationships, and not fully exploiting it in simulating the real world system. The DRBFCM model, on the other hand, is very authentic to the knowledge that has been aggregated. The consequences of the rules are also used, provided that the antecedent is fulfilled: which concept affects the yield, and to what extent?

The differences in predictions are attributed to the generated weights. A recapitulation of weights for the traditional FCM model and DRBFCM are shown in Table IV, where we can clearly see that the influence of Potassium (K) is much lower in DRBFCM (W_{K-Y} =0.22 ± 1.88E-04) compared to the traditional FCM (W_{K-Y} =0.6).

TABLE IV. FCM AND DRBFCM WEIGHTS

	Cotton yield (Y)	
Concept	**FCM**	**DRBFCM** [a]
EC	0.25	0.22 ± 2.04E-04
Mg	-0.4	-0.48 ± 4.27E-02
Ca	0.5	0.48 ± 3.15E-02
Na	-0.7	-0.7 ± 2.00E-15
K	0.6	0.22 ± 1.88E-04
P	0.5	0.49 ± 5.24E-02
N	0.4	0.35 ± 1.51E-02
OM	0.4	0.35 ± 8.23E-03
pH	0.1	0.26 ± 2.37E-02
S	-0.6	-0.5 ± 7.07E-16
Cl	0.5	0.5 ± 5.47E-16

[a] Mean values shown with standard deviation obtained using the 360 cotton yield cases.

The low influence produced by DRBFCM seems to make sense as Potassium produces a 'high' variation when it is 'very high', nevertheless by looking at the 360 cases of cotton yield data, Potassium was classified as either 'medium' or 'low' all the time. Hence, DRBFCM seems to generate weights that are coherent with the model structure and collected knowledge, since it produces predictions that can be interpreted by tracing the rules that contributed to the results.

IV. CONCLUSION AND FUTURE WORK

DRBFCM is a rule-based FCM, where relationships between concepts are expressed in the form of fuzzy "if-then" rules that dynamically determine the influence of one concept on another one, while running a simulation for a specific scenario. In this work, we evaluated DRBFCM numerically using cotton yield knowledge and data. We used 360 entries of measured data, collected during three years in an experimental cotton field in Central Greece. The results revealed an accuracy of predictions of 85.55%, 87.22% and 73.33% for the years 2001, 2003 and 2006, respectively.

In comparison to the conventional FCM approach with Fuzzy Weights, DRBFCM proved, in the cotton yield case study, to predict more accurately the yield while being faithful to the real world model. The knowledge collected from the experts is fed into a standard inference system to map adequately the input space into the output space. Hence, the generated projections are more coherent with the model's collected knowledge, and the use of rules improves interpretation of the produced results.

In this study, we used the inference parameters and membership functions as defined in [8]. As a future work, we would like to perform an uncertainty and a sensitivity analysis to gain insights into the factors that would have an impact on the produced predictions, and to attribute the uncertainty in the output to the uncertainties in the input.

REFERENCES

[1] O. Motlagh, S. H. Tang, N. Ismail, and A. R. Ramli, "An expert fuzzy cognitive map for reactive navigation of mobile robots," *Fuzzy Sets and Systems,* vol. 201, pp. 105-121, 2012.

[2] M. Mendonça, L. V. R. de Arruda, and F. Neves, "Autonomous navigation system using Event Driven-Fuzzy Cognitive Maps," *Applied Intelligence,* vol. 37, pp. 175-188, 2012.

[3] M. Mendonça, L. V. R. Arruda, I. R. Chrun, and E. S. d. Silva, "Hybrid Dynamic Fuzzy Cognitive Maps Evolution for autonomous navigation system," in *2015 IEEE International Conference on Fuzzy Systems (FUZZ-IEEE)*, 2015, pp. 1-7.

[4] M. Mendonça, B. A. Angélico, L. V. R. de Arruda, and F. Neves, "A Subsumption Architecture to Develop Dynamic Cognitive Network-Based Models With Autonomous Navigation Application," *Journal of Control, Automation and Electrical Systems,* vol. 24, pp. 117-128, 2013.

[5] M. Mendonça, I. R. Chrun, F. Neves Jr, and L. V. R. Arruda, "A cooperative architecture for swarm robotic based on dynamic fuzzy cognitive maps," *Engineering Applications of Artificial Intelligence,* vol. 59, pp. 122-132, 2017.

[6] E. I. Papageorgiou and J. L. Salmeron, "A Review of Fuzzy Cognitive Maps Research During the Last Decade," *IEEE Transactions on Fuzzy Systems,* vol. 21, pp. 66-79, 2013.

[7] A. Mourhir, T. Rachidi, E. I. Papageorgiou, M. Karim, and F. S. Alaoui, "A cognitive map framework to support integrated environmental assessment," *Environmental Modelling & Software,* vol. 77, pp. 81-94, 2016.

[8] E. I. Papageorgiou, A. Markinos, and T. Gemptos, "Application of fuzzy cognitive maps for cotton yield management in precision farming," *Expert Systems with Applications,* vol. 36, pp. 12399-12413, 2009.

[9] B. Kosko, "Fuzzy Cognitive Maps," *International Journal of Man-Machine Studies,* vol. 24, pp. 65-75 1986.

[10] A. K. Tsadiras, "Comparing the inference capabilities of binary, trivalent and sigmoid fuzzy cognitive maps," *Information Sciences,* vol. 178, pp. 3880-3894, 2008.

[11] T. J. Ross, *Fuzzy Logic with Engineering Applications*. New York: Wiley, 2009.

[12] L. A. Zadeh, "Fuzzy sets," *Inform. Control, vol.8,* pp. 338–353, 1965.

[13] E. Oja, H. Ogawa, and J. Wangviwattana, "Learning in nonlinear constrained Hebbian networks," in *Artificial neural networks*, T. Kohonen, K. Makisara, O. Simula., and J. Kangas, Eds., ed Amsterdam: North-Holland, 1991, pp. 385-390.

[14] E. I. Papageorgiou and P. P. Groumpos, "A weight adaptation method for fuzzy cognitive map learning," *Soft Computing,* vol. 9, pp. 846-857, 2005.

[15] IEC, "IEC 61131 - Programmable Controllers-Part 7: Fuzzy control programming," ed. Geneva: International Electrotechnical Commission technical committee industrial process measurement and control, 2000.

[16] E. H. Mamdani, "Application of fuzzy algorithms for control of simple dynamic plant," *Electrical Engineers, Proceedings of the Institution of,* vol. 121, pp. 1585-1588, 1974.

Smart Driving Behavior Analysis Based on Online Outlier Detection: Insights from a Controlled Case Study

Igor Vasconcelos[1,2], Rafael Oliveira Vasconcelos[1,2],
Bruno Olivieri[1], Markus Endler[1]
[1]*Department of Informatics*
Pontifical Catholic University of Rio de Janeiro (PUC-Rio)
Rio de Janeiro, Brazil
e-mail: {*ivasconcelos, rvasconcelos, bolivieri, endler*}*@inf.puc-rio.br*
[2]*Department of Informatics*
University Tiradentes (UNIT)
Aracaju, Brazil

Methanias Colaço Júnior
Department of Informatics
Federal University of Sergipe (UFS)
Aracaju, Brazil
e-mail: *mjrse@hotmail.com*

Abstract— **This paper presents an approach for online outlier detection over multiple data streams based on Complex Event Processing (CEP) to enable driving behavior classification. Driving is a daily task that allows people to move around faster and more comfortably. However, more than half of fatal crashes are related to recklessness behaviors. Reckless maneuvers can be detected with good accuracy by analyzing data relating to the driver-vehicle interaction, abrupt turnings, acceleration and deceleration, for instance. In this paper, we investigate if off-the-shelf smartphones can be used to an online detection of driving behavior. To do so, we have adapted the Z-Score algorithm, a classical outlier detection algorithm, to perform online outlier detection as a data stream processing model, which receives the smartphone and in-vehicle sensors data as input. The evaluation of the approach was carried out in a case study to assess the algorithm. Our results indicate that the algorithm's performance is fairly good in a real world case study since the algorithm's accuracy was 84% and the average processing time was 100 milliseconds.**

Keywords-Online Outlier Detection; Complex Event Processing; In-Vehicle Sensing; Online Driving Behavior Detection; Smartphone.

I. INTRODUCTION

Driving is a daily task that allows people to travel more quickly and comfortably. However, a study on road safety conducted by the American Automobile Association [1] reported that 56% of fatal crashes between 2003 and 2007 involved one or more unsafe behaviors typically associated with reckless driving, such as speeding, improper lane changes, making improper turns and weaving in and out of traffic [2][3]. Reckless driving is a particular type of driving behavior defined by Tasca [3] as a behavior that "*deliberately increases the risk of collision and is motivated by impatience, annoyance, hostility or an attempt to save time*".

Nonetheless, current Intelligent Transportation Systems (ITS) still rely on an infrastructure composed of static sensors and cameras installed on roads, making it difficult to collect, aggregate and analyze the data, especially in real time [4]. Moreover, due to the high cost of installation and maintenance, they are usually restricted to certain roads or neighborhoods. In contrast, Internet of Things (IoT) aims to pervasively connect billions of things or smart objects, such as vehicles, sensors, actuators and smartphones. IoT poses an even more complicated challenge in a multi-stream environment where multiple data streams are competing for the available memory and processing resources, especially in resource-constrained systems, such as sensors and mobile devices [5].

Current approaches, such as [2][6][7], use the smartphone to understand and evaluate the driver's driving behavior. Mobile Sensor Platform for Intelligent Recognition Of Aggressive Driving (MIROAD) [2] is a driving style recognition platform that uses only the smartphone as a data source and processing unit. MIROAD uses the Dynamic Time Warping algorithm, originally developed for speech recognition, to classify the maneuvers (driver events) performed by the driver. Join Driving [6] proposes a scoring mechanism to quantitatively evaluate maneuvers and passenger comfort level based on ISO 2631-1-1997 [8]. Quintero, Lopez and Pinilla. [7] use Fuzzy Logic and Neural Networks - the output Fuzzy variables are inserted in a neural network properly trained to classify the behavior of the drivers. However, as the neural network is on a remote server, all Fuzzy variables outputs need to be sent to the remote server that performs the offline analysis and classification of driver behavior. These approaches use models/techniques (e.g., in Neural Network, Fuzzy Theory and Hidden Markov) with good accuracy [9]. In addition, they were not designed for data stream processing [10], and according to Lin et al. [9], they have low processing performance, need a long training phase, require artificial assumptions or require prior knowledge to formulate rules. Moreover, since these approaches are static, they have difficulty to recognize the parameters quick and accurately [9], for instance, neural networks have subjective methods for adjusting their topology (numbers of layers and neurons) and requires a fixed number of input parameters.

The rest of this paper is organized as follows. Section II presents an overview of the key concepts. Section III highlights the definitions and planning of the study case. Section IV addresses the study case operation. Finally,

Section V reviews and discusses the central ideas presented in this paper, and proposes lines of future work on the subject.

II. FUNDAMENTALS

This section presents the main concepts about complex event processing, as well as outlier detection algorithms.

A. *Complex Event Processing*

Complex Event Processing (CEP) is a set of techniques and tools that provides an in-memory processing model upon the asynchronous data stream, in real time (i.e., minimum delay) for online detection of situations of interest [11]. CEP offers [11]: (i) situation awareness through the usage of continuous queries that correlate data from different sensor data streams, (ii) context awareness by subdividing data streams into different views, such as temporal windows or key partitions, and (iii) flexibility since it can specify events at any time, that is, the specification of events may be changed dynamically while the system is running (i.e., on-the-fly).

The CEP central concept is a declarative Event Processing Language (EPL) to express the event processing rules (continuous queries and patterns). These rules are based on event-condition-action triad, and use operators (e.g., logic, counting and temporal) on the input events, searching for correlations, exceptional conditions and pattern occurrence. The CEP central task is to provide mechanisms for Event Pattern Matching, i.e., from hundreds or even thousands of events, to identify significant patterns in the application domain [12]. The event processing and pattern detection are made by so-called event processing agents (EPAs) that process the events' stream. Basically, an EPA filters, separates, aggregates, transforms and synthesizes new complex events from simple events. To be able to detect the pattern of the maneuver, it is necessary to use an important CEP concept called Time Window (or just window). A window is a temporal context that defines which portions of the input data stream are considered during the EPL rule execution [13], e.g., events in the last 30 seconds.

B. *Outlier Detection*

Commonly, outlier detection technics typically assume that outliers in data are rare when compared to normal instances and when outliers do occur, these are observations that deviate significantly from the rest of the sample [14]. However, "meaningful" constitutes a subjective judgment to consider an instance as outlier. For instance, the main grouping pattern are extremely similar in Figure 1(a) and (b). However, there are significant differences outside these major groups. In Figure 1(a), the point *A* clearly deviates significantly from the rest of the points and therefore it is an outlier. However, Figure 1 (b) is much more subjective, since point *A* lies in a sparse region of data. Thus, it becomes more difficult to state with confidence that this data differs significantly from the other points. It is quite likely that this data point represents randomly distributed noise. This is because point *A* seems to fit a pattern represented by other randomly distributed points.

Therefore, although noise detection/removal is important for several application domains, it is not always possible to classify an instance as normal, noise or outlier precisely and choices depend on the specific criteria of each application. In this way, noise can be modeled as the semantic limit between normal and anomalous instances [15]. Thus, some authors use the term weak outlier (noise) and strong outlier to distinguish them [16]. In this paper, the term outlier refers to an instance that can be considered an abnormality or noise.

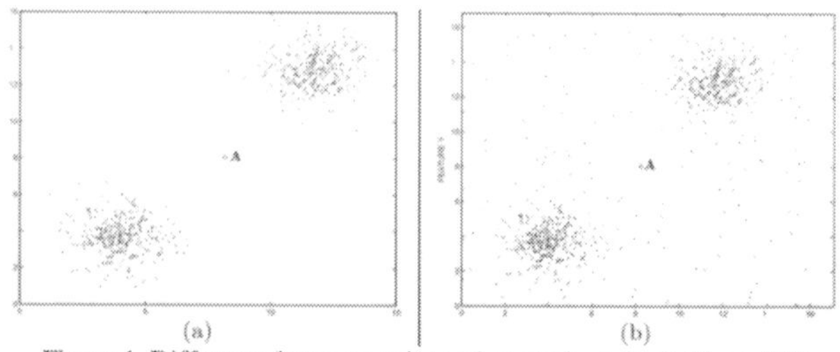

Figure 1. Difference between noise and anomaly. Adapted from [15].

Most anomaly detection algorithms uses scores for measuring the "outlierness", such as density, nearest neighbor clustering or statistical inference [15][17]. Thus, outliers usually have a higher score than the noises [15]. However, Aggarwal and Yu [16] emphasize that approaches based on clustering and density have an expensive computation and are not appropriate for data stream environments.

Statistical approaches were the earliest algorithms used for outlier detection and they assume that normal instances occur in high probability regions, while outliers occur in low probability regions of a stochastic model. The Standard Score (commonly referred as Z-Score) is a simple statistical technique that enables one-pass computation over a data stream to identify outliers. Z-Score describes raw score's location in terms of how far above or below the mean is when measured in standard deviation. A Z-Score of zero means that raw data instance is equal to the mean. Z-Score computation creates a unitless score that is no longer related to the original units (e.g., km/h and m/s²) as it measures number of standard deviation units and therefore can more readily be used for comparisons. After computing the Z-Score for each data instance, the algorithm calculates the Z-distribution, i.e., the relative frequency of the raw Z-Scores of a population or sample.

III. DEFINING AND PLANNING OF THE CASE STUDY

In this section, the case study is presented with the focus on the definition and planning of the objective.

A. *Drivers' and route selection*

Due to the difficulty of recruiting drivers and the costs associated with assessing driving behavior, the process of driver selection was a matter of convenience and sampling was completed by quota. However, it was tried to establish a sample that represented the universe of drivers, preserving the same behavioral characteristics. Thus, 25 drivers were chosen for the study. Sixteen were male and nine female, theirs age ranged from 20 to 60 years. Another important issue is the drivers' experience. In our sample, drivers' experience ranged from 2 to 42 years. Finally, all drivers were familiar with local traffic condition and regulations. This is important so that during the assessment of the drivers, the behaviors reflect the daily behaviors.

Regarding route selection, we defined a paved route comprising streets and avenues ranging from one to three lanes with approximately 14.5 km in Aracaju-SE, Brazil. In addition, the route contains roundabouts, traffic lights, pedestrian crossings and turns. The speed limit on the route was 60 km/h. A pilot study was conducted on the chosen route, and this provided insights about driver's behaviors.

B. *Instrumentation*

The instrumentation process started with the implementation of the Z-Score algorithm, through CEP rules. The algorithm was implemented in EPL, an structured query like language (SQL-like) where streams replace tables as the source of data with events replacing rows as the basic unit of data for running in ASPER, a CEP processing engine based on ESPER and adapted for Android. ESPER is an open source complex event processing engine.

A Brazilian version of manual Citröen C3 was equipped with a Samsung Galaxy SIII 1.4 GHz Quad Core with 1GB of RAM and Bluetooth OBD-II device. Our prototype was installed on the smartphone running the online Z-Score algorithm.

C. *Measurement Metrics*

We calculate five performance metrics, shown in Table I, which will be used to evaluate the algorithm. In addition, as quality metric, we use the **average execution time**, that is, the arithmetic mean of execution times for a given algorithm and algorithms' **average resources consumption**, i.e., Central Processing Unit (CPU) usage and memory consumption.

TABLE I. PERFORMANCE METRICS

Metric
Accuracy is the percentage of instances (evidences) correctly classified.
Recall is the percentage of instances that were correctly classified as positive.
Precision is the percentage of instances classified as positive (evidence) that are actually positive.
F Measure is the harmonic mean of precision and recall, that is, it combines the precision and recall.
Error Rate is the proportion of instances that are incorrectly classified.

IV. OPERATION OF THE CASE STUDY

This section describes the preparation and execution of the real world case study.

A. *Preparation*

For the evaluation, we used the open dataset provided by Bergasa [18]. The dataset provides three axis accelerometer data labeled (as cautious and reckless) based on thresholds given by Paefgen, Kehr, Zhai and Michahelles [19] for acceleration, braking and turning. This dataset contains driving data of six different drivers and vehicles in two different routes, one is 25km in a road with normally 3 lanes on each direction and 120km/h of maximum allowed speed, and the other is around 16km in a secondary road of normally one lane on each direction and around 90km/h of maximum allowed speed. For each driver data, a 3-fold cross-validation was performed, where each driver's data are randomly divided into two pieces of 35% for training and one piece of 30% for testing and checking the subset of data that generated the best results the algorithm. For the Online Z-Score algorithm, the best results were achieved considering a data instance as outlier based on the threshold (Z-score greater than the modulus of three) proposed by Chandola, Banerjee and Kumar [17].

Aiming to be operational in a mobile device, applications need to vary data rates based on available computation resources. Therefore, the Online Z-Score needs to adapt its behavior to perform the outlier detection with good accuracy. Thus, based on this scenario, we define two setups. First, we set the sensor data sample rate to be h = 100Hz and time window Δ = 10s (setup 1). Second, we set the sensor data sample rate to be h = 50Hz and time windows Δ = 20s (setup 2).

B. *Intrinsic Evaluation of The Knowledge Model*

In this subsection, we present the results for the training using the open dataset aforementioned. We repeated each evaluation 5 times and the confidence level for all results is 95%. Table II shows the average Z-Score Online performance. Despite the good overall performance, the Online Z-Score stood out with an average accuracy greater than 98%. In respect to the precision, the Online Z-Score had an expressive result with an average precision of 99.31%. This means that Online Z-Score classifies correctly cautious data instances that are really cautious in an average of 99.31%. Online Z-Score achieved an excellent recall performance in both setups. This means that, on average, Online Z-Score reached true positive rates greater than 99% in setup 1 and greater than 98% in setup 2. Regarding the F Measure, Online Z-Score stood out with the average F Measure greater than 99% in both setups.

TABLE II. OLINE Z-SCORE PERFORMANCE METRICS

Metric	Setup 1	Setup 2
	h = 100Hz and Δ = 10s	*h = 50Hz and Δ = 20s*
Accuracy	98.07%	98.70%
Precision	98.72%	99.90%
Recall	99.33%	98.78%
F-Measure	99.02%	99.33%

Table III shows the Online Z-Score quality metrics. In order to check the algorithms' resource consumption in both setups, we firstly verify the smartphone's memory (in megabytes) and CPU (in percentage) usage in two situations: in standby and collecting data from smartphone's own sensors and OBD-II device, however, without processing them. Through the Table III, it is possible to note that only collecting data increases memory consumption by 12.54% and CPU usage by 60.83%. However, the Online Z-Score consumed only 6.15 and 6.40 MB of the 830 MB available on the smartphone. Disregarding CPU usage for *collecting*, Online Z-Score used only 3.01% and 3.86% of the CPU in setups 1 and 2, respectively. Moreover, a larger time window resulted in a higher memory consumption and processing.

TABLE III. Z-SCORE OLINE QUALITY METRICS

Metric	Setup 1			Setup 2		
	RAM (MB)	*CPU (%)*	*Time (s)*	*RAM (MB)*	*CPU (%)*	*Time (s)*
Standby	4.53	1.41	-	4.53	1.41	-
Collecting	5.18	3.60	-	5.18	3.60	-
Z-Score Online	6.15	6.61	101.6	6.40	7.46	99.58

C. *Execution*

The smartphone was installed in the center of the vehicle windshield. The OBD-II reader device was connected to the OBD-II port of the vehicle and reads a variety of data from the vehicle bus. The OBD-II device sends the data streams via Bluetooth to the smartphone. Thus, the execution of the case study consisted of performing the process of outliers' detection from driving data streams of each driver volunteer.

The driver behavior data were collected in seven sunny days and the drivers drove between 9am and 8pm. Each driver made one trip on the chosen route. Thus, a total of 362.5 km were covered comprising 12.5 hours of driving.

Then, the chosen route was explained in detail and it was asked to the driver drives as usually. The driver volunteer also was informed that a driver expert with 15 years of experience would follow him\her during the case study – similar to an expert-based test administered in initial tests to judge driver performance – but we emphasize that our goal was to analyze and classifies driver's behavior in cautious or reckless and not approve or disapprove him/her. This classification served as a ground truth.

The prototype collects data from smartphone sensors (i.e., accelerometer, gyroscope, magnetic compass and GPS) and from vehicle sensors (i.e., speed, revolutions per minute and throttle position in percentage) through OBD-II device. These sensor data streams are sent to the smartphone via Bluetooth connection. The connection between the smartphone and OBD-II device was performed using a generic mobile middleware [20] for short range communication.

D. *Extrinsic Evaluation of the Knowledge Model*

Unlike the results obtained by Hong, Margines and Dey [21], both cautious and reckless drivers have substantial differences regarding speed. Through an online analysis, it is possible to identify reckless maneuvers that result in significant changes in Z-distribution, as shown in Figure 2. Cautious maneuvers follow the normal distribution.

Figure 3 shows the average revolutions per minute (rpm) Z-distribution. There is a notable Z-distribution difference in reckless maneuvers while performing an online analyzes. For instance, in the maneuver one and two, the total of outlier evidences are 17% and 23.5% respectively. The Online Z-Score algorithm identified quite a different distribution for reckless maneuvers, as shown in Figure 4. For instance, the maneuvers 1 and 2 had respectively 32.67% and 31.14% of evidences classified as outliers.

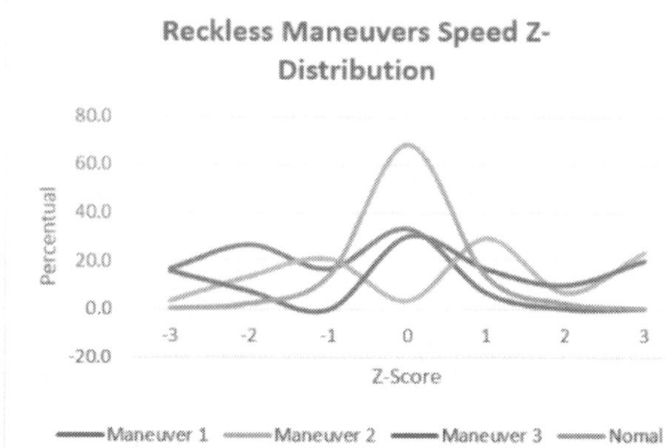

Figure 2. Speed maneuvers Z-distribution comparison

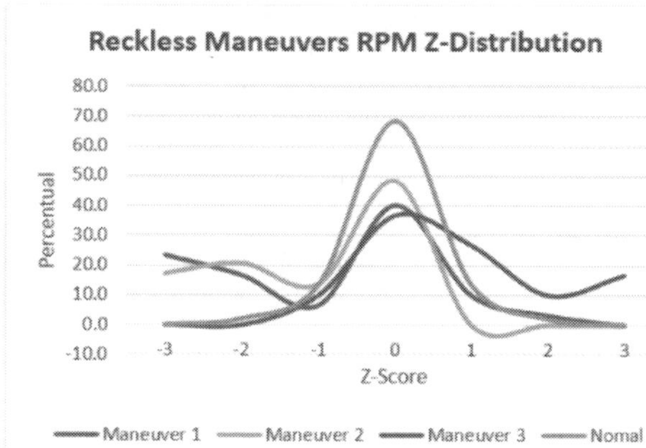

Figure 3. RPM maneuvers Z-distribution comparison

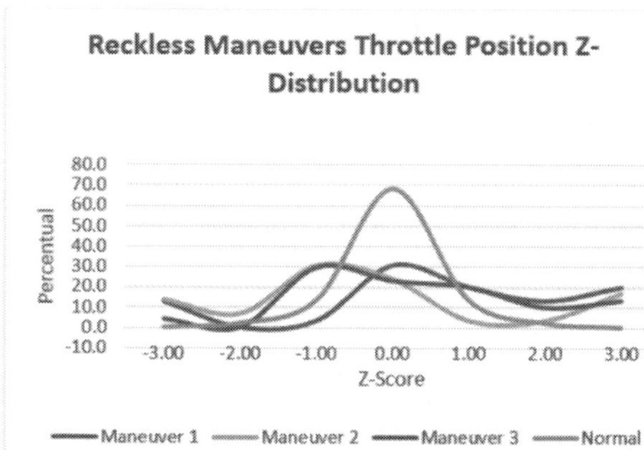

Figure 4. Throttle position maneuvers Z-distribution comparison

Analyzing 3-axis accelerometer data it should be noted that aggressive events Z-distribution is practically equal to the normal curve, as shown in Figure 5. Unlike other studies that consider only the lateral and longitudinal acceleration [21], we decided to consider the 3-axis since in Brazil many of the roads have poor quality. Thus, we believe that an analysis considering the 3-axis depicts more faithfully the Brazilian scene. However, to our surprise and going against the results of several studies, such as [21], evaluating the driver behavior, it was not noticed considerable changes in acceleration Z-distribution in reckless maneuvers as shown in Figure 5. Unlike the data aforementioned, maneuvers 1 and 2 had, respectively, only 9.37% and 7.86% of evidences classified as outliers. However, based on parameters established in ISO 2631-1-1997, which evaluates the effects of human exposure under acceleration, to measure the level of passengers comfort/discomfort. Considering that in our case study a stopped vehicle had acceleration equal to 9.8 m/s², so passengers felt comfortable while acceleration was within a range from 8.9 to 11.2 m/s². Nevertheless, reckless drivers' events, such as sudden lane changes, abrupt accelerations/deceleration and jerks, generated much more uncomfortable feelings for passengers once 75% of the outliers were out of comfortable this range.

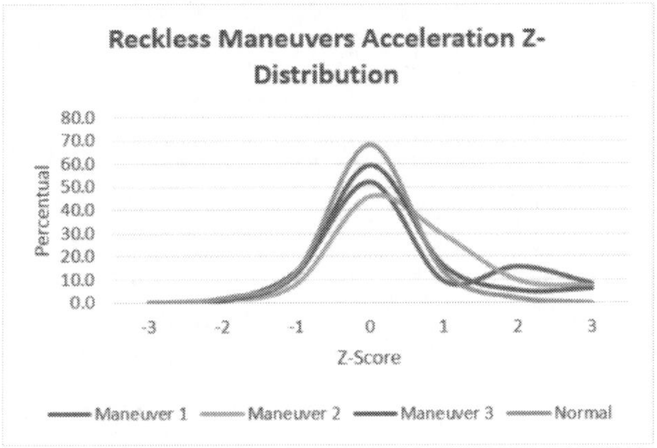

Figure 5. Acceleration Z-distribution comparison

E. *Scoring Driving Behaviors*

In order to score the drivers' behavior, it is necessary to consider that (i) sensors have different acquisition rates. For instance, in this case study, the OBD-II device and the smartphone's accelerometer average acquisition rate was 8 Hz and 140 Hz, respectively. Thus, during the data stream processing, we will have 17.5 times more evidences of acceleration than speed and (ii) certain evidences may have little power for discriminating driver behavior. To this end, we adapted a statistical mechanism used in document mining to evaluate how important a word is to a document in a collection, called inverse document frequency [22], to identify how important a outlier in a data stream.

We defined an outlier frequency (of_d) as the number of outliers that occurs in a dimension d. Furthermore, we defined the inverse outlier frequency (iof_d) of a data instance in dimension d as shown in (1).

$$iof_d = \log\left(\frac{N}{of_d}\right) \quad (1)$$

Thus, the iof_d of a rare outlier evidence is high, whereas the iof_d of a frequent outlier evidence is likely to be low. In order to weighting each outlier evidence in a time window, we combine the definition of outlier frequency and inverse outlier frequency ($ofiof$) as given by (2), where e is the outlier evidence value and d is the dimension. Therefore, a driver' trip score is given through the weighted average of sum of all $ofiof$, as shown in (3), where t is the number of time windows during the trip.

$$ofiof_{e,d} = of_{e,d} * iof_d \quad (2)$$

$$Score = average\left(\sum_{i=1}^{t}\left(ofiof_{e,d}\right)\right) \quad (3)$$

Figure 6 shows the drivers' score. For this case study, drivers with scores greater than 50 were classified as reckless. This threshold was chosen by analyzing data from six other drivers. These drivers drove on the same chosen route, but for three of them were asked to drive cautiously and the others recklessly. The maximum score for cautious drivers was 35 and the minimum one for the reckless was 65. Therefore, we consider the threshold of 50 as the upper bound in the classification of the cautious drivers and as the lower bound in the classification of reckless one. Comparing the algorithm classification with the ground truth, it should be noted an excellent performance, as shown Table IV.

Figure 6. Drivers' score during case study

TABLE IV. OLINE Z-SCORE PERFORMANCE

Metric	Value
Accuracy	84.00%
Recall	76.47%
Precision	100.00%
F-Measure	86.67%
Error Rate	16.00%
RAM	6.35 MB
CPU	7.24%

V. Conclusion And Future Work

In this paper, we introduced an online outlier detection for driver behavior detection approach. Unlike many works that aims to provide a faster outlier detection and to adapt algorithms to perform a distributed processing, our proposal performs an online outlier detection in mobile devices, such as smartphone, with limited computational resources. The main contributions of this paper are (i) a classical offline outlier detection algorithm adapted to perform online outlier detection. In addition, this algorithm is operational on mobile devices and able to adapt their behavior based on available computational resources, that is, change sensors' refresh rate and time window without varying the algorithm accuracy, (ii) a prototype to identify driver behavior based on online outlier detection and (iii) assessment that validates and demonstrates the performance of our proposal.

More research is still needed with this approach. However, considering the encouraging performance results, we are confident that our approach can be used in several others IoT scenarios. For the future, we expect to advance our work along the following lines: (i) perform a comparison with other related works, (ii) adapt the algorithm to scenarios where energy consumption is critical, (iii) perform a distributed online outlier detection, (iv) analyze the effect that different types of windows may generate in the correctness of algorithms and devices' resource consumption and (v) regarding to driver behavior, identify behaviors that precede accidents and to identify the relationship between driving behavior, fuel consumption and air pollution.

References

[1] Safety Foundation for Traffic, "Aggressive driving: Research update," 2009. [Online]. Available: https://www.aaafoundation.org/sites/default/files/AggressiveDrivingResearchUpdate2009.pdf. [Accessed: 28-Apr-2017].

[2] D. A. Johnson and M. M. Trivedi, "Driving style recognition using a smartphone as a sensor platform," in *2011 14th International IEEE Conference on Intelligent Transportation Systems (ITSC)*, 2011, pp. 1609–1615.

[3] L. Tasca, *A review of the literature on aggressive driving research*. Ontario Advisory Group on Safe Driving Secretariat, Road User Safety Branch, Ontario Ministry of Transportation, 2000.

[4] V. Moosavi and L. Hovestadt, "Modeling urban traffic dynamics in coexistence with urban data streams," in *Proceedings of the 2nd ACM SIGKDD International Workshop on Urban Computing - UrbComp '13*, 2013, p. 1.

[5] Q. Xie, J. Zhu, M. A. Sharaf, X. Zhou, and C. Pang, "Efficient buffer management for piecewise linear representation of multiple data streams," in *Proceedings of the 21st ACM international conference on Information and knowledge management - CIKM '12*, 2012, p. 2114.

[6] H. Zhao, H. Zhou, C. Chen, and J. Chen, "Join driving: A smart phone-based driving behavior evaluation system," in *2013 IEEE Global Communications Conference (GLOBECOM)*, 2013, pp. 48–53.

[7] C. G. Quintero M., J. O. Lopez, and A. C. Cuervo Pinilla, "Driver behavior classification model based on an intelligent driving diagnosis system," in *2012 15th International IEEE Conference on Intelligent Transportation Systems*, 2012, pp. 894–899.

[8] I. O. for Standardization, "ISO 2631-1-1997: Mechanical vibration and shock-Evaluation of human exposure to whole-body vibration-Part 1: General requirements," 1997.

[9] N. Lin, C. Zong, M. Tomizuka, P. Song, Z. Zhang, and G. Li, "An Overview on Study of Identification of Driver Behavior Characteristics for Automotive Control," *Mathematical Problems in Engineering*, vol. 2014, pp. 1–15, 2014.

[10] M. Čermák, D. Tovarňák, M. Laštovička, and P. Čeleda, "A performance benchmark for NetFlow data analysis on distributed stream processing systems," in *NOMS 2016 - 2016 IEEE/IFIP Network Operations and Management Symposium*, 2016, pp. 919–924.

[11] D. C. Luckham, *The Power of Events: An Introduction to Complex Event Processing in Distributed Enterprise Systems*. Boston, MA, USA: Addison-Wesley Longman Publishing Co., Inc., 2001.

[12] J. Dunkel, "On complex event processing for sensor networks," in *2009 International Symposium on Autonomous Decentralized Systems*, 2009, pp. 1–6.

[13] G. Cugola and A. Margara, "Processing Flows of Information: From Data Stream to Complex Event Processing," *ACM Comput. Surv.*, vol. 44, no. 3, p. 15:1--15:62, 2012.

[14] V. J. Hodge and J. Austin, "A Survey of Outlier Detection Methodologies," *Artificial Intelligence Review*, vol. 22, no. 2, pp. 85–126, Oct. 2004.

[15] C. C. Aggarwal, *Outlier Analysis*. New York, NY: Springer New York, 2013.

[16] C. C. Aggarwal and P. S. Yu, "Outlier detection for high dimensional data," *ACM SIGMOD Record*, vol. 30, no. 2, pp. 37–46, Jun. 2001.

[17] V. Chandola, A. Banerjee, and V. Kumar, "Anomaly detection," *ACM Computing Surveys*, vol. 41, no. 3, pp. 1–58, Jul. 2009.

[18] L. M. Bergasa, D. Almeria, J. Almazan, J. J. Yebes, and R. Arroyo, "DriveSafe: An app for alerting inattentive drivers and scoring driving behaviors," in *2014 IEEE Intelligent Vehicles Symposium Proceedings*, 2014, pp. 240–245.

[19] J. Paefgen, F. Kehr, Y. Zhai, and F. Michahelles, "Driving Behavior Analysis with Smartphones: Insights from a Controlled Field Study," in *Proceedings of the 11th International Conference on Mobile and Ubiquitous Multimedia*, 2012, p. 36:1--36:8.

[20] L. E. Talavera, M. Endler, I. Vasconcelos, R. Vasconcelos, M. Cunha, and F. J. Da Silva E. Silva, "The Mobile Hub concept: Enabling applications for the Internet of Mobile Things," in *2015 IEEE International Conference on Pervasive Computing and Communication Workshops (PerCom Workshops)*, 2015, pp. 123–128.

[21] J.-H. Hong, B. Margines, and A. K. Dey, "A smartphone-based sensing platform to model aggressive driving behaviors," in *Proceedings of the 32nd annual ACM conference on Human factors in computing systems - CHI '14*, 2014, pp. 4047–4056.

[22] C. D. Manning, P. Raghavan, and H. Schütze, *An Introduction to Information Retrieval*, Online edi. Cambridge, England: Cambridge University Press, 2008.

Development of a Lean Information and Communication Tool to Connect and Digitize Company Departments in Small and Medium-Sized Enterprises

Rainer Müller[a], Matthias Vette[b],
Leenhard Hörauf[c], Christoph Speicher[d] and Dirk Burkhard[e*]
Centre for Mechatronics and Automatisation gGmbH (ZeMA)
Group of Assembly Systems and Automatisation Technology
Eschberger Weg 46, Gewerbepark Geb. 9,
66121 Saarbrücken, Germany
email: [a]rainer.mueller, [b]matthias.vette, [c]leenhard.hoerauf, [d]christoph.speicher, [e]dirk.burkhard@zema.de

Abstract—**Small and Medium-sized Enterprises (SME) see themselves confronted with constant challenges. Globalization, volatile markets and international competition require a focus on key topics such as customer satisfaction and delivery reliability. Key requirements for achieving these aims are lean and reactive business processes, which are obtained through horizontal and vertical networking. To network these business departments a lean shop floor information system, consisting of Smart Devices and a production application is developed. The aim of the system is the recording and needs-based communication of component modifications and technical drawings in SME special machine manufacturers. With the system, reduction of cycle time in projects, timely feedback of errors from the shop floor to the top floor, reduction of mistakes carried over to new projects and reduced time for the completion of the customer documentation can be achieved.**

Keywords-Lean Manufacturing Tool; Production-App; Smart Devices; Industry 4.0; Value Chain Digitization

I. INTRODUCTION

Small and Medium-sized Enterprises (SME) are facing many challenges and have to overcome these, in order to persist in the international competition [1], including challenges such as the individualization of the products and shorter product life cycles [2]. In response to these challenges in production, lean and reconfigurable processes are applied as a solution [3]. The required ability to react more frequently and flexibly can only be achieved, on correct and timely information [4].

Verbal and paper-based information exchange is the most widely accepted form of communication in SMEs even today. In particular, SMEs must accept these challenges, open themselves to new technologies and take advantage of it [11]. The introduction of new technologies is particularly difficult for SMEs, due to non-existent IT capacities and their high specialization in manufacturing and assembly processes of their daily business. In order to be able to react adequately to time-intensive factors, such as production changes and disturbances, it is necessary to develop lean solutions and find new ways to optimize and to digitize production based on existing IT facilities in SMEs.

The article focuses on the connection of shop floor and top floor, especially the connection of design/development department with production entities such as manufacturing and assembly. The presented industrial use case is the change of technical products and drawings during production in special engineering companies. Therefore, a production-app in combination with smart devices and lean processes was developed. Use case and procedure as well as the technical solution are mainly related to SME – machinery and plant engineering companies. Especially companies, which produce individual and special machines, mostly with batch size one, are designated for using the system.

The presented research and development is part of the research project NeWiP. In four different use cases the project analyses industry-related problems and develops solutions for the connection of company departments and production entities. Moreover, solutions for the connection between companies and information exchange are developed.

This paper is structured as follows: in Section II, an overview of related work is given. Furthermore, Section II describes the use case in detail and concludes with the advantages and aims of the presented procedure and the technical solution - the shop floor information application (SIA). Section III describes the procedure and used tools during the analysis of the initial situation. In Section IV the resulting requirements are described. Both analysis and requirement were taken into account during the development of the optimized process and the design of the production application. Optimized process and technical solution are finally outlined in Section V. It leads to the description of main functionalities of the developed production-app in combination with the smart devices in Section VI. Finally, Section VI concludes with a summary and gives an outlook on future work.

II. RELATED WORK AND PROBLEM DESCRIPTION

Efficient management of flexible processes is hardly possible without supporting systems and the provision of decision-relevant information [3]. Cyber-Physical Systems (CPS), Manufacturing-Executive-System (MES) and Enterprise-Resource-Planning (ERP) systems are designed to bridge the media gap between the physical and virtual world, providing up-to-date and comprehensive information. Components equipped with sensors, actuators and computing capacities can transfer information about themselves and their environment from reality to IT systems [5]. These CPS offer an opportunity to close the gap between the real world and the virtual world [6]. CPS gather physical data via sensors, control processing units and communication devices [7] [8]. By linking barcode, quick response code or RFID, the media gap between the object and information level can mostly be reduced [6].

The technologies associated with Industry 4.0 have not yet taken a comprehensive approach to production, especially in SMEs [9].

During industrial production, a variety of information, e.g., product-, process-, and project-related information occurs. For these types of information, there are several methods and systems of information gathering and exchange. At the shop floor area, information is transferred via verbal, written or computer-related communication. Production Data Acquisition (PDA), Machine Data Acquisition (MDA), Shop Floor Programming (SFP), Computerized Numerical Control (CNC) and Tool Management Systems (TMS) are the most frequently used computer-related applications in the shop floor area. Some systems have grown historically as isolated applications, without suitable interfaces that enable the integration of further systems. In addition, these systems are stationary and often not very intuitive. Declared goal of research and industry is a consistent shared use of data and a complete integration of all systems, as well as a uniform structure of information to ensure data exchange among each other [10].

The usage of CPS and digitalization is providing up-to-date and comprehensive information, which help to optimize the production process, to support employees in various company departments and to close media gaps between the physical and virtual world along the value chain. The focus is on socio-technical systems, in which people and machines are networked at different levels. Information are collected by means of suitable technical systems and software solutions. These are distributed to the respective specialists in a context-based manner so they are able to make their decisions.

A. *Problem Description*

The use case for the communication tool is the connection of shop floor and top floor departments in SMEs special machine manufacturers, where the transmission and recording of information is still largely paper-bound. The customer-specific special machines are planned in the design/development department. Then, they are manufactured, assembled and commissioned in the company's shop floor facility and later at the customer's plant.

During the execution of a project (development to commissioning of a special machine), a large number of employees of various business departments are involved. Main subject of the use case is the change process of technical drawings. For clarification, the process as it is today is described in the following: the design/development department creates the technical drawings, which are forwarded to the shop floor upon approval of the project leader in analogue form. Occasionally, design and drawing mistakes occur, which have to be corrected both on the product itself and the CAD data (3D and 2D data). Certain employees in the shop floor are qualified to make these alterations if it becomes necessary. These are handwritten on the technical drawings. At the end of the production process, all technical drawings of a project are transferred to the design/development department, in order to create the complete project and customer documentation. Since all of these technical drawings are received in the design/development department at the same time and after completion of the special machine, they have to be updated successively. This procedure is personal intensive and causes delays.

Moreover, handwritten changes on technical drawings increase the risk of media breaks between shop floor and design/development. During these projects, mistakes and errors have to be reported and corrected timely, so that they are not repeated in new projects. The result is that these mistakes might be carried over to new projects running in parallel, if the incorrect machine modules have not been updated in CAD programs in time. Figure 1 shows the initial situation and the aim of developing and implementing a production-app.

B. *Objective*

The objective of the communication tool SIA is the reduction of media breaks in the presented use case. On the technical side, this becomes possible by using Smart Devices and a production-app to digitize changes on technical drawings and modules. Furthermore, there are changes/adaptations of the business processes.

If technical changes and process adaptations are combined, new change/business processes become possible so that the design/development department is enabled to update (modules) changes simultaneously to the production process. This reduces the time until changes are noticed and - more important - corrected. So design mistakes on machine modules can be updated timely to their detection in shop floor, resulting in a reduced probability of repeating an error in new projects. Besides, it also improves the planning of required personal capacities in the design/development department.

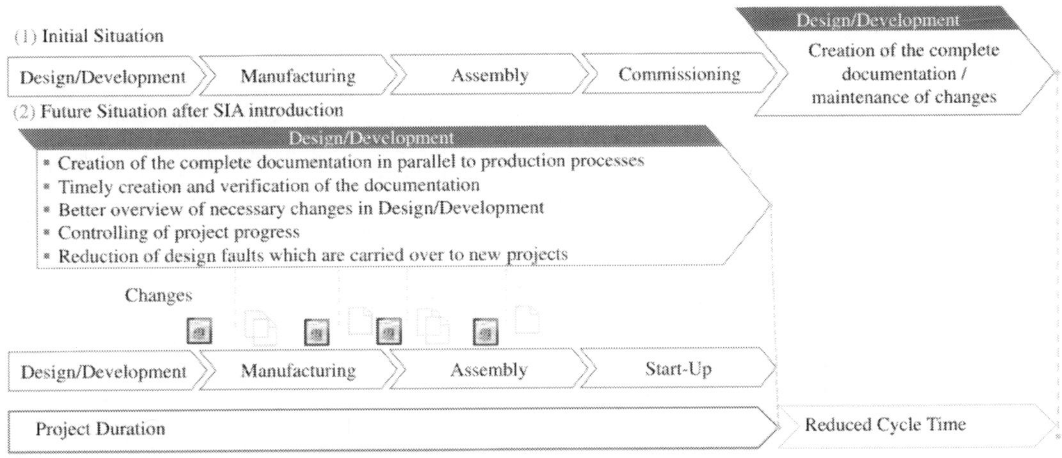

Figure 1: Advantages by using the shop-floor-information-application (SIA)

By directly digitizing technical drawings on the shop floor, media breaks are avoided. The shop floor information application (consisting of Smart Devices and production-app) provides necessary functionalities with the following advantages:

- Reduction of cycle time of a customer project
- Timely feedback of errors from shop floor to top floor
- Reduction of mistakes carried over to new projects
- Improved planning capacity in development and design/development department
- Reduced time for the completion of the customer documentation

III. Analysis of the Initial Situation

In the development and production of special machines, interdisciplinary project-teams are involved. Especially in interdisciplinary teams, it is not guaranteed that all participants will understand a statement in the same way. Therefore, a uniform understanding of the initial problems and requirements is necessary. A starting point is constituted by a user-story. In the development phase, the project objective is divided into definable and independent subgoals, which are described in an easy and understandable way [12]. Acceptance criteria should be identified and named, in order to increase the willingness of users for technological change. Acceptance criteria are for instance ergonomics, mobility, robustness and tolerance. During the development of the technological solution, these acceptance criteria must be noted and their degree of performance should be checked. In addition to these criteria, quality requirements should be identified and named. These requirements describe the features of the system to be developed according to ISO / IEC 9126. Characteristics such as functionality, reliability, usability, efficiency, maintainability and transferability have to be considered.

Nowadays, information should be provided at the right time, in the right place and in sufficient quality to the user. Therefore, lean and smart production processes and short information flows within the organization are needed [13]. Real improvements in business-, core-, support- and management processes can only be achieved if current processes and information flows are analyzed. The main reasons for modeling of the actual state are following:

- The modeling of processes is the starting point for the detection of weak points and the elaboration of improvements.
- Without an accurate understanding of the actual process, fault causes and possible potentials for improvement cannot be localized precisely.
- The documentation of the actual state generates process knowledge, which is available to all project participants.
- Media breaks can be better recognized.

The scope of analysis is always project-specific. There are among others four survey methods for analyzing the actual situation. In advance, by viewing and analyzing all process relevant documents, a high degree of information can be generated. Often, documents are created regarding to certifications DIN EN ISO 9001 and are already existing. By analyzing the value chain, beginning from shipping area on to receiving area, further process relevant information is gathered through observation and interview of the process owner. In team workshops, more detailed information about specific production processes and information flows can be acquired. Open questions and further issues can be discussed. In specific single interviews with employees, remaining questions can be answered and high detailed knowledge about processes, production as well as information and material flow can be collected.

A variety of different languages for process modelling are available. Common modelling languages are for instance Event-driven Process Chain (EPK), Unified Modeling Language (UML) or Business Process Execution Language (BPEL) or Business Process Modeling Notation 2.0 (BPMN2.0). BPMN2.0 was chosen for the use case because it is suited for the requirements of a structured and formalized mapping of business processes and information flows. In this language, activities, gateways and events are represented by BPMN basic elements. Primary goal of the BPMN2.0 is to provide a notation, which is easy to understand for all participants in business process management [14]. During analysis of the initial situation, the BPMN2.0 was used to document the current business processes in an understandable way for the project team. With an analysis of the important business processes for the project, the future business process was developed in BPMN2.0, so everyone in the project team got a clear view of the future business process and the requirements and functions for the production-app. Moreover, the documentation in BPMN2.0 is understandable and expressive enough to be used in future DIN EN ISO 9001 documentations.

Following the analysis of the current state, the requirements for the system and the app as well as the Smart Device are derived.

IV. REQUIREMENTS TO THE SYSTEM

The following fields of action, such as the mastery of information and communication technologies, the economic introduction of new technologies and processes, the involvement of employees in this new form of industrial production, have become key success factors.

Challenge - Information Technology: IT-systems are developed to support business processes and production processes. Due to constantly changing influencing factors, an adaptation of these systems is indispensable. However, it is difficult for producing SMEs to cope with necessary changes in complex programs and architectures because of their own limited resources and their high specialization in manufacturing and assembly. This circumstance has resulted in isolated applications that are optimally suited to the execution of a specific business process, but can only be integrated into the IT infrastructure of the company in a highly resource-intensive manner [11]. Therefore, a requirement of the developed system and application was the integration into an existing architecture without endangering other systems.

Challenge - Cost-Effectiveness: The key factors of production, labor, land and capital, are some of the input factors of any industrial production. The output, on the other hand, is e.g., simply valued over the product price. The desired transparency and responsivity, a key target of industry 4.0, is achieved only on the basis of information. Information as such is not quantifiable and does not represent a typical characteristic for the economic consideration of an investment project in producing SMEs. Collection of context-related information on the shop floor is the main function of the developed system. For the economic assessment of the system, quantifiable factors such as improved personnel utilization, reduced error avoidance of the same components and a shortened project running time can be mentioned.

Challenge - Employees: Industry 4.0 introduces a paradigm shift to an enhanced network of intelligent production technology. The main focus of this development is the human being, as a link between process and equipment. This human-machine interface requires a rethinking of all existing forms of work organization and efficient workplace design. In order to meet the requirements of an efficient workplace design, factors such as user characteristics, environmental factors, social and organizational environment, factors of work tasks, as well as factors of work equipment were taken into account in the development of the system [15]. On the basis of this, a prototypical conceptual design (drawing, low-fidelity prototype and high-fidelity prototype) took place. Particular attention was paid to the creation of an ergonomic human-machine interface and a lean integration of the system into existing business processes as well as a lean design of main functionalities for the multimodal gathering of information. In the design of the main functionalities, the seven principles of dialogue design, task adequacy, self-describability, controllability, expectation conformity, fault tolerance, individualization and learning support according to DIN EN ISO 9241-110 were considered. Further methods like discussion-, simulation-, version-, and prototyping methods can be of use for the participation of users in software development and increasing the willingness for using the new system. In order to evaluate the design, functionality and content in an early phase of the project, the solutions are implemented in different prototypes. With increasing project progress, the prototypes change in kind of their build effort. Therefore, low-fidelity prototypes were developed at the beginning of the project. This type of prototyping is relatively resource saving and allows short and low time consuming changes in the design [16]. The design was developed with the standard software Microsoft Visio. Even before programming the app, all responsible users could discuss the rudimentary functions. In further iterative loops, the design and functions could be changed with low effort. After the rough plan period, the application was build up in detail. These are high-fidelity prototypes and illustrate precise functionalities and structures as well as the design of the application. Therefore, the prototype software Axure was used.

V. CONCEPT OF THE COMMUNICATION TOOL

After an initial state- and requirements analysis a concept for networking shop floor and top floor area was developed. By using the system, employees can be supported during their daily work, without additional burden or additional processes, physical and ergonomical restrictions. The developed system and its application in the business process are shown in figure 2. The optimized process in business departments of the treated use case follows steps (1) to (6):

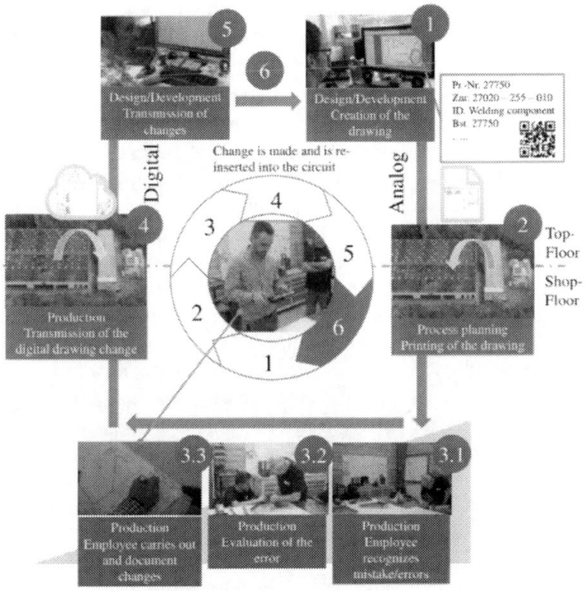

Figure 2. Optimised process by using the production application

(1) In design/development department, an auto-ID code (QR-Code and Dot-Paper) for the technical drawing has to be generated. The printed pattern consists of small dots whose diameter is 100 µm. By the combination of these points and their position at the intersections of a four-sided right angle grid, coordinates can be formed. This allows the Smart-Pen to determine position on the paper [17]. In Smart-Pen a camera is integrated, which record and protocol movement of the Smart-Pen. The generation of the QR-Code is done automatically. This is achieved by a developed plug-in for computer aided design programs (e.g., Solidworks, NX, Inventor, AutoCAD). The QR-Code contains relevant information such as the drawing number, project number, name and index of the drawing and is used for identifying the technical drawing via Smart Device. By means of the QR-Code, which is printed onto the analogue technical drawings on the shop floor, analog technical drawings can be digitized by reading the machine-readable code with the Tablet-PC without much effort.

(2) The approved technical drawings are stored in the operational data management system and provided to the work preparation as a PDF file. In the work preparation department, the technical drawings of a project are still printed out and placed in a project folder. The analogue version is often still a must-have in shop floor. With this restriction several ways to document a virtual twin are possible, see chapter VI. This analogue project folder runs through the production and serves as a sole work instruction for the worker. The digital twin of the technical drawing is stored and can be used any time after QR-Code scan.

(3) Hand-picked employees are equipped with the Smart Device (Tablet-PC), Smart-Pen and the production-app. When the employee makes a change to the components and to the technical drawing, as described in the application scenario, he/she has several functions to document the changes. After a personalized log-in to the application, the operator scans the QR-Code with the camera of the Tablet-PC. The QR-Code scan loads the digital twin and further information of the technical drawing. The application provides the employee with four multimodal functionalities, to document the changes on the parts or technical drawings: Smart-Pen, Tablet-Pen, Take Picture, 3D-Model.

After documentation, there are an analogue and digital twin of the technical drawing. The analogue version runs further with the modified part through production, whereas the digital version is forwarded to the design/development department for documentation and correction.

(4) The employee finishes the changes and sends the digital technical drawing with its changes to the design/development department by using a predefined mail.

(5) In the design/development department, the incoming information includes the technical drawings as well as a description of the problem and the priority. These are sighted by the manager of the department and arranged according to their urgency. With this information, he/she is able to improve capacity planning and can direct the changes to employees according to priorities and available capacities.

(6) The design/development department maintains the modifications. After this, a new release of the mechanical drawing and CAD data is stored in the Operational Data Management System. The work preparation department has now access to the blueprint`s PDF-version and is able to attach a printed copy of it in the project`s file folder. Furthermore, all relevant changes are done and CAD data is updated for new projects.

VI. Functionalites of the Application

To achieve the above mentioned change process, the production-app is developed, offering several functions, which are described below:

Through specifications and requirements as stated in the previous sections, several functionalities like Tablet-Pen, Take Picture, Smart-Pen and 3D-Model were included in the production-app as shown in Figure 3. After a first log-in of the employee on the app, the secondary function QR-Scan (1) is executed. The employee moves the Tablet-PC over the QR-Code on the technical drawing. After identification, a data download of the digital technical drawing (the virtual twin) from a server to the temporary memory of the Tablet-PC is carried out. As a result, the previously analogue drawing is loaded and visualized on the Tablet-PC. At this point, the user has the option to choose between the main functionalities (2) Tablet-Pen, (3) Take Picture, (4) Smart-Pen and (5) 3D-Model. After the information has been completed by one of the main functions, the changes noted on the technical drawing are sent to the development/design department. The transmission of the information is performed by the secondary function (6) Send Email.

(1) Scan QR: The QR-Code is used to digitize analogue technical drawings on the tablet by reading the code on the drawings. The QR-Code is generated in the development/design department. It is associated with the technical drawing and has information about the project, drawing, etc.

(2) Tablet-Pen: With the functionality, the employee can process the technical drawing using a Tablet-Pen. Via a Tablet-Pen, the employee can perform the following elementary tasks according to DIN EN ISO 9241-420:2011: drawing, accurate pointing, fast pointing, selecting and pulling. After the completion of the information gathering, the technical drawing, including all changes, is sent to the design/development department via email.

Figure 3. Main functionalities of the production-app

(3) Take Picture: The Take Picture function module allows the employee to capture images from the technical drawing. It is conceivable that he takes a snapshot of a component that is still in production. The image of the component can thus be coupled with the technical drawing. After confirming the suitability of the recording, the image appears on the Tablet-PC's user interface. The picture is automatically provided with the recording date and time. Thus, a later termination of the recording is possible. Analogous to the Tablet-Pen function, alphanumeric information can also be recorded here.

(4) Smart-Pen: Handwritten changes on an analogue drawing are immediately digitized by the Smart-Pen. When the change has been completed, the specialist can view the change on the Tablet-PC. In turn, the digital twin can be further prepared with the surface pen and sent to the development and design department. The Smart-Pen is based on a common ballpoint pen. When the pen is placed on the paper, the ink mine leaves an ink trace on the paper. Simultaneously, the data is recorded as soon as the Anoto-patterned paper is being written on. The pencil records each stroke and point as it is made by the employee, and then transfers the data to the processing system [17]. The data is stored on the pen until it is transferred to an FTP server via a docking station. If there is a need for a change in the drawing by the employee, the changes on the technical drawing are recorded (drawing is provided with Dot-pattern) with the Smart-Pen. After completion of the handwriting modification with the Smart-Pen, a digital twin of the analogue technical drawing is generated on the Tablet-PC.

(5) 3D-Model: This is a functionality to provide the employee with additional information of the machine component in manufacture or assembly. This function loads a 3D-Model of the component onto the Tablet-PC. The model can be changed in size and orientation by the employee.

(6) Send Email: Communication between the employee and the developer/designer takes place via the standard e-mail account (Microsoft Outlook) of the employee. A content system is integrated into the function module in order to spare the employee the writing of an email and to ensure a standardized information content of the email. The employee is given the opportunity to define the responsible persons, the originator of the changes and the urgency of the change by means of two dialog windows. With this standardized information system, the employee can finish and send his report with three clicks in the production app. The email is received by the design/development department manager. The information gives him an overview on changes in the project. Considering all information and current projects, he can perform his capacity planning for his team. In the future, the production-app shall be extended with a capacity planning tool.

VII. Summary and Outlook

The presented shop floor information application, which consists of Smart Devices and a production-app is developed to gather changes on the shop floor in real time and communicate these to organizational departments.

The system targets at first the design/development, in which a QR-Code is generated. The QR-Code is copied on the digital technical drawing by a plug-in in the four software-supported CAD programs used. The QR-Code is a qualifier to digitize the analogue technical drawings on the shop floor without much effort. In addition, a so-called dot-paper is created in the design/development. By the dot-paper a further form of digitization is provided via the Smart-Pen. Accordingly, the technical drawing is provided with two auto-ID codes for digitization. In production planning, the analogue technical drawing is printed for the run through reduction. If the employee has to make a change to the components or to the technical drawing, he uses a Smart Device (Tablet PC) to scan the QR-Code. A lean developed application is installed on the Tablet-PC, which provides the employee with four functionalities for gathering and communicate changes to the components. The aim of SIA is the reduction of media breaks between shop floor and top floor. The digitization results in improvements by timely creation and verification of the device documentation and reduction of design faults, which are carried over to new projects. Furthermore, creation of the complete documentation in parallel to production processes and controlling of project progress will be possible.

The shop floor information application will be implemented in future in the company. During implementation phase, the system and processes will be evaluated and adapted iteratively. Results and experiences of the use case will be used to develop the system further and to refine methods for networking and digitizing of the value chain.

ACKNOWLEDGMENT

This paper was written in the framework of the research project NeWiP, which is funded by the Federal Ministry of Education and Research (BMBF) and supervised by the lead partner PTKA-Karlsruher Institut für Technologie under the funding code 02P14B203.

REFERENCES

[1] R. Müller, Strategies and trends in assembly technology and organization, editor: C. Brecher, L. Schlapp, Apprimus Verlag, Aachen 2009.

[2] G. Schuh et al., Technology roadmapping for the production in high-wage countries, *Production Engineering*, Volume 5, issue 4, pp. 463 - 473. 2011.

[3] G. Reinhart et al., "Cyber-physical production systems: productivity and flexibility increase through networking of intelligent systems in the factory," in *wt Werkstattstechnik online* - version 2-2013 special edition industry 4.0, pp. 84 - 89, 2013.

[4] J. Kletti, Manufacturing Execution System – MES, Springer, Berlin, 2007.

[5] Acatech: *Cyber-Physical Systems-Driving force for innovation in mobility, health, energy and production.* [Online]. Available from: http://www.acatech.de [accessed: 26-April-2017].

[6] D.-M. Lucke, Ad hoc information procurement using context-based systems in the multi-variant batch production, dissertation, Universität Stuttgart, 2013.

[7] J. Kletti, MES-Manufacturing Execution System: Modern production requirements, Berlin: Springer, 2015.

[8] C. Alvaro, "Secure Control: Towards Survivable Cyber-Physical Systems," in the 28th International Conference on Distributed Computing Systems Workshops . 2008.

[9] D. Steegmüller and M. Zürn, Reconfigurable production systems for the future automotive industry. in, T. Bauernhansl, M. Hompel, B. Vogel-Heuser, Industry 4.0 in production, automation and logistics. pp. 103 - 119, Springer Vieweg, Wiesbaden, 2014.

[10] A. Neuschwinger, Multimodal, information-based workplace communication system, Dissertation, Ruhr-Universität Bochum, 2003.

[11] A. Bildstein and J. Seidelmann, Industrie 4.0-Readiness: Migration to industry 4.0 manufacturing. in, T. Bauernhansl, M. Hompel, B. Vogel-Heuser, Industry 4.0 in production, automation and logistics. pp. 581 - 597, Springer Vieweg, Wiesbaden, 2014.

[12] M. Cohn, User Stories Applied – For Agile Software Development, Addison-Wesley, Boston, 2004.

[13] G. Fischer, Context-aware systems: the "right" information, at the "right" time, in the "right" place, in the "right" way, to the "right" person, AVI '12 Proceedings of the International Working Conference on Advanced Visual InterfacesPages 287-294, 2012.

[14] P. Wohed, On the Suitability of BPMN for Business Process Modelling, Springer, Berlin, 2006.

[15] J. Ziegler, Wearables in industrial applications - Capable of mobile IT-supported work through distributed portable user interfaces, TUDpress, Dresden, 2016.

[16] M. Walkter, L. Takayama, J. A. Landay, "High-fidelity or low-fidelity, paper or computer? Choosing attributes when testing web prototypes," in *proceedings of the human factors and ergonomics society 46th annual meeting*, 2002.

[17] R. Boldt, T. Pietsch, Digital Pen & Paper, equbli, Berlin, 2014.

UAV Integration Into IoIT: Opportunities and Challenges

Mariana Rodrigues*, Daniel F. Pigatto†, João V. C. Fontes*,
Alex S. R. Pinto ‡, Jean-Philippe Diguet § and Kalinka. R. L. J. C. Branco*
*University of Sao Paulo (USP)
São Carlos, São Paulo, Brazil
e-mail: rodrigues.mariana@usp.br, joao.fontes@usp.br, kalinka@icmc.usp.br
†Federal University of Technology Parana (UTFPR)
Curitiba, Paran, Brazil
e-mail: pigatto@utfpr.edu.br
‡Federal University of Santa Catarina (UFSC)
Blumenau, Santa Catarina, Brazil
e-mail: a.r.pinto@ufsc.br
§Lab-STICC, UBS Research Center
Lorient, France
e-mail:jean-philippe.diguet@univ-ubs.fr

***Abstract*—Unmanned Aerial Vehicles (UAVs) have been applied in many fields such as military, traffic management, natural disaster prevention and assistance, and agriculture. Due to their characteristics, they are natural candidates to integrate the Internet of Intelligent Things (IoIT), a network composed of devices that are autonomous and mobile and have both sensing and action taking capabilities. The insertion of UAVs into IoIT infrastructure brings new dimensions to UAV applications and at the same time introduces new challenges. In this paper, we outline some opportunities and challenges brought by the insertion of UAVs into IoIT.**

Keywords–Unmanned Aerial Vehicles; UAV; Unmanned Aircraft Systems; UAS; Internet of Intelligent Things; IoIT; Challenges

I. Introduction

Due to the development of processing, sensing and communication technologies, many once simple devices are now able to perform more complex tasks and communicate with other devices or systems. This is the base of the Internet of Things (IoT) paradigm, whose core concept revolves around ubiquitous, uniquely identifiable everyday objects equipped with sensing, networking and processing capabilities that communicating with each other to achieve a common goal [1][2].

The IoT paradigm is being applied in several study fields; it is easy to find in the literature many applications in healthcare, industry, smart farms and cities, environmental monitoring and others. In some cases, application-specific networks are considered IoT branches, such as the Internet of Vehicles [3] or the Internet of Mobile Things [4]. The Internet of Intelligent Things (IoIT) is said to be composed of devices that are autonomous and mobile and have both sensing and action taking capabilities [5].

Popularly known as drones, Unmanned Aerial Vehicles (UAVs) are natural candidates to integrate with IoIT. Their integration with other vehicles and systems enables more complex missions, in which acquired data is up-to-date and intelligent actions can be taken either remotely or locally in cooperation with other devices — all with remote supervision. This integration, however, brings new challenges to be addressed regarding public safety and privacy, standardisation and technical aspects.

In this paper, we present some UAV applications that can be boosted by being integrated with IoIT, as well as new opportunities brought by connected UAVs, and challenges that need to be addressed so that the integration can be done seamlessly. Section II brings background information on UAVs and IoT. Section III present some related work. Section IV presents the opportunities in inserting UAVs into IoIT. Section V outlines some challenges that arise by UAV and IoIT integration. Finally, Section VI presents the paper conclusion.

II. Background

In this section, some background concepts covering Unmanned Aircraft Systems, Flying Ad hoc NETworks and the Internet of Things are presented.

A. *Unmanned Aircraft System (UAS)*

UAVs are gaining popularity in both military and civilian segments, with the technology being successfully used in applications such as surveillance, disaster control and response, infrastructure and environmental monitoring, among others. Usually, an Unmanned Aircraft System (UAS) is composed by UAVs, the Ground Control Station (GCS) and the communication links [6][7]. Despite UAVs being usually considered resource-constrained devices, they also benefited from technology development and are now able to provide more complex functionality that lead to more sophisticated missions.

In recent years, the use of multi-UAV solutions in civilian applications has increased [8] since it presents numerous advantages. Multi-UAV systems have higher scalability (larger covered area) and survivability (the mission can still be performed even if one UAV fails), usually complete missions faster than a single UAV and have lower acquisition and maintenance costs [8][9][10].

Establishing efficient communication in a multi-UAV system, however, is a major challenge. Opposed to single-UAV systems, in which the communication can easily be done through a GCS or satellite connection, multi-UAV systems that use the infrastructure for inter-vehicle communication can experience disturbances in link maintenance due to environmental conditions or terrain topology, and the mission target area is limited by the network coverage. Therefore, an ad hoc approach is generally applied for multi-UAV systems, forming a Flying Ad hoc NETwork (FANET) [11][10].

B. Flying Ad hoc NETworks (FANETs)

An ad hoc network is a collection of nodes forming a temporary network with no infrastructure or centralised administration that is able to operate stand-alone or connected to the Internet. When nodes are mobile, the network is called MANET (Mobile Ad hoc NETwork). In this case, network topology is dynamic and may change as the nodes (or routers) move. If nodes are vehicles, the network is called VANET (Vehicular Ad hoc NETwork), and, if vehicles are UAVs, the network is called FANET.

Even though they may seem similar, FANETs have some characteristics that differ them from other types of ad hoc network [10]. Firstly, node mobility is usually much higher in FANETs due to node moving speed. Also, nodes in a FANET are usually kilometres apart and may have their course altered due to UAV movements, environmental changes or mission updates, resulting in a very uncharacteristic mobility model. All these facts contribute to a more frequently topology change due to UAV loss or UAV injection or even because of variations in the communication link/channel quality. Finally, some FANET protocols may need accurate localisation data faster than the one provided by a GPS (Global Positioning System). In these cases, the UAV must have other means to acquire this information (for instance, an Inertial Measurement Unit — IMU). Also, when considering small UAVs, computational capabilities and power consumption constraints must be taken into account. Routing and administration protocols must be energy-efficient to prolong the network lifetime [8].

C. Internet of Things (IoT)

Even though the Internet of Things theme has been vastly explored over the last few years, it still lacks a wide-accepted definition. The general idea of IoT is a large amount of everyday objects pervasively integrated in our environment, equipped with identifying, sensing, networking and processing capabilities, and able to communicate among themselves in order to complete a common task [1][2]. This results in a very distributed network system composed by entities that both provide and consume data from the physical world through sensors and actuators [12]. The application realm of IoT is really large, including areas such as health-care, smart environments (smart homes, factories or cities), environmental monitoring, and disaster alert and recovering [1][2][13][14][15].

Different technologies are involved in enabling IoT systems. *Identifying techniques* are crucial for uniquely address each connected device, ensuring the identification reliability and persistence. *Communication technologies* in general play a major role in these applications. New protocols and network strategies are necessary so that devices with both power and computational resources constrains can be integrated into the IoT. *Middleware* systems will be necessary to make the abstraction of all devices or *things* and make them available to users and applications. Also, it is expected that IoT systems will generate a large amount of data, making *data storage* a key technology for IoT and *Big Data* strategies essential for knowledge extraction [1][16][17]. *Cloud platforms* are being considered an important part of IoT systems and have gained interests in research recently [16][18]. The merge of IoT with cloud computing provides easy access to virtually unlimited processing and storage capabilities on demand and at a low cost, enhancing IoT scalability and performance [13][18]. Given its portability, the cloud is very suitable for IoT architecture, being able not only to aggregate, analyse and distribute collected IoT data continuously and securely but also to remotely manage and control systems. Moreover, it can concentrate services from different providers and bring them to the users in an easy, intuitive way [13][19].

Considering the amount of aspects and technologies involved, it is not surprising that IoT technology also comes with many challenges. *Scalability* can be considered a very onerous task given the large number of connected devices. How to locate, identify, authenticate, use and maintain them in a reliable manner is a hard problem to solve [12][16][20]. *Interoperability* issues will also arise due to a variety of devices supporting different protocols and platforms, or very resource-constrained devices that do not support any communication protocol. These problems must be considered by both developers and manufacturers since system inception so that device integration is done without compromising performance [12][16]. *Data sharing policies* among different applications also have to be considered. Deciding which data will be available to which application, as well as who has the higher priority has to be done carefully in order to ensure system trust and avoid application conflicts [12][20]. The *lack of standardisation* of both architecture and protocols is a major obstacle for IoT implementation, preventing both universal integration of devices — creating a "Babel Tower Effect" among them — and the creation of a competitive market in which all-size players can provide quality products for customers [16]. *Security and trust* of communication and data are a key challenge to address not only to guarantee system functionality, but also to have it accepted by the general public [12][16][20]. The *integration with the cloud* also brings its own challenges: the cloud must support a large number of users, providing at the same time real-time responses that meet system requirements; be prepared to deal with contextual and non-structured data, as well as resource-constrained devices and unreliable connectivity; and offer easy means for developing and deploying IoT applications. Data and communication security must also be addressed, as well as standardisation of IoT-supporting architecture, and device virtualization [16][17][18].

III. Related Work

The integration of UAVs and the Internet/cloud is a fairly recent research topic and is primarily focused in providing UAV telemetry information though a cloud platform or a service-oriented architecture that virtualizes UAVs and make them accessible through a cloud/IoT infrastructure. Some examples are discussed in this section.

In [21], a cloud-supported UAV application framework in which a client hosted at the UAV responsible for image acquisition, which are sent to a server in the cloud for image processing and data storage. The results are sent to a control centre to be evaluated by a human operator.

Authors in [22] propose an emergency-management service. A cloud platform manage UAVs that can be invoked by threatened citizens through a smartphone app. When the UAV reaches the person, a real-time video streaming is provided to security authorities, which can remotely operate the UAV in order to assess the danger and take necessary actions.

In [23], a cloud-based architecture for mission control called Dronemap is proposed. The cloud infrastructure is used to realise UAV virtualization and perform resource-demanding computations. In this architecture, the user requests a mission, performed by one or more UAVs selected by the user or automatically by a cloud manager. While the mission is being executed, relevant data are reported real-time to the user.

Authors from [24] present a framework to offer UAV as a Service (UAVaaS), in which UAVs are hired by a different set of users trough an Internet interface to execute a task. While waypoints and video feeds are available to the users, control and navigation functionality are handled by UAV's on board flight controller. A cloud coordinator handles all communication between the users and UAVs in order to provide better security and optimize resource usage.

In [25], the authors propose a technique to control UAVs using the Cloud — the user inputs only the state of the flight (for instance, altitude, direction and speed) and the system makes the necessary control adjustments so that user requirements are met. The communication between UAVs and the cloud is made by the remote ground station, which has the ability to connect to the cloud through Internet and to the UAVs using a wireless communication link (radio system).

Authors in [26] propose an UAV-Cloud platform in a Resource-Oriented Architecture in which UAVs act as servers whose resources can be accessed by APIs, applying a broker architecture for scalability. A proof of concept is provided using Arduino devices as UAVs and RESTful APIs to access their resources.

The work presented in [27] present a softwarization of the network so that the UAV infrastructure is decoupled from control. A controller layer virtualizes the infrastructure to the higher layers, while an orchestration layer manages the mission. A loosely coupled architecture is used to connect UAVs and sensors, with a middle layer managing the cooperation between the two.

IV. UAVs into IoIT: Opportunities

So what happens when we integrate UAVs into IoIT and connect them to the cloud? First of all, UAVs will have at their disposal the virtually unlimited cloud processing and storing capabilities, allowing the use of smaller, cheaper UAVs in missions. One must be careful, however, about how much processing will be done within the cloud. Processing primary tasks as obstacle avoidance remotely will bring a latency for the system not acceptable for aircraft [28]. Therefore, the cloud must be used for tasks that demand high computational power and can afford a quasi-instantaneous response.

Also, UAV telemetry and captured data will be available to the user through the cloud, making new data readily available and enabling real-time operations and decision making from any location. Thus, the cloud can also be used for the execution of machine learning techniques and algorithms, improving the overall operation by using the acquired experience.

The connection of UAVs will also be boosted. Aircraft will be able to communicate among themselves and share data, network resources, and services even with no line-of-sight (LoS), enhancing UAS collaboration and cooperation.

UAVs are likely to be considered as systems of systems. Every internal aircraft module necessary to fly (e.g., motors, actuators) or perform missions (e.g., cameras, thermal sensors) can be considered a single system. Such a view leads to a next-level-approach where every aircraft module is a *thing* on an IoT network that is fully capable of providing real-time information and take actions. The UAV can be considered a network of things (1st order) connected to the IoIT infrastructure, and the UAV itself would also be a node on the IoIT network (2nd order). Moreover, such modules can be considered not simply *things*, but also smart and intelligent things that can be connected as an independent network node and even provide cloud-based services to users nearby, e.g., local sensing, computation and decisions capabilities or remote resources. That is a potential achievement that inherits important characteristics from the fly by wireless paradigm [29].

The integration of UAVs and IoIT and the consequent UAV availability to other systems in real-time can enhance UAV performance in many situations, as described in this Section. Moreover, the possibility of moving a set of sensors (such as a vehicle) to an area that lacks in IoIT coverage will provide more precise services delivery, improved Quality of Service (QoS) and better sensors positioning.

Regardless of the application, UAVs as intelligent things are able to perform self-diagnosis in order to verify whether they are capable of performing the required task or providing the requested service. If unexpected events during the mission generate failure or unavailability, the IoIT redundancy offers replacement possibilities.

A. Emergency Applications

Emergency situations are always a trial for the city infrastructure. In some cases, the situation happens in an area of difficult access, delaying the emergency personnel response and in some cases jeopardising the victim's medical care. IoIT can improve emergency response by integrating UAVs and other devices in emergency situations.

UAVs in particular can be used to perform a first assessment sense and detect victims, specially in areas of difficult access such as mountains or very large areas like the ocean. Once the victim is located, the UAV can send through IoIT infrastructure the precise victim location to the emergency response team together with video feed for a quick evaluation of the situation. If needed, the same UAV or a different one can be used to deliver supplies such as bottled water or first-aid resources for immediate use until emergency personnel arrives.

Victim rescue can also benefit from IoIT. The UAV positioned near the victim can send weather conditions and terrain topology data so that the emergency response infrastructure can decide in advance if the rescue will be done by air or ground, optimising the emergency resources usage. In case of ground rescue, the UAV can also scout the area in order to identify blocked roads and other access difficulties, aiding the team to decide which path to take to reach the victim.

UAVs and other IoIT participants can also be used to improve the communication network in case it suffered damage during the emergency. Papers such as [30] and [28] propose the use of UAVs to build a temporary, mobile network infrastructure to be used by emergency personnel or the population in general until communication services are operating normally.

B. Smart Cities Applications

Smart Cities are becoming a topic of great interest in research. The objective of Smart Cities is to provide better quality of life with efficient infrastructure at reduced costs by integrating multiple assets such as transportation systems, power plants, law enforcement and others [31].

Figure 1. Smart Farm applications taken to the next level: (A) Surveillance in real-time; (B) Services integration; and (C) Identification of unexpected issues.

UAVs can perform several tasks in a smart city when connected to the IoIT. They can monitor in real-time the city infrastructure such as power lines, bridges, roads and railroads, reducing maintenance costs. Law enforcement can also be aided by patrolling, monitoring crowds or following a person of interest during a chase. They can also monitor the traffic flow and communicate the Intelligent Transportation System (ITS) about road accidents, as well as providing video images for emergency personnel. Finally, UAVs can also function as network infrastructure for city areas in which the connection link is limited, integrating them to the rest of the city and expanding the range of smart services.

C. Industry & Retail Applications

Industries have a lot to benefit from IoIT and its interface with other connected devices. The integration of smart machines in smart factories, smart storage facilities and smart supply chains will allow to automate the entire product chain, from production to delivery. For instance, a smart storage can detect if the sales of a particular product have increased and trigger a higher production so that this specific product is always available. In retail, smart supply chains will be able to provide real-time information for both suppliers and costumers, increasing the efficiency and customer experience.

In industries, UAVs can be used for real-time supervision of outdoor areas of the factory or for infrastructure inspection such as building structures or transportation ducts in oil and gas industry. When considering retail, UAVs are already being used in delivery of goods for major players such as Amazon [32], and can provide great customer experience by notifying the delivery and allowing it to be supervised in real-time.

D. Smart Farm Applications

Smart Farms also have great benefit potential from IoIT. The use of autonomous vehicles together with ubiquitous sensors for planting, monitoring crops and cattle and harvesting can increase efficiency of production by reducing its costs. Figure 1 presents examples of smart farm applications such as: (A) Surveillance in real-time; (B) Services integration; and (C) Identification of unexpected issues.

UAVs in particular can be used in many different ways in a smart farm [31]. UAVs can monitor farm borders for intruders or wildlife predators, promptly sending an alert for farm owner and calling law enforcement through IoIT infrastructure if necessary or dispersing the animals before they damage the crops or cattle. Monitor tasks can also extend to fields and cattle conditions, triggering suitable actions if a problem is encountered. They can also search for missing cattle and inspect the farm infrastructure such as silos or barn roofs. In plantation process, UAVs have been used for chemicals spraying, which can be optimised by the use of soil data gathered by IoIT connected sensors in the ground.

E. Government Applications

Border protection and surveillance is a task performed by different means, from human surveillance to walls and monitoring cameras. With the use of IoIT, this task can be automated and performed by unmanned vehicles (ground, aerial and aquatic) in cooperation, responding real-time to a remote control station that can perform the necessary protocol when an anomaly is detected. Specifically, UAVs can also be used to monitor forests and areas of environmental protection to identify problems such as forest fire or areas of illegal logging and notify the competent authority so that proper actions can be taken.

F. Vehicular Sensors as a Service

The integration of mobile objects (flying, driving, floating, rolling, diving, walking, etc.) to IoIT networks will provide means of moving sensors to the right place at the right time. That leads to the possibility of enabling modules as potential providers of cloud-based real-time services to nearby networks and users, improving targeted information delivery. This approach has great potential on providing flexible intelligent mapping, efficient goods delivery, and search and rescue services with high precision.

G. Environmental monitoring

Environmental monitoring is another promising domain for unmanned vehicles connected to the IoIT. There is a growing necessity to monitor great barrier reef or pole ice regarding climate changes. The application of Unmanned Underwater Vehicles (UUV) and Unmanned Surface Vehicles (USV) directly connected to satellites or somehow supported by UAVs will provide IoIT connectivity that can improve such activities with real-time information and services both ways.

V. UAVs into IoIT: Challenges

As seen before, the integration of UAVs into IoIT brings a lot of opportunities. However, there are many challenges that need to be overcome — some of them well known by the unmanned vehicle community, others emerging due to the connection of vehicles to an infrastructure such as IoIT. In general, these challenges are classified in three categories: public safety and privacy, standardisation and technical.

A. Public Safety and Privacy Challenges

Confidentiality issues regarding the data acquired by UAVs is a major concern — particularly if there is critical information being collected — and will play a starring role in public acceptance of the technology. There is a tendency to store as much data as possible into the UAV main memory in order to ensure availability [33], which ends up being a critical security weakness [34]. If the UAV is stolen or has its control taken, it can be used as a gateway to probe sensitive information from the secured network it is authenticated in. IoIT could improve security by transferring sensitive data to the cloud. However, providing data distribution in a secure manner on UAVs or other resource-restricted devices is another challenge.

Another concern for the general population would be snooping — a UAV can take unauthorised video or photos and share them online, making them nearly impossible to be removed and very difficult to identify the perpetrator. It is likely that governments will enact legislation to UAV registration and to prevent privacy invasion, as done in some states in the US [35]. Moreover, providing vehicular sensors as a service will increase risks, leading to the demand for more precise information security approaches.

B. Regulation & Standardisation Challenges

Certification is a must for insertion of UAVs into the airspace and prevent the technology of being used for nefarious purposes, such as physical assault, drug smuggling and others [36]. UAV safety plays a major role in this regulations, since a UAV out of control can cause damage to property or harm people. Because of that, many regulation agencies such as FAA [37] and EASA [38] have started to regulate the UAV market.

As with IoT, standardisation is also a major challenge for IoIT, and must involve both the industry and governments. From a technical point of view, standardisation is necessary to ensure all devices are able to communicate, preventing a "Babel Tower Effect" in which devices become split into disjoint subsets (for instance, all devices from the same manufacturer) that can only talk to others from the same subset. From a social and economic point of view, standardisation will favour the entrance of small and medium companies in the market, stimulating entrepreneurship and competition, benefiting the final customer and spreading the use of the technology.

C. Technical challenges

There are many technical issues in UAVs being integrated into IoIT. For starters, UAVs are resource-constrained devices. Hardware and software design must take into account limited memory, storage and processing capabilities, as well as a limited power source. Thus, algorithms and communication protocols must be as energy-efficient as possible. This aspect demands a local intelligence to decide how to partition computation and data over local and remote resources that can also be temporally unreachable because of wireless connection outage.

Also, IoIT will be formed with a variety of devices developed for various platforms and using different communication protocols, which can lead to compatibility and interoperability issues. Furthermore, the inclusion of vehicular sensors as *things* on the IoIT network will increase the complexity of the entire system, since the communication links can be performed directly from sensors belonging to different vehicles. This heterogeneity will also extend to the acquired data, that will most likely be non-structured. How data is gathered, distributed, stored and recovered has to be planned carefully in order to ensure real-time and security requirements.

Apart from certification, there is also a rising concern with GPS security. GPS spoofing attacks have become more frequent. Such attacks can cause the aircraft to completely lose control, which is a very critical issue. The GPS spoofing may help attackers to hijack UAVs, another issue that is strongly related to man-in-the-middle attacks.

Security is always a challenge in any communicating system and relate to all other aspects aforementioned. Limited resources demand efficient security algorithms that do not compromise performance or resource/power consumption; heterogeneity defies the idea of implementing a global security policy for all devices and data storage must also be covered by security in case the communication is interrupted or the physical integrity of the device compromised. Therefore, security solutions must permeate all layers of the architecture — reducing the breaches throughout the layers will consequently reduce the overall chances of attacks to the network.

Safety is another important aspect for the devices, which must be able to determine the "health" and the authenticity of both its internal and external components [11] — something even more challenging if the internal components are also connected wirelessly.

VI. Conclusion

IoIT is a network composed of autonomous and mobile devices equipped with both sensing and action taking capabilities. UAVs are natural candidates to be integrated into IoIT, which enable a new degree of collaboration between devices and real-time supervision of missions. One promising opportunity is the use of vehicles and sensors as services allowing a better integration of all *things*, leading to an environment composed by everything, updated every-time and available everywhere. This integration, however, introduces new challenges to be addressed regarding public safety and privacy, standardisation and technical aspects. Despite the challenges, the integration of UAVs into IoIT is a promising research topic with high chances of applicability. In this paper, we presented how UAV integration to IoIT can improve applications, as well as the current challenges.

By proposing solutions to the identified challenges, the development of IoIT integrated with autonomous vehicles should be facilitated in order to achieve relevant advances in this research area. Moreover, the challenges presented here are only a sampling of potential issues that might be faced in this new paradigm. Besides the number of challenges, the several different missions and applications pointed out that can be performed in the near future are exciting. This is why not only the military but also the civilians, the academics, and the industry are enthusiastic about novel uses and applications of autonomous vehicles and IoIT.

Acknowledgements

The authors acknowledge the support granted by CAPES and FAPESP under processes 2012/16171-6.

References

[1] L. Atzori, A. Iera, and G. Morabito, "The Internet of Things: A Survey," Computer Networks, vol. 54, no. 15, 2010, pp. 2787–2805, ISSN: 13891286.

[2] A. Whitmore, A. Agarwal, and L. Da Xu, "The Internet of Things A Survey of Topics and Trends," Information Systems Frontiers, vol. 17, no. 2, 2015, pp. 261–274, ISSN: 1387-3326.

[3] O. Kaiwartya et al., "Internet of Vehicles: Motivation, Layered Architecture, Network Model, Challenges and Future Aspects," IEEE Access, vol. PP, no. 99, 2016, ISSN: 21693536.

[4] L. E. Talavera et al., "The Mobile Hub concept: Enabling applications for the Internet of Mobile Things," in International Conference on Pervasive Computing and Communication Workshops (PerCom Workshops), March 23-27, 2015, St. Louis, USA. IEEE, Mar 2015, pp. 123–128, ISBN: 978-1-4799-8425-1, URL: http://dx.doi.org/10.1109/PERCOMW.2015.7134005 [accessed: 2017-01-09].

[5] Y. Chen and H. Hu, "Internet of intelligent things and robot as a service," Simulation Modelling Practice and Theory, vol. 34, 2012, pp. 159–171, ISSN: 1569190X.

[6] K. P. Valavanis and G. J. Vachtsevanos, Handbook of Unmanned Aerial Vehicles. Dordrecht: Springer Netherlands, 2015, ISBN: 9789048197064.

[7] S. G. Gupta, M. M. Ghonge, and P. M. Jawandhiya, "Review of Unmanned Aircraft System (UAS)," International Journal of Advanced Research in Computer Engineering & Technology, vol. 2, no. 4, 2013, pp. 1646–1658, ISSN: 2278-1323.

[8] L. Gupta, R. Jain, and G. Vaszkun, "Survey of Important Issues in UAV Communication Networks," IEEE Communications Surveys & Tutorials, vol. 18, no. 2, 2016, pp. 1123–1152, ISSN: 1553-877X.

[9] O. K. Sahingoz, "Mobile networking with UAVs: Opportunities and challenges," in International Conference on Unmanned Aircraft Systems (ICUAS), May 28-31, 2013, Atlanta, USA. IEEE, May 2013, pp. 933–941, ISBN: 9781479908172, URL: http://dx.doi.org/10.1109/ICUAS.2013.6564779 [accessed: 2016-03-31].

[10] I. Bekmezci, O. K. Sahingoz, and S. Temel, "Flying Ad-Hoc Networks (FANETs): A survey," Ad Hoc Networks, vol. 11, no. 3, 2013, pp. 1254–1270, ISSN: 15708705.

[11] D. F. Pigatto et al., "HAMSTER - Healthy, Mobility and Security-based Data Communication Architecture for Unmanned Aircraft Systems," in International Conference on Unmanned Aircraft Systems (ICUAS) May 27-30, 2014, Orlando, USA. IEEE, May 2014, pp. 52–63, ISBN: 9781479923762, URL: http://dx.doi.org/10.1109/ICUAS.2014.6842238 [accessed: 2016-05-10].

[12] D. Miorandi, S. Sicari, F. De Pellegrini, and I. Chlamtac, "Internet of things: Vision, applications and research challenges," Ad Hoc Networks, vol. 10, no. 7, 2012, pp. 1497–1516, ISSN: 15708705.

[13] A. Botta, W. de Donato, V. Persico, and A. Pescapé, "Integration of Cloud computing and Internet of Things: A survey," Future Generation Computer Systems, vol. 56, 2016, pp. 684–700, ISSN: 0167739X.

[14] H. Arasteh et al., "Iot-based smart cities: A survey," in 16th International Conference on Environment and Electrical Engineering (EEEIC) June 7-10, 2016, Florence, Italy. IEEE, Jun 2016, pp. 1–6, ISBN: 9781509023202, URL: http://dx.doi.org/10.1109/EEEIC.2016.7555867 [accessed: 2016-09-14].

[15] R. Kumar and A. Pandey, "A Survey on Security Issues in Cloud Computing," International Journal of Scientific Research in Science, Engineering and Technology (IJSRSET), vol. 2, no. 3, 2016, pp. 506–517, ISSN: 2394-4099.

[16] A. Al-Fuqaha, M. Guizani, M. Mohammadi, M. Aledhari, and M. Ayyash, "Internet of Things: A Survey on Enabling Technologies, Protocols, and Applications," IEEE Communications Surveys & Tutorials, vol. 17, 2015, pp. 2347–2376, ISSN: 1553-877X.

[17] J. Gubbi, R. Buyya, S. Marusic, and M. Palaniswami, "Internet of Things (IoT): A Vision, Architectural Elements, and Future Directions," Future Generation Computer Systems, vol. 29, no. 7, 2013, pp. 1645–1660, ISSN: 0167739X.

[18] E. Cavalcante et al., "On the Interplay of Internet of Things and Cloud Computing: A Systematic Mapping Study," Computer Communications, vol. 89-90, 2016, pp. 17–33, ISSN: 01403664.

[19] J. Singh, T. Pasquier, J. Bacon, H. Ko, and D. Eyers, "Twenty Security Considerations for Cloud-Supported Internet of Things," IEEE Internet of Things Journal, vol. 3, no. 3, 2016, pp. 269–284, ISSN: 2327-4662.

[20] J. A. Stankovic, "Research Directions for the Internet of Things," IEEE Internet of Things Journal, vol. 1, no. 1, 2014, pp. 3–9, ISSN: 2327-4662.

[21] C. Luo, J. Nightingale, E. Asemota, and C. Grecos, "A UAV-Cloud System for Disaster Sensing Applications," in 81st Vehicular Technology Conference (VTC Spring), May 11-14, 2015, Glasgow, Scotland. IEEE, May 2015, pp. 1–5, ISBN: 9781479980888, URL: http://dx.doi.org/10.1109/VTCSpring.2015.7145656 [accessed: 2016-04-23].

[22] G. Ermacora et al., A Cloud Based Service for Management and Planning of Autonomous UAV Missions in Smart City Scenarios. Springer International Publishing, 2014, pp. 20–26, ISBN: 9783319138237_3.

[23] B. Qureshi, A. Koubaa, M.-F. Sriti, Y. Javed, and M. Alajlan, "Dronemap - A Cloud-based Architecture for the Internet-of-Drones," in International Conference on Embedded Wireless Systems and Networks (EWSN) February 15-17, 2016, Graz, Austria, Feb 2016, pp. 255–256, ISBN: 9780994988607, URL: http://www.ewsn.org/file-repository/ewsn2016/255_256_qureshi.pdf [accessed: 2016-04-02].

[24] J. Yapp, R. Seker, and R. Babiceanu, "UAV as a service: Enabling on-demand access and on-the-fly re-tasking of multi-tenant UAVs using cloud services," in 35th Digital Avionics Systems Conference (DASC), September 25-19, 2016, Sacramento, USA. IEEE, Sep 2016, pp. 1–8, ISBN: 9781509025237, URL: http://dx.doi.org/10.1109/DASC.2016.7778007 [accessed: 2017-01-20].

[25] S. Majumder and M. S. Prasad, "Cloud Based Control for Unmanned Aerial Vehicles," in 3rd International Conference on Signal Processing and Integrated Networks (SPIN), February 11-12, 2016, Noida, India. IEEE, Feb 2016, pp. 421–424, ISBN: 9781467391979, URL: http://dx.doi.org/10.1109/SPIN.2016.7566731 [accessed: 2016-12-19].

[26] S. Mahmoud and N. Mohamed, "Toward a Cloud Platform for UAV Resources and Services," in Fourth Symposium on Network Cloud Computing and Applications (NCCA), June 11-12, 2015, Munich, Germany. IEEE, Jun 2015, pp. 23–30, ISBN: 9781467377416, URL: http://dx.doi.org/10.1109/NCCA.2015.14 [accessed: 2016-04-23].

[27] S. Mahmoud, I. Jawhar, and N. Mohamed, "A Softwarization Architecture for UAVs and WSNs as Part of the Cloud Environment," in International Conference on Cloud Engineering Workshop (IC2EW), April 4-8, 2016, Berlin, Germany. IEEE, apr 2016, pp. 13–18, ISBN: 9781509036844, URL: http://dx.doi.org/10.1109/IC2EW.2016.17 [accessed: 2016-09-25].

[28] M. Cochez, J. Periaux, V. Terziyan, K. Kamlyk, and T. Tuovinen, "Evolutionary Cloud for Cooperative UAV Coordination," Department of Mathematical Information Technology, University of Jyväskylä, Jyväskylä, Finland, Tech. Rep., 2014, ISBN: 9789513957292, URL: http://www.cs.jyu.fi/ai/papers/UAV_report.pdf [accessed: 2016-04-16].

[29] D.-K. Dang, A. Mifdaoui, and T. Gayraud, "Fly-By-Wireless for next generation aircraft: Challenges and potential solutions," in IFIP Wireless Days (WD), November 21-23, 2013, Dublin, Ireland, Nov 2012, pp. 1–8, ISBN: 9781467344043, URL: http://dx.doi.org/10.1109/WD.2012.6402820 [accessed 2017-01-22].

[30] S. Morgenthaler, T. Braun, Z. Zhao, T. Staub, and M. Anwander, "UAVNet: A Mobile Wireless Mesh Network Using Unmanned Aerial Vehicles," in IEEE Globecom Workshops, December 3-7, 2012, Anaheim, USA. IEEE, Dec 2012, pp. 1603–1608, ISBN: 9781467349413, URL: http://dx.doi.org/10.1109/GLOCOMW.2012.6477825 [accessed: 2016-04-02].

[31] F. Mohammed, A. Idries, N. Mohamed, J. Al-Jaroodi, and I. Jawhar, "UAVs for smart cities: Opportunities and challenges," in International Conference on Unmanned Aircraft Systems (ICUAS) May 27-30, 2014, Orlando, USA. IEEE, May 2014, pp. 267–273, ISBN: 9781479923762, URL: http://dx.doi.org/10.1109/ICUAS.2014.6842265 [accessed: 2017-01-20].

[32] "Amazon makes its first drone delivery in the U.K." URL: http://money.cnn.com/2016/12/14/technology/amazon-drone-delivery/ [accessed: 2017-01-17].

[33] K. Hartmann and C. Steup, "The vulnerability of UAVs to cyber attacks - An approach to the risk assessment," in 5th International Conference on Cyber Conflict (CyCon) June 4-7, 2013, Tallinn, Estonia. Tallinn, Estonia: IEEE, Jun 2013, pp. 1–23, ISBN: 9781479904501, URL: http://ieeexplore.ieee.org/xpls/abs_all.jsp?arnumber=6568373 [accessed: 2016-04-16].

[34] Q. Jing, A. V. Vasilakos, J. Wan, J. Lu, and D. Qiu, "Security of the Internet of Things: perspectives and challenges," Wireless Networks, vol. 20, no. 8, 2014, pp. 2481–2501, ISSN: 1022-0038.

[35] Y. Kim, J. Jo, and S. Shrestha, "A Server-Based Real-Time Privacy Protection Scheme against Video Surveillance by Unmanned Aerial Systems," in International Conference on Unmanned Aircraft Systems (ICUAS) May 27-30, 2014, Orlando, USA. IEEE, May 2014, pp. 684–691, ISBN: 9781479923762, URL: http://dx.doi.org/10.1109/ICUAS.2014.6842313 [accessed: 2016-08-12].

[36] N. Hossein Motlagh, T. Taleb, and O. Arouk, "Low-Altitude Unmanned Aerial Vehicles-Based Internet of Things Services: Comprehensive Survey and Future Perspectives," IEEE Internet of Things Journal, vol. 3, no. 6, 2016, pp. 899–922, ISSN: 2327-4662.

[37] "Unmanned Aircraft Systems," URL: https://www.faa.gov/uas/ [accessed: 2017-01-20].

[38] "Unmanned Aircraft Systems (UAS) and Remotely Piloted Aircraft Systems (RPAS)," URL: https://www.easa.europa.eu/unmanned-aircraft-systems-uas-and-remotely-piloted-aircraft-systems-rpas [accessed: 2017-01-20].

D-Joseph: An Efficient Approach for Dynamic Software Reconfiguration in Data Stream Processing Systems

Rafael Oliveira Vasconcelos[1,2], Igor Vasconcelos[1,2], Markus Endler[1]
[1]*Department of Informatics Pontifical Catholic University of Rio de Janeiro (PUC-Rio)*
Rio de Janeiro, Brazil
email: {*rvasconcelos, ivasconcelos, endler*}@*inf.puc-rio.br*
[2]*Department of Informatics*
University Tiradentes (UNIT)
Aracaju, Brazil

***Abstract*— While many data stream systems have to provide continuous (24x7) services with no acceptable downtime, they also have to cope with changes in their execution environments and in the requirements that they must comply (e.g., moving from on-premises architecture to a cloud system, changing the network technology, adding new functionality or modifying existing parts). On one hand, dynamic software reconfiguration (i.e., the capability of evolving on the fly) is a desirable feature. On the other hand, stream systems may suffer from the disruption and overhead caused by the reconfiguration. Due to the necessity of reconfiguring (i.e., evolving) the system whilst the system must not be disrupted (i.e., blocked), consistent and non-disruptive reconfiguration is still considered an open problem. This paper presents and validates D-Joseph, a non-quiescent approach for dynamic software reconfiguration that preserves the consistency of distributed data stream processing systems. Unlike many works that require the system to reach a safe state (e.g., quiescence) before performing a reconfiguration, the proposed approach enables the system to smoothly evolve (i.e., be reconfigured) in a non-disruptive way without reaching quiescence. The evaluation indicates that the proposed approach supports consistent distributed reconfiguration and has negligible impact on availability and performance. Furthermore, the implementation of the proposed approach showed better performance results in all experiments than the quiescent approach and Upstart.**

Keywords-Online Dynamic reconfiguration; Adaptability; Software adaptation; Data Stream Processing.

I. Introduction

Many stream processing systems have to provide services for 24x7, with no acceptable downtime [1]. However, they commonly have to cope with changes in their execution environment (e.g., moving from on-premises architecture to cloud architecture or changing the network technology) and in the requirements that they must comply with [2] (e.g., adding new functionality or modifying existing parts). The authors [2] further emphasize that changes are hard to predict at design time. The continuous service execution makes it difficult to fix bugs and add new required functionality on-the-fly as this requires non-disruptive replacement of parts of a software version by new ones [3]. Ertel and Felber [3] further explain that prior approaches to dynamic reconfiguration (a.k.a. dynamic adaptation, live update or dynamic evolution) require the starting of a new process and the transfer of states between the components being swapped [4]. However, some authors argue that the cost of redundant hardware may be considerable high [5].

Despite extensive research in dynamic software reconfiguration, safe reconfiguration is still an open problem [1]. A common approach is to put the component that has to be updated into a safe state, such as the quiescent state [6], before reconfiguring the system [7]. Thus, a safe reconfiguration must drive the system to a consistent state and preserve the correct completion of on-going activities [2]. At the same time, dynamic reconfiguration should also minimize the interruption of the system's service (i.e., disruption) and the delay with which the system is updated (i.e., its timeliness) [6]. Furthermore, coordinating (i.e., orchestrating) the restart of all the exchanged or added components is very challenging if the system's service must not be interrupted [3].

Aligned with the aforementioned requirements, applications in the field of data stream processing require continuous and timely processing of high-volume of data, originated from a myriad of distributed sources, to obtain online notifications from complex queries over the steady flow of data items [8]. Intelligent Transportation Systems, Network Monitoring, Stock Exchange, Smart Cities, Smart Energy management and logistics are some examples of application areas that require processing data streams. Thus, while dynamic reconfiguration is a desirable feature, such systems shall not suffer performance degradation due to the potential disruptions and overhead caused by the reconfiguration.

In order to enable dynamic software reconfiguration for stream based systems, our work allows the concurrent execution of multiple versions of a software component. Concisely, the proposed approach is based on the idea that a tuple (a.k.a. message) has to be entirely processed by a specific version of each component. However, there is no problem in updating a component C while a tuple T traverses the system as long as the system keeps the previous and the new versions of C (and of its dependent components) until all previous' version tuples are flushed (i.e., draining the tuples between the source and sink nodes).

The remainder of the paper is organized as follows. Section II presents an overview of the key concepts and system model used throughout this work. Section III delves into details D-Joseph. Section IV summarizes the main results of the assessment conducted to evaluate the proposal. Finally, Section V reviews and discusses the central ideas presented in this paper.

II. FUNDAMENTALS

This section presents the main concepts about data stream processing, as well as our system model and related works.

A. *Data Stream Processing*

Data stream processing is a computational paradigm [9] that is focused at sustained and timely analysis, aggregation and transformation of large volumes of data streams that are continuously updated [8]. Data stream is a continuous and online sequence of unbounded items where it is not possible to control the order of the data produced and processed [10][11]. Thus, the data is processed on-the-fly as it travels from its source nodes downstream to the consumer nodes, passing through several distributed processing nodes [12], that select, classify or manipulate the data. This model is typically represented by a graph where vertices are source nodes that produce data, operators that implement algorithms for data stream analysis, or sink nodes that consume the processed data stream, and where edges define possible data paths among the nodes (i.e., stream channels).

In order to cope with the high processing demand, stream processing systems typically employ Single Instruction, Multiple Data (SIMD) parallelism and use multiple instances of an operator (i.e., processing units), where each operator instance is responsible for processing a subset of the data stream independently of the remaining data stream, and hence without need to manage communication or synchronization among those operators [13]. Therefore, many stream processing systems are inherently distributed and may consist of dozens to hundreds of operators distributed over a large number of processing nodes [12], where each processing node executes one or several operators.

B. *System Model*

Our notion of a stream processing system is a directed acyclic graph that consists of multiple operators (i.e., components) deployed at distributed device nodes. More formally, the graph G = (V, E) consists of vertices and edges. A vertex represents an operator and an edge represents a stream channel. An edge $e = (v1, v2)$ interconnects the output of vertex *v1* with the input of vertex *v2*. Vertices without input ports (i.e., without incoming edges) are referred as source vertex. Correspondingly, vertices without output ports are called sink vertices. Finally, vertices with both input and output ports are called inner vertex. A tuple $t = (val, path^*)$ consists of a value (*val*) and an execution path (*path**) that holds the operators, and their versions, that a tuple *t* traveled through G. For instance, a tuple *t* that traveled from source vertex SO1 to sink vertex SI1 via operators O1 and O2 holds *path* = {SO1, O1, O2}. The tuple's *val* field is transformed (i.e., processed) along the graph. A stream s = (t*) between *v1* and *v2* consists of an ordered sequence of tuples t* where t1 < t2 represents that *t1* was sent before *t2* by a node *n1*. A vertex is composed of f^{select}, f^{output} and f^{update} functions. When a vertex *v1* generates a tuple (i.e., sends it via the output port), its succeeding vertices (i.e., the vertex that receive the stream from *v1*) receives such tuple via the function f^{select}, which is in charge to select, or not, this tuple to be processed by the function f^{update}.

In order to standardize the terms and notations used throughout this work, an operator (a.k.a. graph vertex) [14] will be generically referred to as a component. A node is any physical device node (e.g., desktop and smartphone) that executes a component. A Processing Node (PN), in turn, is a node that holds at least one inner operator (i.e., an operator with input and output ports). Furthermore, as data stream systems must be elastic to adapt to variations in the volume of the data streams [15], we consider that some PNs share their workload [16].

Taking into account that many current distributed systems follow the mobile-cloud architectural paradigm [17][18], our model is composed of Client Nodes (CNs), which may be mobile or stationary nodes, and PNs deployed in the cloud. The CNs are interconnected to the cloud through a Gateway (GW), which in turns forwards the stream to the PNs. Considering that we model our system as distributed data stream system, some software components are concerned with communication issues, while other are concerned with processing issues (i.e., the analysis, aggregation and transformation the data stream). The GW, for instance, is a node in charge of forwarding the data stream from/to the CNs to/from the PNs and interconnecting the CNs to the Reconfiguration Manager (RM). Conversely, a CN has some communication component for enabling the interaction with the GW while CN may also have a processing component that performs some pre-processing on the produced data before sending the stream to the cloud.

In addition to these nodes, the RM manages software component deployments, and coordinates the execution of the reconfiguration by the nodes. The RM is responsible for coordinating (i.e., initiate and orchestrates the execution of all the operations that encompass a distributed reconfiguration) the system-wide reconfiguration process (e.g., deployment of new software components) on many CNs. For example, if the reconfiguration is the deployment of a new component version, the RM sends the code that implements the new component to the nodes and then verify whether all of them successfully deployed it. The red dashed lines represent the reconfiguration control channel between the RM and the other nodes, while the black lines represent the system data flow. Thus, all reconfigurations performed at the nodes are driven and orchestrated from the RM.

C. *Related Work*

Software reconfiguration at runtime is a research topic that combines issues and approaches from areas, such as software engineering, programming languages and operating systems. However, a common problem is the identification of states in which the system is stable and ready to evolve [2]. The authors Ertel and Felber [3] propose a framework for systems that are modeled using (data)flow-based programming (FBP) [19]. The idea behind FBP is to model the system as a directed acyclic dataflow graph where the operators (vertices) are functions that process the data flow and the edges define de input and output ports of each operator. Since the messages are delivered in order, this proposal forwards special messages informing when a component (a.k.a. operator) is safe to be reconfigured [3]. Despite the advantages, the problem with the work is that either all components will perform the reconfiguration or none of them can proceed with the reconfiguration, similar to a transaction.

The seminal work by Kramer and Magee [6] proposed and proved that the *quiescence* criterion guarantees the system consistency over the update process. Their model represents the distributed system as a directed graph whose nodes interact by means of transactions (i.e., a sequence of messages that should be atomically executed). The weakness of their work is that it causes a high disruption since it blocks all potentially dependent computation during system evolution.

III. D-Joseph

This section presents D-Joseph, our approach to enable dynamic reconfiguration in distributed stream processing systems. Differently from other works, D-Joseph does not need to wait for the system to reach a quiescent state (or safe state) to reconfigure a f^{update} function.

Each component has one or more f^{select}, f^{update} and f^{output} functions and components have interdependencies. The advantage of enabling a component to have more than one f^{update} function executing concurrently is that, in face of a reconfiguration, the new function is able to process part of the data stream while the old one is still in use and thus cannot be deactivated. Accordingly, when a tuple T is received by an f^{select} function, it has to choose the right f^{update} to process T. To do so, the f^{select} function verifies the *path* of T when there is more than one f^{update}, otherwise there is no need to verify the path since there is only one f^{update}. The f^{select} and f^{output} represent the input and output ports, respectively, of a component, whereas the f^{update} is the algorithm in charge of processing the transformation on the incoming data stream. Thus, we are able to reconfigure the algorithms that process the data streams (i.e., f^{update} functions) and the system's topology by means of reconfiguring the f^{select} and f^{output} functions.

A. Management of Multiple Versions

In the example of Figure 1, the f^{select} function of the *Processor* component has to know the version of the f^{update} applied at the *Pre-Processor* component in order to avoid inconsistency. Figure 1 shows the partial data flow of a tuple *T* when the system has the f^{update} functions A1, D1 and E1 of *Pre-Processor*, *Processor* and *Post-Processor* components, respectively. Figure 2 shows that the versions A2, D2 and E2 were added to the system and that *Processor D1* (i.e., the f^{update} function of *Processor D1*) and *Post-Processor E1* transformed the tuple *T* in order to maintain the system consistency. Thus, when *T* arrives at the f^{select} function of the *Processor* component, the f^{select} function verifies that *T* comes from *Pre-Processor A1* and then uses the *Processor D1* to transform *T*. The same happens at *Post-Processor* component. Thus, every component has to be aware of its dependency to be able to choose the right f^{update} function.

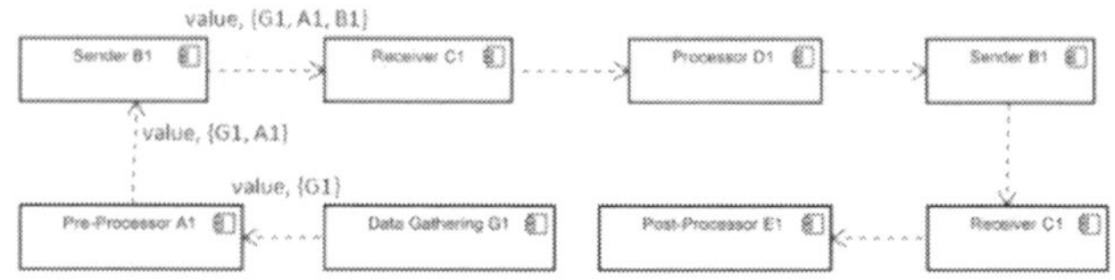

Figure 1. Teste Partial data flow of the motivating scenario where data is to be received by Receiver C1

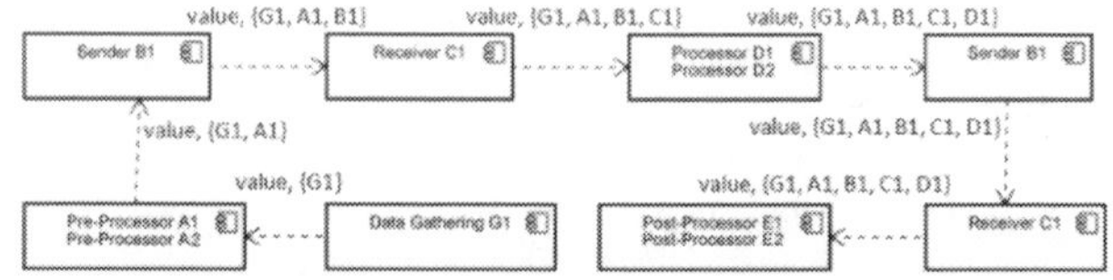

Figure 2. Execution path of the data in a partially reconfigured system

The dependencies can be managed using two approaches, static or dynamic dependency management. The former, which is the simplest one, does not take into account the "downstream" dependent components to generate the execution path of a tuple. Thus, whenever a component processes a tuple *T*, the f^{update} function's version of such component is added into the tuple's execution path, as illustrated by Figure 1 and Figure 2. Finally, when *T* arrives to a downstream component, such as the Processor component, its f^{select} function verifies the execution path of *T* to decide which is the correct f^{update} function to process *T*. To do so, each component has a list of all its upstream dependent components. Conversely, the latter approach verifies if there is any dependent component before adding the version of the f^{update} function into the execution path. If there is no dependent component, the version is not added into the execution path. Furthermore, at each component, the execution path is evaluated to check and discard the versions that have no more dependent components. In Figure 3, for instance, G1 is removed from the execution path at the Pre-Processor component since there is no dependent component of Data Gathering after Pre-Processor.

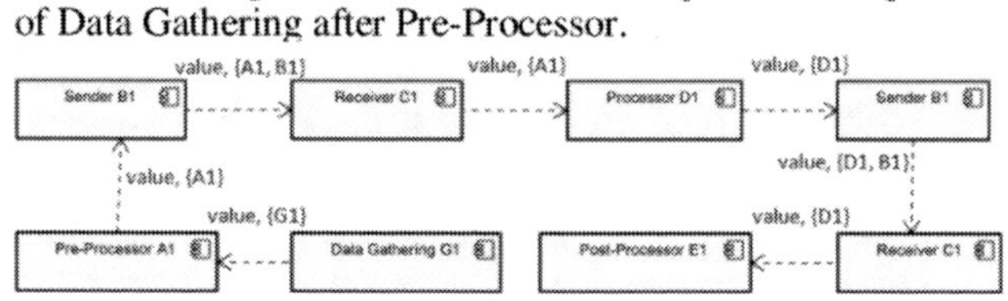

Figure 3. Execution path using the dynamic management

The advantage of applying the static dependency management is that it is simple, has a low execution cost and the dependency changing (e.g., insertion or removal of components) does not affect the system since the execution path field holds all components that a tuple traversed. Thus, a reconfiguration is performed in a simpler and faster way. However, if the execution path grows in size (i.e., there are numerous inner components between the source and the sink nodes), it may degrade the system's performance due to the network and memory costs. On the other hand, the dynamic dependency management has the advantage that does not waste network and memory since the execution path field holds only useful information, which is an advantage for huge paths. The weakness is the complexity introduced to keep the execution path field as short as possible. At each component, all downstream dependency has to be evaluated to remove the unnecessary information in the execution path field.

B. Distributed Reconfiguration

If one (e.g., the system administrator) needs to change the Pre-Processor and Processor component types for some reason the new Processor instances must be deployed before the new Pre-Processor instances. Thus, the reconfiguration execution of all instances has to be coordinated by the RM. Whenever the system administrator needs to replace some components, the administrator uses the RM to start the dynamic software reconfiguration. To replace the Pre-Processor and Processor component types, the RM first deploys the new version of such component on the affect nodes and then activates the instances. After that, it deactivates and removes the previous instances.

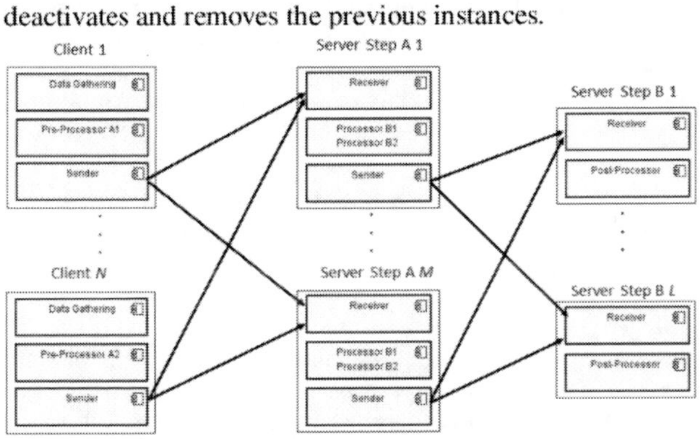

Figure 4. Partial consistent reconfiguration

Figure 4 shows that the servers must have both versions (i.e., Processor B1 and B2) while the system is partially reconfigured because some clients are not yet reconfigured. As soon as the clients are reconfigured, and there are no tuples in transit from Pre-Processor A1, the Processor B1 instances are removed from the servers at step A and the reconfiguration terminates. Therefore, our approach guarantees that the servers are able to handle data stream from any client, reconfigured or not.

IV. Performance Evaluation

In this section, we present the evaluation of D-Joseph. We also have measured the update time and the disruption caused by our reconfiguration approach varying the number of CNs and rate (i.e., frequency) of tuple production, as well as the overhead in terms of throughput imposed by our approach.

Our hardware test was composed of six Desktops Intel i5, 4GB DDR3 and gigabit Ethernet running Windows 7 64 bit, and a gigabit switch. We used three computers to emulate the CNs, and the other three computers to run the PNs and the RM. Our prototype application used for evaluation has been implemented using the Java programing language and Scalable Data Distribution Layer (SDDL), a middleware for scalable real-time communication [20].

Our evaluation scenario consists of a hospital that monitors patients. Each patient has a mobile equipment, composed of some sensors, that continuously monitor each patient vital signs (e.g., temperature, blood pressure, respiratory rate and systolic blood pressure). The mobile equipment sends the patient's vitals (i.e., tuple) to the hospital servers every second where the tuples must be processed as seamless data flow [21][22] in order to generate timely alerts to the medical staff. The success of such application depends on the continuous and timely monitoring of the patients [23].

In order to measure the update time and the service disruption, we varied the number of CNs from three to 300 and the system's tuple production rate from 150 tuples/s (tuples per second) to 15,000 tuples/s, using static and dynamic dependency management. The JAR file that encapsulates each deployed component has nearly 4 kilobytes (KB). The first reconfiguration performed is optimizing the system to discard the tuples that do not meet a criterion (i.e., if the patient vitals do not meet the SIRS criteria, they also will not meet the other criteria) and the second one is changing the temperature unit from Fahrenheit to Celsius.

Regarding consistency of the reconfiguration approach, all reconfigurations were performed consistently. This means that all tuples were properly *processed exactly once* by the right f^{update}. Thus, we were able to achieve global system consistency while the system is being reconfigured.

A. Update Time

The update time experiment measured the Round-trip Delay (RTD), which encompasses the time interval from the instant of time the RM sends the reconfiguration to the nodes until it receives an acknowledgment informing that all nodes completed the execution of the reconfiguration. In other words, it is the time from the first message sent by the RM until all components are reconfigured correctly (i.e., the system has gone from a version v1 to v2). The tuple production rate informs the production rate of the entire system, and not for each CN (i.e., the system has the same production rate in the first three scenarios of Table 1). In the case of 30 CNs and 150 tuples/s, for instance, each CN produces five tuples each second (i.e., the tuple production rate of each CN is 5 tuples/s).

As expected since our approach does not need to wait for a safe state to proceed the reconfiguration, the update time is considerably stable. It ranges from 24.07ms in the scenario with three CNs, production rate of 150 tuples/s to 26.69ms in the scenario with 300 CNs and 15,000 tuples/s, both using the static dependency management. On the other hand, with the dynamic dependency management, the update time ranges from 24.07ms to 26.48ms in the same scenarios.

TABLE I. UPDATE TIME FOR EACH SCENARIO

# CNs	Tuple Production Rate (tuples/s)	Static Dependency Management	Dynamic Dependency Management
		Update Time (ms)	Update Time (ms)
3	150	24.29	24.07
30	150	24.18	25.20
300	150	24.88	24.75
3	1,500	25.18	25.2
30	1,500	24.60	21.36
300	1,500	25.62	23.62
3	15,000	25.05	25.63
30	15,000	26.87	26.27
300	15,000	26.69	26.48

B. *Service Disruption*

In the service disruption experiment, we measured the impact that a reconfiguration causes on the system's throughput and latency, i.e., the time interval between the tuple being sent by the source node until it is received by the sink node. In order to measure the service disruption, we assess the throughput and the latency with 300 CNs and a tuple production rate of 15,000 tuples/s. We performed two reconfigurations, at moments T1 and T2, and at each of them, we compared the throughput of the system with the throughput a second before these reconfigurations took place.

According to our experimental results, the service disruption related to the throughput was negligible. The throughput for the static dependency management had a minor increase at the reconfiguration time T (i.e., the moment in which the reconfiguration was performed) when compared with $T - 1$ (i.e., one second before the reconfiguration), from 14,795 tuples/s to 15,019 tuples/s at reconfiguration T1 and from 14,869 tuples/s to 14,924 tuples/s at reconfiguration T2. For the dynamic dependency management, the throughput varied from 15,060 tuples/s to 15,030 tuples/s at reconfiguration T1 and from 15,073 tuples/s to 15,043 tuples/s at reconfiguration T2. In both dependency management, the throughput was not significantly affected by the reconfiguration, i.e., the experiments demonstrate that our approach causes just a marginal decrease (lower than 0.2%) in the system's throughput.

The reconfiguration may affect the latency when the system has a considerable high workload (e.g., high CPU – Central Processing Unit – usage). In both static and dynamic dependency managements, the reconfiguration T1 from *v1* to *v2*, which reduces the system's workload by discarding the tuples that do not meet some criteria, interfered the tuples' latency for a short period. However, after optimizing the system and thus reducing its workload, the reconfiguration T2 had minor impact on latency ($\approx$ 2ms) in both cases.

C. *Overhead*

We also measured the overhead that D-Joseph imposes on the prototype application when no reconfiguration is performed. To do this experiment, we assessed the time required by the application to generate and process 100,000 tuples, as well as the throughput and latency, with and without the reconfiguration mechanism. Concerning the required time to complete the computation of all tuples, the static dependency management imposed 3.83% of overhead while the dynamic one imposed 8.98%. The throughput was reduced by 2.38% and 2.84% using the static and dynamic dependency management approaches, respectively. Finally, the latency was impacted by 6.57% and 12.50% % using the static and dynamic dependency management approaches, respectively. Thus, for such prototype application, the better choice is the static dependency management.

D. *CN Disconnection*

Due to the possibility of disconnections of mobile CNs, we assessed the amount of time required to complete a reconfiguration after an MN becomes available again. To do so, we have forced a CN to disconnect before the reconfiguration and reconnect after the reconfiguration. The reconnection time encompasses the time interval from the instant of time the CN reconnects until it completes the execution of the reconfiguration. As the number of CNs and the tuple production rate has minor impact on the update time (see Section 4.1.1), we conducted this experiment with 1,000 CNs and 1,000 tuples/s. As soon as the CN reconnects, it took 31.50ms to complete the reconfiguration.

V. CONCLUSION AND FUTURE WORK

In this paper, we proposed and validated D-Joseph, a non-quiescent approach for dynamic reconfiguration that preserves global system consistency in distributed data stream systems. Unlike many works that require blocking the affected parts of the system to be able to proceed a reconfiguration, our proposal enables the system to smoothly evolve in a non-disruptive way.

We are aware that more work and research is still needed. However, considering the encouraging preliminary performance evaluation, we are confident that our approach can be used for development of reconfigurable data stream processing systems. In a scenario with 300 CNs and 15,000 tuples/s, our reconfiguration prototype was able to reconfigure the entire system in 24.07ms, while the service disruption in terms of throughput was lower than 0.2% due to a reconfiguration. On the other hand, the tuples' latency may increase due to a reconfiguration. When comparing the reconfigurable with the non-reconfigurable version of the application prototypes, the reconfiguration capabilities imposed an overhead of only 3.83% and 8.98% on the latency using the static and dynamic dependency approaches, respectively. Our prototype middleware reduced at most 2.84% of the system's throughput and increased at most 12.50% the system's latency when compared to the corresponding system without reconfiguration support.

Problems such as parametric variability and reconfiguration making, which is responsible for deciding when an reconfiguration is required, which alternative best satisfies the overall system goal, and which reconfigurations are needed in order to drive the system to the next state (i.e., an optimal state or state with a new functionality), are not covered by our research. Security is also an important concern for many real systems, particularly for distributed systems since nodes are potentially exposed on the Internet. Therefore, authenticity, integrity and confidentiality emerge as key aspects. Thus, ensuring that only the system administrators, or the system itself, have the ability to drive a software reconfiguration will avoid unauthorized component deployments, such as viruses, on the nodes. However, security aspects are beyond the scope of our current work.

REFERENCES

[1] C. Giuffrida, C. Iorgulescu, and A. S. Tanenbaum, "Mutable Checkpoint-restart: Automating Live Update for Generic Server Programs," in *Proceedings of the 15th International Middleware Conference*, 2014, pp. 133–144.

[2] X. Ma, L. Baresi, C. Ghezzi, V. Panzica La Manna, and J. Lu, "Version-consistent dynamic reconfiguration of component-based distributed systems," in *Proceedings of the 19th ACM SIGSOFT symposium and the 13th European conference on Foundations of software engineering - ESEC/FSE '11*, 2011, p. 245.

[3] S. Ertel and P. Felber, "A framework for the dynamic evolution of highly-available dataflow programs," in *Proceedings of the 15th International Middleware Conference on - Middleware '14*, 2014, pp. 157–168.

[4] C. M. Hayden, E. K. Smith, M. Hicks, and J. S. Foster, "State Transfer for Clear and Efficient Runtime Updates," in *Proceedings of the 2011 IEEE 27th International Conference on Data Engineering Workshops*, 2011, pp. 179–184.

[5] C. M. Hayden, E. K. Smith, M. Denchev, M. Hicks, and J. S. Foster, "Kitsune: Efficient, General-purpose Dynamic Software Updating for C," in *Proceedings of the ACM International Conference on Object Oriented Programming Systems Languages and Applications*, 2012, pp. 249–264.

[6] J. Kramer and J. Magee, "The evolving philosophers problem: dynamic change management," *IEEE Trans. Softw. Eng.*, vol. 16, no. 11, pp. 1293–1306, 1990.

[7] M. Ghafari, P. Jamshidi, S. Shahbazi, and H. Haghighi, "An architectural approach to ensure globally consistent dynamic reconfiguration of component-based systems," in *Proceedings of the 15th ACM SIGSOFT symposium on Component Based Software Engineering - CBSE '12*, 2012, p. 177.

[8] G. Cugola and A. Margara, "Processing flows of information: From data stream to complex event processing," *ACM Comput. Surv.*, vol. 44, no. 3, pp. 1–62, Jun. 2012.

[9] H. Schweppe, A. Zimmermann, and D. Grill, "Flexible On-Board Stream Processing for Automotive Sensor Data," *IEEE Trans. Ind. Informatics*, vol. 6, no. 1, pp. 81–92, Feb. 2010.

[10] L. Golab and M. T. Özsu, "Issues in Data Stream Management," *ACM SIGMOD Rec.*, vol. 32, no. 2, pp. 5–14, 2003.

[11] B. Babcock, S. Babu, M. Datar, R. Motwani, and J. Widom, "Models and issues in data stream systems," in *Proceedings of the twenty-first ACM SIGMOD-SIGACT-SIGART symposium on Principles of database systems - PODS '02*, 2002, p. 1.

[12] M. Cherniack *et al.*, "Scalable distributed stream processing," in *2003 Biennial Conference on Innovative Data Systems Research (CIDR 2003)*, 2003, p. 12.

[13] R. O. Vasconcelos and M. Endler, "A Dynamic Load Balancing Mechanism for Data Stream Processing on DDS Systems," M.Sc Thesis, Departamento de Informática, PUC-Rio - Pontifícia Universidade Católica do Rio de Janeiro, Rio de Janeiro, 2013.

[14] B. Gedik and H. Andrade, "A Model-based Framework for Building Extensible, High Performance Stream Processing Middleware and Programming Language for IBM InfoSphere Streams," *Softw. Pr. Exper.*, vol. 42, no. 11, pp. 1363–1391, 2012.

[15] R. O. Vasconcelos, M. Endler, B. Gomes, and F. Silva, "Autonomous Load Balancing of Data Stream Processing and Mobile Communications in Scalable Data Distribution Systems," *Int. J. Adv. Intell. Syst.*, vol. 6, no. 3&4, pp. 300–317, 2013.

[16] W. Kleiminger, E. Kalyvianaki, and P. Pietzuch, "Balancing load in stream processing with the cloud," in *2011 IEEE 27th International Conference on Data Engineering Workshops*, 2011, pp. 16–21.

[17] Q. Zhang, L. Cheng, and R. Boutaba, "Cloud computing: state-of-the-art and research challenges," *J. Internet Serv. Appl.*, vol. 1, no. 1, pp. 7–18, Apr. 2010.

[18] D. J. Cook and S. K. Das, "Pervasive computing at scale: Transforming the state of the art," *Pervasive Mob. Comput.*, vol. 8, no. 1, pp. 22–35, Feb. 2012.

[19] J. P. Morrison, *Flow-Based Programming, 2nd Edition: A New Approach to Application Development*. Paramount, CA: CreateSpace, 2010.

[20] L. David, R. Vasconcelos, L. Alves, R. André, and M. Endler, "A DDS-based middleware for scalable tracking, communication and collaboration of mobile nodes," *J. Internet Serv. Appl.*, vol. 4, no. 1, p. 16, 2013.

[21] S. I. Lee *et al.*, "Remote patient monitoring: what impact can data analytics have on cost?," in *Proceedings of the 4th Conference on Wireless Health - WH '13*, 2013, pp. 1–8.

[22] Forbes, "4 Interesting Tech Trends In Patient Monitoring," 2014. [Online]. Available: http://www.forbes.com/sites/robertszczerba/2014/12/10/4-interesting-tech-trends-in-patient-monitoring. [Accessed: 14-Jul-2016].

[23] H. Catalyst, "The Year of Healthcare Data Analytics," 2014. [Online]. Available: https://www.healthcatalyst.com/2014-Year-Healthcare-Data-Analytics. [Accessed: 14-Jul-2016].

AUTHOR INDEX

**International Academy, Research,
and Industry Association (IARIA)**
412 Derby Way
Wilmington, DE 19810

ISBN 978-1-5108-4298-4
9 781510 842984

CURRAN ASSOCIATES INC.
proceedings.com

Seventh International Conference on Sensor Device Technologies and Applications (SENSORDEVICES 2016)

Held at NetWare 2016

Nice, France
24 - 28 July 2016

IARIA